Fundamentals of Enterprise Architecture

Proven Frameworks for
Effective Architecture Decisions

Tanusree McCabe

Beijing · Boston · Farnham · Sebastopol · Tokyo

Fundamentals of Enterprise Architecture

by Tanusree McCabe

Published by O'Reilly Media, Inc., 1005 Gravenstein Highway North, Sebastopol, CA 95472.

O'Reilly books may be purchased for educational, business, or sales promotional use. Online editions are also available for most titles (*https://oreilly.com*). For more information, contact our corporate/institutional sales department: 800-998-9938 or *corporate@oreilly.com*.

Acquisitions Editor: Louise Corrigan
Development Editor: Corbin Collins
Production Editor: Gregory Hyman
Copyeditor: nSight, Inc.
Proofreader: Helena Stirling

Indexer: Ellen Troutman-Zaig
Interior Designer: David Futato
Cover Designer: Karen Montgomery
Illustrator: Kate Dullea

September 2024:   First Edition

Revision History for the First Edition

2024-09-05:   First Release

See *http://oreilly.com/catalog/errata.csp?isbn=9781098159375* for release details.

978-1-098-15937-5

[LSI]

Table of Contents

Preface

Once upon a time, a respected colleague declared that enterprise architecture, as we knew it, was dead. With unprecedented transformations such as cloud and artificial intelligence, it did appear that enterprise architecture in its original form was too archaic to add value. How could a function formalized in the 1980s hope to not only keep up with such rapid technological changes, but also to ensure that such changes would lead to positive business outcomes?

Yet having witnessed reboots and resets, and having driven changes to architecture myself, I have come to the conclusion that enterprise architecture, when delivered effectively, is still undoubtedly essential to any organization seeking to deliver technology solutions better, faster, and cheaper.

Enterprise architecture aligns business's strategies, processes, and technologies to achieve business goals. As if that weren't enough, enterprise architecture also defines the structure and operation of an organization's technology. Enterprise architecture establishes architecture principles and practices to guide organizations through the business, information, process, and technology changes necessary to execute their strategies, and ensures that systems and processes are efficient, effective, and cohesive while allowing scalability and flexibility in changing business needs.

Organizations that try to fulfill business needs without first defining their enterprise architecture strategy are at risk of experiencing siloed delivery and arbitrary uniqueness. Without an effective enterprise architecture practice, investments are made without a defined purpose, and problems are solved without understanding the full implications of the solution. The best architects and engineers can only get so far on their own without an effective enterprise architecture practice.

This book is a defense of enterprise architecture, and a guide to establishing enterprise architecture so that it operates effectively. Throughout this book, I cover proven frameworks from my experiences that you can tailor to meet your own needs.

Who Should Read This Book?

This book is for anyone involved in delivering software products. Architects, engineers, product managers, executives, data scientists—all are necessary in effective enterprise architecture.

This book is especially relevant for those undertaking the challenge of leading or performing enterprise architecture. By the end of this book, you will understand what enterprise architecture is and why it is important to have an effective enterprise architecture practice, and who needs to be involved to make enterprise architecture successful. You will learn about common pitfalls through my presentation of case studies that inhibit effective enterprise architecture. You will be able to assess the current state of your organization's enterprise architecture practice to identify opportunities for improvement, establish your own enterprise architecture strategy, and strengthen your ability to help yourself and others make great architecture decisions.

Any organization seeking to use modern technology with a cogent strategy can benefit from adapting the frameworks and applying the concepts presented in this book.

Conventions Used in This Book

The following typographical conventions are used in this book:

Italic
> Indicates new terms, URLs, email addresses, filenames, and file extensions.

This element signifies a tip or suggestion.

This element indicates a warning or caution.

O'Reilly Online Learning

 For more than 40 years, *O'Reilly Media* has provided technology and business training, knowledge, and insight to help companies succeed.

Our unique network of experts and innovators share their knowledge and expertise through books, articles, and our online learning platform. O'Reilly's online learning platform gives you on-demand access to live training courses, in-depth learning paths, interactive coding environments, and a vast collection of text and video from O'Reilly and 200+ other publishers. For more information, visit *https://oreilly.com*.

How to Contact Us

For updates and information on this book and the topics it covers, please visit the author's website at *https://www.funeabook.com*.

You can also address comments and questions concerning this book to the publisher:

O'Reilly Media, Inc.

1005 Gravenstein Highway North

Sebastopol, CA 95472

800-889-8969 (in the United States or Canada)

707-827-7019 (international or local)

707-829-0104 (fax)

support@oreilly.com

https://oreilly.com/about/contact.html

We have a web page for this book, where we list errata, examples, and any additional information. You can access this page at *https://oreil.ly/fundamentals-enterprise-architecture*.

For news and information about our books and courses, visit *https://oreilly.com*.

Find us on LinkedIn: *https://linkedin.com/company/oreilly-media*

Watch us on YouTube: *https://youtube.com/oreillymedia*

Acknowledgments

I'd like to thank my daughter, Ashley, for inspiring me to take a chance and my son, Ryan, and husband, David, for their love, support, and confidence in me. Similarly, thank you to my sister, Mamani, my parents, Kalpana and Dipankar, and my in-laws, Susan and Michael, for being my biggest champions.

I'd also like to extend my gratitude to Aaron Rinehart, who opened up doors.

This book is a culmination of many years of experience, and I appreciate all the people that I learned from, and worked with, to shape my views and perspectives. I extend my gratitude to Brandee Pierce, David Geen, Allison Boulais, Arjun Dugal,

Mark Pender, Zach Blizzard, John Andrukonis, Pete Davies, Kiran Ramineni, Joe Reunthirisak, Keith Gasser, Tony Reynolds, Kathleen Devalk, Lakshmi Seetharaman, Vince Gutosky, Tariq Shaikh, Todd Safford, Parvez Naqvi, Liz Ashton, Alejandra Rios, Jeanine McGinniss, Michael Arroyo-Young, Anantha Bangalore, Keith McCloskey, John Hughes, Dan Katz, Prashant Sarambale, and Alok Awasthi.

Thanks to Doron Beit-Halahmi, Doug Holland, Naveen Krishnaraj, and Sivakumar Ponnusamy for giving the manuscript a read for technical accuracy. Also, thank you to the O'Reilly publishing and editing team for all your hard work and constructive feedback.

Thank you to all the architects who work so hard to make a difference and to all of their partners who are allies in the quest to achieve value through architecture. Last but not least, thank you to readers who have taken the time to learn more about effective enterprise architecture.

CHAPTER 1

Key Enterprise Architecture Concepts

What does the word *architecture* mean to you? Perhaps it brings to mind visions of Renaissance art and Gothic cathedrals, or if you've ever done a home remodel, blueprints of houses and rooms. Perhaps you're civically oriented and you start thinking about maps of cities and designs of buildings.

Whatever comes to mind, I have a strong hunch that *design* was part of it. So, we can then say that architecture definitely has something to do with designing something new. In the context of modern information technology (IT) organizations, the *something* is typically a software-based system.

How well does architecture help you and your organization deliver software? Perhaps you've had bad experiences with ineffective architecture, and the first words that come to mind are things like *ivory tower*, *out of touch*, or *behind the times*. Perhaps architecture seems like an archaic relic of the past, something that's no longer needed in a modern organization as it attempts to keep pace with rapidly changing technology and business demands.

On the other hand, maybe you've had great experiences with architecture, and the first words that come to mind are things like *clarity*, *strategy*, and *shared*. Architecture may have provided the clarity needed to set forth a shared strategy with clear goals and blueprints to achieve them. Perhaps architecture allowed for great decisions that met business goals, kept customers happy, and also allowed for innovative technology, or maybe architecture provided the way to connect business to technology strategy.

This book aims to set you up for great experiences with architecture. Specifically, it aims to provide you with a path to successfully establish a strong enterprise architecture practice, where *enterprise* means across the entire company.

To do that, let's first look at the value proposition of enterprise architecture. Why should you, or anyone in your organization, care to invest in enterprise architecture?

Why Enterprise Architecture?

Enterprise architecture is critical to an organization's ability to operate effectively with a clear technology strategy that fulfills business objectives. Where *architecture* as a general function solves problems, *enterprise architecture* solves complex problems that impact the *enterprise* and changes the enterprise as a whole. Where architecture in general seeks to deliver well-designed software, enterprise architecture provides the principles, standards, and best practices that enable all software engineering teams to deliver reusable, cost-effective, secure, scalable software that meets business needs.

It may be easier to understand the value proposition of enterprise architecture if I first talk about what happens to organizations that don't have strong enterprise architecture.

Organizations without a strong enterprise architecture practice typically fall victim to the development of silos, chaos, and technical debt.

Avoiding Silos

You may be in a siloed organization if Figure 1-1 looks familiar. In Figure 1-1, each organizational unit makes decisions independently of others. There are only vertical decisions, no horizontal decisions.

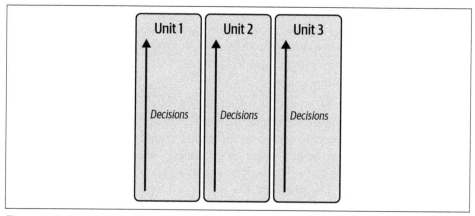

Figure 1-1. Decisions made within each vertical organizational unit, illustrating siloed decision making

Organizational units race to meet their specific business objectives, each thinking that they have unique problems to solve. While they do deliver results in the form of software products, these results are optimized for each organizational unit rather than the enterprise as a whole. This means that the company ends up needing to maintain several similar yet slightly different solutions, and/or outright duplication of solutions, and/or solutions that are unable to effectively integrate with each other. This is both a waste of the company's resources and an impediment to connected experiences.

You see, typically customers don't want to know the complexity of all of the organizational units behind a product or service that they use; they want a seamless experience across them, and it takes an enterprise perspective to stitch that together. For example, suppose there is a company made of multiple business units. Both business unit A and business unit B need to reach customers with mobile devices. Business unit A decides to build a new mobile app. Since the company is siloed, so does business unit B. Each business unit accomplishes its specific goal of reaching customers via mobile apps. However, given that the units share a customer base, customers are quite perplexed about why the same company was offering two mobile apps with two experiences. Customer loyalty declines as customers decide to try out competition C, which has a much more integrated, seamless mobile app experience.

 Siloed decisions made with myopic vision lead to shortsighted focus on tactics to resolve near-term fires, rather than strategic investment in the end game. An enterprise perspective allows for making decisions across silos.

Avoiding Chaos

The second symptom of a weak enterprise architecture practice is chaos. Chaos is a consequence of lacking a clear set of technology standards, as shown in Figure 1-2. Chaos in this context means that each software delivery team makes their own choices, and while there is some benefit in allowing for innovation and competition, there are often significant issues that occur in such an environment.

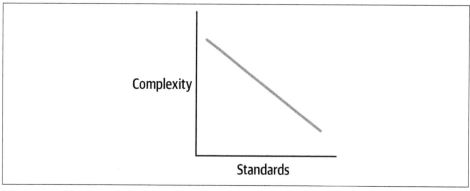

Figure 1-2. The fewer standards there are, the more technology sprawl occurs to increase complexity

One issue is in impeding the ability to scale talent. You need to hire and train talent that understands how to use the various technologies that the teams decided to build with, whether that's a mainstream industry-leading contender or an esoteric niche product. It can also be difficult to build fungible skill sets and engage in team mobility. This is because teams that use different technology choices cannot easily transfer their knowledge of one technology to another. It can also make it difficult to attract new talent, if there isn't enough new modern technology in use.

Another issue is with sustaining and scaling cybersecurity and governance support and oversight. For each technology in use, typically there are requirements around securing it, and that can be technology specific. For example, the ability to scan software for cybersecurity vulnerabilities: for every software language in use, that's one more capability needed. There is a cost to maintaining cybersecurity and governance oversight and assurance for each technology choice.

A third issue is in inhibiting operational gains or reducing an organization's agility in terms of adapting and interoperating technology. When standards are introduced after disparate technology is already in use, organizations often have a tough time adapting and adhering to those standards, and in many cases have to invest in refactoring and rearchitecting their software applications.

As an example, imagine a company that falls in love with DevOps. Enamored with the idea of automated continuous integration (CI) and continuous delivery (CD), each of the company's 5,000 teams decides to invest in its own DevOps solutions. Six months later, the company has not one, not two, not even a hundred CI/CD pipelines, but at least one pipeline per team. Five thousand teams had to design, develop, debug, troubleshoot, and maintain 5,000 pipelines. Each team had to go through the learning and change curve to manage its own pipeline, from start to finish. The company retroactively declares a standard to centralize the pipeline instead. Adding standards after 5,000 slight deviations had already been made proves to be quite painful.

Proactive standards accelerate development efforts. Reactive or no standards cause chaos.

Avoiding Technical Debt

The third symptom of an ineffective enterprise architecture practice is burgeoning technical debt that stifles true innovation and inhibits business agility. While, generally speaking, architecture decisions require the acceptance of trade-offs and risks, *technical debt* refers to the cost to remediate or refactor technical issues in the future that are caused by shortsighted decisions. Without clear architecture principles and decisioning practices or criteria, architecture decisions are at risk of being made only to fulfill an immediate need. Applications are then bogged down with technical debt that inhibits them from adapting to changing technology and/or evolving business needs.

A classic example of technical debt is in cloud migrations. Let's say a company decides to migrate their applications to the cloud. Their applications were originally designed for data centers, not for the cloud. As a result, they do not horizontally scale, and they do not use technology that has parity with managed services in the cloud. They may even hardcode IP addresses. The company is under a tight timeline, though, so it decides to lift and shift its applications rather than refactoring or rearchitecting them. *Lift and shift* refers to migrating an application as is, without changes. Since the applications are not optimized to operate in the cloud, costs increase and they are still unable to scale to peak demands. The company is surprised when its newly cloud-hosted applications can't actually reap the rewards of the cloud.

If you have to live with technical debt, understand the implications of it. Better yet, don't introduce technical debt.

Summarizing the Benefits

Just as you wouldn't build a house without a blueprint, you wouldn't want to stake your company's technology future on whims, without a technology strategy. An effective enterprise architecture practice enables the definition of that technology strategy, at every level of the enterprise organization, to deliver the right, unique solutions. It creates shared vision across all impacted stakeholders, across business, technology, product, engineering, cybersecurity, and so on. When everyone has the same objective and marches toward that objective together, it becomes easy to reconcile priorities and deliver effectively. Products are delivered for the common good of the company, and here's the key business benefit: delivery is better, faster, and cheaper since people are working together in an optimal way.

Effective enterprise architecture defines standards that provide guardrails for safe, secure, and scalable innovation. When standards are defined proactively, and teams understand what needs to be true, it becomes easy to deliver against these standards and enable reuse of common solutions. Instead of solving the same problem many times over, teams can adhere to standards to accelerate their development. From a business perspective, this is critical because it enables agility and prevents duplicative cost.

It results in modern applications that are future-proofed. Technology advances at a blistering pace, and applications that are constrained with yesterday's technology can drag down an organization's ability to innovate and excel with tomorrow's technology. This allows for competitive advantage—key to any business.

A Note on "Effective"

You may have noticed that I keep qualifying enterprise architecture with the key word *effective*. This is because there are many times when operationalizing enterprise architecture in an organization does not deliver the intended business value. Organizations that try to overcome silos, chaos, and technical debt must be aware of the pitfalls of failed or ineffective enterprise architecture implementations.

Given that a primary aim of an effective enterprise architecture practice is to avoid silos, it is both ironic and detrimental when enterprise architecture itself becomes a siloed operation. This scenario is often referred to as *ivory tower architecture*, a term that implies that the enterprise architecture decisions made to establish strategy, standards, and processes, and to recommend solutions for complex enterprise problems, are made without adequate context. They are lofty and abstract, without alignment or a feasible way to achieve the recommended solution, and so separated from the reality of execution that they end up being ineffective and adding no business value. You must deliberately ensure that the enterprise architecture practice is grounded in real technology and business needs and is solving actual business problems.

As discussed, another aim of an effective enterprise architecture practice is to avoid chaos. The cautionary note here is to also avoid the other extreme—so much standardization and prescription that innovation itself is stifled. Hubristic organizations have so little trust and confidence in their engineering and development talent that they restrict too many choices, and force all teams, all use cases and solutions, to conform to the standards. Enterprise architecture in this type of organization becomes a hated foe, a dictator that tells you what to do, that is just asking for talent to rebel against it. As soon as teams believe that architecture is against them—a bottleneck instead of an enabler of delivering great solutions—it is time to seek a transformative change to overcome this perception. Ineffective enterprise architecture strangles

---

teams' creativity and innovation through heavy-handed standards and the need to ask for permission for every decision. You must promote enterprise architecture as an enabler: one that accelerates teams through rightsized standards.

Last but not least, let's revisit the goal around reducing technical debt. While in an ideal world, there is no technical debt, in the real world, there is always a trade-off and a risk-based decision to consider. Ineffective enterprise architecture struggles to guide risk-based decisions and with the ability to define good enough or imperfect recommendations in such a way that the implications are clear enough to understand what risks are being accepted. You must advocate enterprise architecture as a vehicle to solve complex problems in such a way as to avoid the most impactful rework yet balance business value with business acceptance of technology risk.

Now that you see why we pursue enterprise architecture, let's dive into what enterprise architecture means.

What Is the Practice of Enterprise Architecture?

Let's first differentiate between *practice* and *roles*. The *practice* of enterprise architecture refers to enabling both the ability to solve complex enterprise-wide problems and the ability to deliver reusable, cost-effective, secure, scalable software that meets business needs. The *roles* are elaborated in a later section and refer to the people who perform the practice of architecture.

To understand what the practice of enterprise architecture is, or rather, what it should be, let me take you through its vision and mission.

The Vision

A *vision statement* typically declares what you want to achieve in the future. To put it simply, enterprise architecture defines the north star for an organization. The *north star* is the strategic direction that guides all technology investment in a way that connects business to technology. Creating a shared destination state across business, technology, and architecture for a given set of capabilities and the technology solutions that provide them consistently is the ultimate goal of enterprise architecture.

Knowing that ultimately we want to define that north star throughout the enterprise organization, here's an example vision statement for an effective enterprise architecture practice:

> Define technology strategy that transcends organizational differences to connect different aims into common business goals.

If a vision is what you want to achieve, then how do you go about achieving it? Enter the mission statement.

The Mission

A *mission statement* typically declares how a vision is to be achieved. To achieve the vision above, where enterprise architecture as a practice can effectively output a clear north star that aligns stakeholders across the company, it is necessary to establish a foundation of trust-based decision making. It is through great architecture decisions that organizations decide on their business and technology strategy, break through siloed decision making to find commonalities, and do what is right not for any given team or organizational unit, but for the company itself.

Here's an example mission statement for an effective enterprise architecture practice:

> Enable great architecture decisions to deliver great solutions as one team.

Word choice in a mission statement matters, and different words may resonate differently in your organization. For this example mission statement, I want to emphasize a few key word choices:

Enable
> Provide the ability to make architecture decisions—not actually make all of the architecture decisions.

Great
> Great meaning sustainable, solves the problem, and meets business needs, yet not necessarily perfect because architecture decisions require identifying, understanding, and accepting trade-offs.

One team
> An objective enterprise perspective is unique to enterprise architecture and is what enables enterprise architecture as a function to bring teams together across silos to accomplish common aims.

Later chapters do a deep dive on why these things are key. For now, let's look at the functions of enterprise architecture.

What Are the Functions of Enterprise Architecture?

To establish the practice of enterprise architecture, it is necessary to have some sort of an enterprise architecture organization. The exact nature of this organization can vary company to company but should at minimum include the functions illustrated in Figure 1-3, as these allow for executing the mission and achieving the vision.

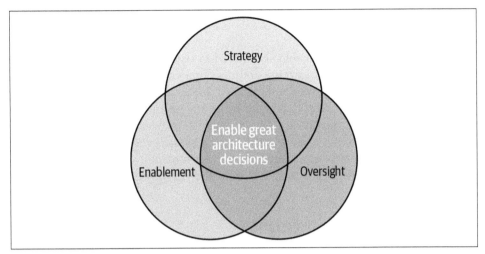

Figure 1-3. Enterprise architecture functions

Let's start by expanding on the enterprise architecture strategy function.

Enterprise Architecture Strategy

Strategy in general refers to planning or directing actions to achieve a major business goal. Enterprise architecture strategy applies this concept to providing the guidance and direction necessary to achieve the goals of an effective enterprise architecture practice. It does so by defining all of the strategies, standards, policies, principles, and processes necessary to operationalize and perform architecture across the company.

This function requires senior technology leaders who are experts in technology, deeply understand business needs, and are capable of influencing alignment at senior levels across the enterprise organization. In short, enterprise architecture strategy defines what to do for an effective enterprise architecture practice.

Knowing what to do is but the first step. Next, you need to know how to do it! That brings us to the enterprise architecture enablement function.

Enterprise Architecture Enablement

The standards and processes that are defined by the enterprise architecture strategy function need to be operationalized for usage by architecture roles (defined in a later section). To operationalize effectively, an enterprise architecture enablement function should be established to provide tools and training, independent albeit integrated with the enterprise's software delivery tools and training. The reason for independence here is because the customers of these tools and training cater to different personas (as described in the following roles section) and different needs. The reason for integration is because there is overlap in how these tools and training are used to deliver software. See Chapter 4 about embedded and accessible architecture for elaboration on this reasoning.

This enterprise architecture enablement function requires product and engineering talent to deliver tooling, and learning and development talent to deliver training. It must be both customer and results focused to deliver effective tooling and training. As sophisticated and successful as enterprise architecture enablement can be to enable the architecture practice, it's still necessary to provide assurance and verification that the architecture practice as implemented actually met the requirements and goals defined by the enterprise architecture strategy function. This assurance and verification is the purview of the next function, the enterprise architecture oversight function.

Enterprise Architecture Oversight

The standards and processes that are defined by the enterprise architecture strategy function also need to be enforced to ensure that they are adequately followed, and that opportunities for improvement can be identified and implemented. While the details of technical enforcement may vary, from a functional perspective, the enterprise architecture oversight function retains accountability for the effectiveness of all of its standards, policies, procedures, processes, and *controls*. A *control* refers to a process or technical policy that provides assurance that a requirement is met in a compliant manner.

This oversight carries three parts:

Governance
    Architecture governance ensures that processes and oversight are in place to align with architecture standards.

Risk
    Architecture risk identifies, mitigates, and manages all risks associated with practicing architecture in accordance with the architecture standards.

Compliance
    Architecture compliance manages and monitors all activities and controls necessary to adhere to architecture requirements as defined in architecture standards.

The degree, complexity, and human labor needed to perform oversight depends greatly on an organization's maturity and automation levels for defining, implementing, and monitoring controls. Controls can be centrally executed or federated down to an organizational unit or even a team. It is up to the enterprise architecture oversight function to work in partnership across the enterprise organization's risk and audit functions to ensure a highly performant and efficient suite of effective architecture controls. It is also necessary for the enterprise architecture oversight function to work hand in hand with the enterprise architecture enablement function as directed by the enterprise architecture strategy function to rightsize the rigor of the oversight with the need for engineering teams to deliver software solutions better, faster, and cheaper.

By now, you may be wondering "What about the enterprise architects themselves? Aren't they part of the enterprise architecture organization? And what about design? You said architecture was about design!" And so it is. The functions of enterprise architecture enable architecture *roles* to do what they do best: make good design decisions that clarify the target state. Enterprise architect is a role, and the placement of enterprise architects in an organizational structure is a key decision that has to be made. So, let's now look into typical architecture roles.

What Are Typical Architecture Roles?

In the IT industry there are a wide variety of architecture roles. In practice, I have found that the minimum set of roles discussed in the following subsections work well. The enterprise architecture strategy function should partner with senior leaders to define and tailor the architecture roles that are needed at an organization.

The first role that I'll mention is the enterprise architect role.

Enterprise Architect Role

The enterprise architect role is focused on strategic enterprise-impactful decisions such as technology standards and architecture patterns that are directly tied to business outcomes. This is typically a senior-level person who has strong communication, influence, and impact skills, and a broad understanding across several areas.

Successful enterprise architects are technology leaders who are also strategic thinkers who operate at the enterprise level. This combination is hard to find, because you need both someone who can lead and influence change, where that change can span across technology, process, and culture, and someone who has the technical expertise and strategic ability to figure out what the change is supposed to be, when looking at a strategic time horizon three to five years out. They can define that strategy as well as the tactics and trade-offs necessary to achieve it, and they can communicate that vision in simple terms.

Also, successful enterprise architects are able to provide an objective, holistic perspective into decision making, such that they deeply understand the needs of the overall corporation's business and how technology can be used to satisfy it across the entire enterprise. They can solve problems that transcend domains or divisions. They can establish trust based on technical credibility and communication skills, and use that to influence both business and technology leaders, typically at an executive level, to align on making a change.

Enterprise architects solve problems such as:

- How do we converge identity solutions across the enterprise?
- What should our modernization strategy be?
- What should our approved software languages technology standard be?

Next, let's look at the solution architect role.

Solution Architect Role

The solution architect role brings both a business and technology focus, in that they marry capabilities to technology solutions while evolving both toward business outcomes. This is typically a senior-level person with strong communication, influence, and impact skills and a deep understanding in a particular subject. Often, subjects are represented as *architectural domains*, which are groups of capabilities that are provided by solutions in support of business processes. Check out Chapter 8 for more elaboration on domains.

Successful solution architects straddle both business and technology. They understand business objectives and business needs, and moreover what business capabilities are necessary to fulfill those needs. They may be adept in domain-driven design (DDD) to define logical boundaries and contexts to bring clarity and understanding to those capabilities. They also understand technology, and they know how to think through trade-offs and perform analysis of alternatives to recommend technology usage to provide a given capability. They are well versed with architecture principles and standards to inform architecture decisions. They collaborate well with others, both business and technology leaders. They can mine solutions to identify new patterns. They become experts for a given domain, knowing both the business and technology of that domain inside out.

Solution architects solve problems such as:

- Would this capability be better serviced by a product, a platform, or a service?
- Where do we need to invest in new capabilities or deprecate existing capabilities?
- How should solutions integrate to support a new business use case?

Now, let's look at the application architect role.

Application Architect Role

The application architect role is focused on technology with an understanding of business. Application architects provide technical expertise to design systems, applications, and platforms. The level of this person ranges depending on the complexity and criticality of the application or system that they are supporting. A mission-critical system should have a more senior-level application architect, whereas a noncritical system can have a more junior-level application architect. These architects typically have strong problem-solving and technical backgrounds, with a deep understanding of patterns and analysis.

It is worth noting that there is currently an industry trend to merge this role with that of a tech lead or senior engineer on an engineering team. This tech lead or senior engineer essentially expands responsibilities to cover application architecture scope in addition to their responsibilities around executing the engineering delivery for their software product.

A successful application architect is an expert with the technologies used by the engineering delivery team. They are also able to understand architecture standards and patterns and how to apply them or adapt them to a particular application. They view themselves as part of the engineering team, and work with them throughout the design and delivery process, rather than being a hands-off consultant.

Application architects solve problems such as:

- How can this application be highly available to provide four nines (99.99%)?
- Should this application use a microservices architecture or not?
- What is the best method of integration between this application and another?
- Where does this application have a critical dependency on another, and how can that dependency be mitigated?

Now that you've learned about the three typical roles, let's look at how they compare and contrast.

Comparing Typical Architect Roles

To better understand how these roles are differentiated and where they overlap, let's take a look at a few key characteristics and how they compare. The first characteristic is described in Figure 1-4 to show the type of architecture that the architect role concentrates on delivering. *Conceptual architecture* refers to the most abstract level of architecture, where concepts and business capabilities are used to describe an architecture solution. *Logical architecture* is primarily concerned with the functional units and boundaries of solutions. *Physical architecture* focuses on the technical implementation details of an architecture solution.

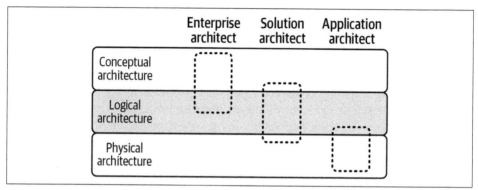

Figure 1-4. Typical architecture roles spanning types of architecture

The next characteristics are described in Figure 1-5 to illustrate the *scope* and *volume* of architecture decisions that these roles make. *Scope* means both the breadth of context that must be considered in making the decision as well as the impact of the changes caused by the decision. *Volume* refers to the amount and frequency of decision making. As shown in Figure 1-5, the enterprise architect role operates at the enterprise level to influence enterprise-impactful changes; these are infrequent in number compared with other types of architecture decisions. The solution architect role operates at a domain level; while some domains are themselves enterprise impactful, others are not. The application architect role operates at the most granular level of a given application or solution; some solutions are themselves enterprise impactful, others are not.

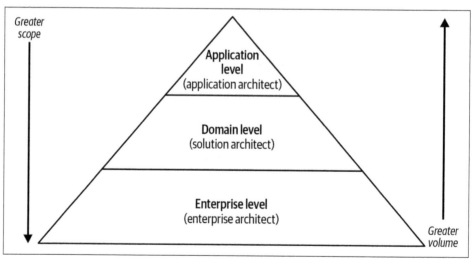

Figure 1-5. Typical architecture roles in terms of scope and volume of decision making

Thus, given the level of seniority and breadth needed for an enterprise architect, they tend to be the fewest in number in any given organization. Next in terms of numbers are solution architects, and then the greatest number is application architects. The exact number of each depends on an organization's needs.

All of these architect roles have common traits, as follows:

Trust
> The ability of an architect to establish trust with business and technology leader counterparts is paramount to their success in being able to influence decisions from inception through execution to realize tangible business outcomes.

Expertise
> The technical acumen of the architect is unquestionable. What is truly unique, though, is the ability to understand business needs and know how technology can be used in service of those.

Problem-solving
> As mentioned in the beginning, effective enterprise architecture solves complex problems. The architect roles are the performers of the functions of architecture to solve problems in objective, meaningful, lasting, and substantive ways.

Leaders
> Architects have to be able to influence outcomes, more so than with positional authority. As a result, they must be perceived as technology leaders and inspire others to drive an agenda of changes.

So far, I've discussed these roles generically. Next, let's look at how to apply them in a specific context.

Specialized Functions

Enterprise architects, solution architects, and application architects may be required in a particular subject matter area to fulfill business needs. There are several specialized functions that can be coupled with each of these roles, and following is a nonexhaustive list:

Security
> Brings a deep understanding of cybersecurity and threat analysis to problem-solving. A security-focused enterprise architect may lead a data protection strategy. A security-focused solution architect may solve a domain-specific problem, such as endpoint protection. A security-focused application architect may use threat modeling techniques to define the security architecture of an application.

Network
> Brings a deep understanding of network design and constraints to problem-solving. A network-focused enterprise architect may define a zero trust strategy. A network-focused solution architect may solve a domain-specific problem, such as establishing routing patterns. A network-focused application architect may solve specific network problems, such as fixing virtual private networks.

Cloud
> Brings a deep understanding of cloud architecture and patterns to their problem-solving. A cloud-focused enterprise architect may define a multicloud strategy. A cloud-focused solution architect may solve a domain-specific problem, such as defining the cloud execution environment for all applications. A cloud-focused application architect may use cloud architecture frameworks to design a highly available cloud native application.

Site reliability
> Brings a deep understanding of operational automation to enable teams to swiftly recover from incidents. A site reliability–focused enterprise architect may define an observability strategy. A site reliability–focused solution architect may define standard tooling to use for monitoring, alerting, and logging. A site reliability–focused application architect may understand business needs to define service-level objectives (SLOs) and service-level indicators (SLIs) for a specific application.

Data
> Brings a deep understanding of data structures, data modeling, and data management, as well as knowledge of different types of databases to their problem-solving. A data-focused enterprise architect may define data management standards. A data-focused solution architect may define a domain-specific problem, such as establishing a data lake or lakehouse. A data-focused application architect may define the right data stores and data replication strategy to meet the business needs of eventual consistency for a specific application.

Additionally, there are specific instantiations of the enterprise architect roles:

Enterprise chief architect (ECA)
> This is the head of enterprise architecture, with approval authority to make enterprise architecture decisions. This is usually a senior-level executive who reports to the CIO or CTO.

Divisional chief architect (DCA)
> This is the head of an organizational unit's architecture team. They are accountable for all the architects consistently delivering high-quality architecture decisions in their organizational unit. They are also responsible for approving divisional decisions, escalating enterprise-impactful divisional decisions for

enterprise review, and providing input into enterprise architecture decisions from a divisional impact, feasibility, and adoption perspective.

Now that we've reviewed what the typical architect roles are, let's take a look at how they can be operationalized in your organization.

Organizational Model

Organizational design needs to be carefully considered to meet the needs and abide by the culture, engagement model, size, and complexity of an organization. Let's look at the most common models that are implemented for architecture organizations, starting with centralized.

Centralized Architecture

Centralized architecture refers to an organizational design in which there is a team of architects, typically fully dedicated in their role, that is consolidated or central to the organization, and/or to an organization unit. This consolidated team concentrates decision-making powers. Figure 1-6 illustrates this concept further to show architecture teams centralized at the enterprise level, and at the divisional or organizational unit levels. These central teams support their particular layer; meaning the enterprise architecture team supports the enterprise, and the organizational unit's architecture team supports that organizational unit.

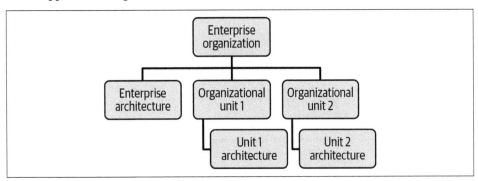

Figure 1-6. Centralized architecture organization

As with any architecture decision, there are trade-offs to consider. Pros of a centralized architecture organizational design include the following:

- Preserves objective viewpoints necessary to advise decisions that weigh the common good more highly than individual benefit. This objectivity is retained because the centralized architect is independent and therefore neutral from the chain of command of the delivery team.

- Facilitates efficient, consistent decision making against a clear vision, because the centralized team shares the same vision and can easily collaborate with one another to ensure consistency.

- Fosters more efficient collaboration across business units and stakeholder groups and overcomes siloed decision making by design. A centralized team is in an optimized position to collaborate with other centralized teams.

On the other hand, here are some cons of a centralized architecture organizational design:

- Further from the customer/business, therefore architects need extra effort to be perceived as valued partners of the engineering teams that they are guiding rather than bottlenecks that cause delays in delivering work.

- Not as scalable in terms of number of people since typically the centralized team follows a matrixed support model.

The opposite of centralized architecture is *federated* or *decentralized* architecture.

Federated Architecture

Federated architecture refers to an organizational design in which the architect role is completely decentralized and embedded into the delivery teams, typically as part-time in their role. The teams themselves are empowered to make the architecture decisions. Figure 1-7 illustrates this concept further, where the architect roles are embedded into the teams themselves and there is no central architecture team at either the organizational unit or enterprise level.

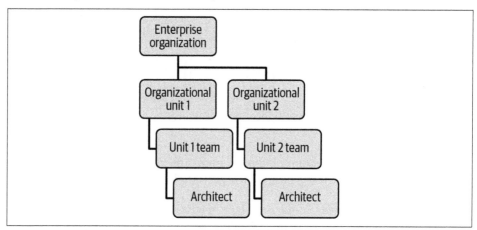

Figure 1-7. Federated architecture organization

The following are pros of the federated architecture organization design:

- Able to scale in terms of decision making since there are more teams with more people to scale with.
- Ability to upskill teams to empower them to make decisions since the decision-making power rests with the team themselves.

Whereas the cons of the federated architecture organization design include the following:

- Can lose objectivity due to being motivated to decide in the team's favor based on incentivization structure, rather than the greater good.
- Can be detrimental for performance management unless architecture outcomes are well understood to be adding tangible business value, since the architect's deliverables are different and not as easily measurable as the engineer's.
- Can duplicate efforts and be more prone to siloed decision making, since each team is deciding independently of one another.

In practice, though, neither centralized nor federated organizational designs are the full answer when it comes to the question of what works best for an effective enterprise architecture practice. Usually, what works best is the combination of both—hybrid architecture.

Hybrid Architecture

Hybrid architecture refers to an organizational design where some architect roles are centralized, and some architect roles are federated. Figure 1-8 illustrates this concept.

Hybrid is usually the model that works the best in a given organization, though again, the organization's size and scale, specific business needs and strategy, and company culture need to be weighed in the decision of organizational design. The enterprise architecture organization that provides the functions of enterprise architecture strategy, enablement, and oversight is typically centralized. The solution architecture organization may be centralized, federated, or both depending on the company. For example, one implementation could be to centralize the enterprise solution architects and federate the domain or divisional-specific solution architects. Another could be to federate all of the solution architects but centralize at the divisional level. The application architect is the most decentralized, usually being federated into the delivery teams. The risk of siloed decision making at the application architect level is mitigated by the presence of strong standards and processes defined by the centralized enterprise architecture organization to yield consistent quality of decisions.

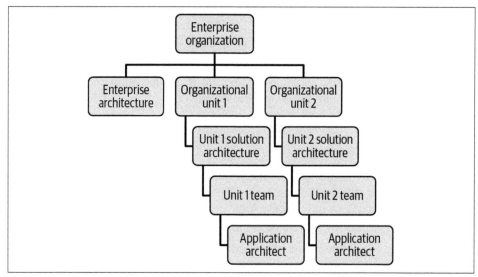

Figure 1-8. Hybrid organization, a mixture of centralized and federated

For an architect to be successful in any organizational model, they require a strong partnership with the following roles:

Technology lead
> At senior levels, this would be an accountable executive. This is the role that has approval authority to align technology development with architecture decisions.

Business lead
> At senior levels, this would be an accountable executive. This is the role that has approval authority to align business goals with architecture decisions.

Product lead
> At senior levels, this would be an accountable executive. This is the role that has approval authority to align product priority and roadmaps with architecture decisions.

It is essential that these three roles agree that they, too, are part of the architecture process and work hand in hand with their counterpart architecture role to define and deliver the shared destination state. Without this partnership, an architecture deliverable is nothing more than a piece of paper. It is this partnership among business, technology, product, and architecture that takes the ideas and decisions documented on that piece of paper into reality.

Speaking of deliverables, let's now take a look at a few essential ones.

What Are Typical Architecture Deliverables?

While there is a wide variety of standard architecture deliverables, and a number of different standards that can guide their creation, this section outlines what I've found to work well in practice. The enterprise architecture strategy function is accountable to create the templates, principles, and standards that guide the formation of these deliverables. I recommend taking a look at industry frameworks like The Open Group Architecture Framework (TOGAF) (*https://oreil.ly/8lsJb*) and the C4 (Context, Containers, Components, and Code) model (*https://c4model.com*) to reuse industry best practices.

Let's start with the architecture decision deliverable.

Architecture Decision Deliverable

Architecture decisions document a recommendation; the context, goals, and constraints to inform that recommendation; the analysis of alternatives conducted to make the decision; and who made the decision and when.

This deliverable provides a documented rationale for why a decision was made that can be reviewed for posterity and inform future decisions to avoid rework. It serves as a mechanism for collaboration among all stakeholders that are impacted by a decision to help create alignment on that decision. This deliverable supports governance processes where decisions must be documented to record the rationale for deviation from a standard.

Architecture decisions are so essential to every architecture role that we'll deep dive on them in just a little while. But first, let's turn our attention to another common deliverable, the architecture pattern.

Architecture Pattern Deliverable

Architecture patterns document a solution to a problem and typically come in two forms: design, which is technology agnostic, and implementation recommendation, which is technology specific. They include documentation of issues and considerations for using the pattern.

This deliverable provides a reusable blueprint to follow to implement a solution. It defines best practices that provide a standard way to do something. To define best practices, it must be proven through implementation and not just theoretical.

Ideally, an architecture pattern can be codified in a form that makes it reusable. For instance, a *reference architecture* may be created as a documented blueprint to provide an example of how several patterns can be used together to design a particular type of application solution. This reference architecture can then be codified as a *reference implementation* that is running software that implements the reference architecture.

Another example is *patterns as code*, where software templates, snippets, modules, and/or libraries are used to codify the pattern.

Architecture patterns are typically output by an enterprise architect role. Next, let's look at a common deliverable for the solution architect role: the capability target architecture.

Capability Target Architecture Deliverable

Capability target architectures document a shared destination state for a group of capabilities and the solutions that provide them. This group is often called an architecture domain, as elaborated in Chapter 8.

This deliverable includes analysis and documentation of solution architecture decisions at this domain level, such as what to invest in versus what to deprecate, where emerging technologies are needed, and where there is opportunity for convergence and consolidation. It is a strategic document that provides a documented target state for how domains will evolve over time. It can include one or more views that illustrate the capability target, such as the following:

Conceptual architecture
Domain broken down into conceptual business capabilities.

Logical architecture
Domain broken down into logical units, mapped to the conceptual architecture.

Physical architecture
Logical architecture mapped to the physical architecture of the solutions that provide the logical functions.

Sequence diagrams
Views written in industry standards such as PlantUML to describe how logical or physical units interact with one another in a specific workflow.

Architecture decisions
Yes, this is the same deliverable mentioned above, but in this context, it refers to decisions made at the domain level.

Next, let's look at a common deliverable for the application architect role: the application target architecture.

Application Target Architecture Deliverable

The application target architecture documents the description and various diagrams of an application, that at minimum includes the following:

Context view
> This describes how the application interacts with others.

Component view
> This describes the logical breakdown of the application into functions and how they interact with one another.

Deployment view
> This describes how the application will be deployed and the resilience and security characteristics therein.

The application target architecture includes analysis and documentation of architecture decisions at the application level. It provides documented design for the application's target state, enabling decisions around changes from current to future state. It also provides visuals that are easy to understand to review the application's architecture and determine any risks.

You may have noticed that architecture decisions were mentioned both as an output of the mission of enterprise architecture, and as a deliverable. As promised, let's deep dive on them a bit.

What Is an Architecture Decision?

An *architecture decision* is simply a decision that is created as a result of an architecture process. These decisions are made by an architecture role in partnership with technology, business, and product counterparts.

Overview

Although formats vary, through experience I have learned that the anatomy of an architecture decision record should include the following elements:

Identifier
> A unique naming convention is necessary to distinguish decisions.

Description
> A human-readable description of what problem the decision is solving is helpful to search for relevant decisions.

Metadata
> The taxonomy of metadata tags or labels can vary from organization to organization, but it is helpful to establish a consistent one up front to enable transparency, visibility, and searchability across an organization, both top to bottom and across.

Stakeholders

Explicitly stating who is accountable, responsible, consulted, or informed by the decision is helpful to ensure that all relevant stakeholders were included in the decision making.

Status

Knowing the status of the decision makes it clear whether it is in effect or not.

Date

Knowing the date of the decision allows for refresh.

Problem statement

Explicitly documenting the problem that this decision solves avoids ambiguity.

Alternatives

This shows what options were considered for the decision, and the pros and cons, or trade-offs, of those options.

Rationale

This describes why a certain option was selected. And if the decision changes over time, this provides the reasoning for that, too.

Implications

This describes the results of implementing the decision, and it should also highlight any technical debt and risk that is accrued.

Sample Template

Templates can differ depending on your desired format. Here is a simple format that I've found to work well:

Decision ID: Unique identifier for the decision record

Title: Brief title, used for search and filtering

Status: Status of decision record, such as draft, in progress, approved

Approval date: Date decision was approved

Approver: Role and name of accountable approver

Contributors: Roles and names of consulted stakeholders

Informed: Roles and names of informed stakeholders

Problem statement: Describe the problem that this decision addresses

Context: Provide background information, define assumptions and constraints, and identify factors considered in options analysis

For each factor considered in the option analysis, add a row to define associated pros and cons. For each solution option, add a column. You can also switch the table to have options listed horizontally and factors listed vertically, depending on your view preference.

Factor	Option 1 (describe option 1)	Option 2 (describe option 2)
Factor 1	+ Pro	+ Pro
	− Con	− Con
Factor N	+ Pro	+ Pro
	− Con	− Con

Recommendation: Describe the option chosen and the rationale for choosing it

Implications: Describe implications of the decision, including technical debt, trade-offs, and impacts

---

Example Architecture Decision

Decision ID: 001

Title: My Application's Compute

Status: Approved

Approval date: 06/10/24

Approver: Public Cloud Enterprise Architect—Tanusree McCabe

Contributors:

- Security—Betty McCormick
- Engineering Lead—Linda Patterson
- Product Manager—Sanjay Gupta

Informed: Finance—Watson Lamb

Problem statement: What compute choice works best for my application?

Context: My application is migrating to the public cloud and needs to modernize to optimize its cloud usage. Approved compute choices include:

- Virtual machines (VMs)
- Containers

Note: functions are not an approved service at this time.

My application uses a microservices architecture that can scale horizontally.

Factors considered in the options analysis include:

Cost
    The total cost of ownership, inclusive of labor and resources, implied by the option

Scalability
    The ability of the option to scale up or down in response to changing demands

Sustainability
    The ability of the option to be maintained

Factor	Option 1 VMs	Option 2 Containers
Cost	– Rightsizing VMs can be difficult. VMs generally cost more than containers.	+ Only pay as you go for cost of container task if using a container management service.
Scalability	+ Can automatically scale with cloud native configurations. – Limited by IP (Internet Protocol) space available in subnet.	+ Can automatically scale based on cluster manager. + Less risk of IP space constraints.
Sustainability	+ Team skilled in support and can patch. + DevOps toolchain supports – VM is less portable to other clouds.	+ Team skilled in support and can patch. + DevOps toolchain supports. + Container artifact is portable (note: cloud native integrations are not).

Recommendation: Option 2, containers, is recommended due to its ability to scale better and be cloud agnostic.

Implications: My application's support team will need to be upskilled in monitoring and maintaining container-based applications.

Summary

When you build a house, you expect it to be built upon a high-quality architecture that meets both regulations and your needs. Similarly, when you deliver technology, you need an effective enterprise architecture practice to lead the way and define the north star. This north star manifests as a cogent technology strategy that permeates every level of your organization. This north star is created by a series of shared, aligned, high-quality architecture decisions that lay the groundwork for the sustainable design and implementation of technology to meet business aims.

To yield optimized results, whether it be for an enterprise technology strategy, a particular set of capabilities, or a specific solution or application, having the right architecture standards, practices, and disciplines in place, along with the right talent in the right roles, is necessary. An effective enterprise architecture is what defines and manages those architecture practices in such a way as to overcome siloed decision making, chaos from technology sprawl, and technical debt from shortsighted decisions:

- Effective enterprise architecture provides a clear vision for an organization to create and clarify a shared destination state, a clear mission to enable great architecture decisions, and powers the productivity of all architecture functions and roles.

- Enterprise architecture functions span strategy, governance, risk, compliance, tooling, and training.

- Enterprise architecture is what defines all the standards, processes, and tools necessary to perform architecture across an organization.

- Architecture roles perform the practices of architecture, which include business-minded roles that make decisions across the enterprise (enterprise architect), an architectural domain (solution architect), or a particular solution (application architect).

- A key decision for any organization is whether to centralize, federate, or do some combination thereof for architecture roles.

- For architecture roles to be successful, it is essential to engage and partner with roles across technology, business, and product.

- Architecture decisions and solutions are the key byproducts of an effective enterprise architecture practice.

Now that you've seen why enterprise architecture is necessary, what it is, and what it drives, in the next chapter we'll turn our attention to how you can establish a strategy to actually implement a strong, effective enterprise architecture practice in your organization.

CHAPTER 2

Key Strategy Objectives

So far, you've read that a strong, effective enterprise architecture practice provides the *north star*, or strategic direction, to define an organization's technology roadmap through a series of architecture decisions. It may not come as a surprise, then, that a strategy is also needed to guide and establish an effective enterprise architecture practice itself.

If you're asking, "How do I get started?" you're in luck, because that's precisely the question this chapter answers. All strategies start by defining their objectives, so this chapter discusses the objectives of an effective enterprise architecture strategy. Although details of implementation may vary and will be tailored based on unique characteristics of your organization, the objectives will, I hope, resonate with you.

Overview

To share the key objectives of an effective enterprise architecture strategy, I have found that the *objectives and key results* (OKR) framework—which was defined in the 1970s and popularized by Google—is very helpful. What I find special about the OKR framework is that rather than just defining transparent and aspirational goals, the OKR framework includes *measurement* as a key characteristic.

It is measurement that is novel to architecture. Traditionally, architectural outcomes are perceived in terms of artifacts or deliverables, such as those described in Chapter 1. As a result, it is difficult to qualitatively (let alone quantitatively) tie architecture work to business value. This, in my opinion, is the number one reason it can be so hard to answer the question of what is the value of architecture. And this is why it can be so difficult for architects to be valued by an organization. When all you see is a deliverable, likely to be in document form, but not the business results that the deliverable is driving, then it is very easy to dismiss that deliverable's value and all the work that it took to create that deliverable.

For example, let's say a software engineering team was able to significantly reduce cloud storage costs by implementing an architecture pattern. By following this pattern, the team changed the storage class of less frequently accessed objects and implemented a hygiene policy that deleted unused data after a period of time. Who gets credit for the cost savings result? The software engineering team? The architect who contributed the pattern? Ideally, it would be both: the team for making the engineering choice and the architect for providing a reusable solution that benefited the business with cost reductions. Thus, it is necessary to place a business value on the architecture pattern itself—both for what it could save and for what it does save. To measure what it does save requires having a mechanism to track pattern adoption.

Here's another example. Let's say it took a solution architect six months to get all relevant stakeholders to agree on a strategy that combines their efforts to build a common platform to provide an enterprise-level service. Now, let's say it takes a couple of years to build this common platform. What happens? Does the architect get rewarded for delivering the strategy before the platform is built, because it was their leadership that allowed for an agreed-upon impactful outcome? Does the architect get no credit at all, or have to wait to get recognized, because strategy isn't as tangible a deliverable as the platform itself? Ideally, the strategy is recognized as a key technical deliverable, and furthermore, all stakeholders adhere to the strategic decisions to implement the solution to realize the projected business outcomes. Thus, it is necessary to quantify the benefits and impacts of the strategy itself. What were the benefits of converging on a platform solution, and what were the milestones that demonstrate incremental progress, and therefore incremental business value, for getting to that final destination? These need to be defined as part of the strategy.

So, starting with the effective enterprise architecture strategy itself, bringing in measurability from the onset is key to success. Understanding that the value of architecture is the business outcomes that the architecture drives, and articulating that in a measurable way, are the first key steps to establishing an effective enterprise architecture strategy.

Measurements are intrinsic to OKRs, since they include two types of key results (KRs):

Outcome-based
    Measures quantifiable outcomes of a process, task, or activity

Effort-based
    Measures the success of a particular initiative or effort

Outcome-based KRs also tend to be *key performance indicators* (KPIs). KPIs are metrics that a company can use to measure the success of its objectives. Moreover, KPIs drive behaviors, so they must be carefully thought through to incentivize the right behaviors. *Leading* indicator KPIs are metrics that indicate future behavior or impact. *Lagging* indicator KPIs are metrics based on events that have occurred in the past.

To complete the definition of a KPI and measure KRs, you must also establish the following:

Clear data sources
Explicitly stating the measurement's data source(s) and transformation logic ensures that there is no ambiguity on the logic used to measure. This exercise may also identify opportunities to create the data source or extract from an existing source.

Clear ownership
Explicitly stating the owner of the measurement clarifies who is accountable and responsible within your organization to ensure that the KPI is delivered.

Frequency
Establishing the frequency of the measurement allows an organization to also react to the KPI results on a periodic basis. While many operational KPIs use monthly as a best practice, given that architecture is a more elongated activity, quarterly tends to be sufficient.

Metrics drive behavior. So don't measure things like this:

Number of architecture standards
If you measure this, the behavior that is incentivized is the number of standards that exist, not the quality or efficacy of those standards. So you may very well see an increase in the number of standards, but they may not add true business value.

Number of architecture artifacts
If you measure this, you may increase coverage and get more artifacts. However, this doesn't cover the true objective of why there was effort put into those artifacts.

Number of compliant applications
If you only measure this, you may increase the amount of applications that are compliant, which is good, but not good enough, because you don't see the business benefit of that compliance. You will get compliance for compliance's sake, rather than the true goal, which is likely around risk mitigation.

Instead, measure outcome-based indicators to incentivize the behaviors that will drive your organization to the business outcomes achieved with an effective enterprise architecture strategy. The following sections provide examples of such indicators while elaborating on each objective recommended for an effective enterprise architecture strategy.

The first objective focuses on the keyword *shared*.

The Shared Alignment OKR

The first objective of an effective enterprise architecture strategy is to *create shared alignment*, where all relevant stakeholders not only agree with the architecture decisions, but also really believe in adhering to them. Regardless of corporate culture, it is human nature that if a human has buy-in to a decision, they will be more motivated to willingly adhere to it. Without buy-in, a human with less authority can still abide by the decision but may not do so with as much aplomb or diligence.

Here's a real-life example. If I make a decision that it's time for homework, my kids, if in the middle of an exciting game, will pause the game and do their homework. However, they may do it grudgingly, and rush things, and not really get any joy out of the learning that occurs. Homework will get completed, but not with high quality. On the other hand, if I make learning fun and allow my kids some input on exactly when the homework gets completed, then they have more buy-in to do it. They will more likely complete it calmly and with focus, and the outcome will likely be better than just having the homework done. You see, the true objective wasn't actually to complete the homework. It was to ensure that learning occurred.

I have seen this behavior a thousand times over in my career, if not more. When decisions are made, and mandates are handed down, professionals will abide by them, especially if there are also mechanisms to enforce the mandates. But the true quality of the outcome depends on how much buy-in they have. Hence, the more *shared* the decision is, the better.

With that in mind, it is critical that the first objective of an effective enterprise architecture strategy is creating shared alignment across all major stakeholders, inclusive of business and technology leaders. *Shared alignment* means that all of these major stakeholders are aligned to adhere to the decision, even if they did not fully agree with it. The scope and degree of shared alignment depends on the impact of the decision. An enterprise-impactful decision ideally has shared alignment across the leadership team and throughout the organization. An application-specific decision, on the other hand, only needs local alignment for the affected application team. The specific details of which stakeholders are necessary to include in decision making are elaborated upon in Chapter 3.

 A culture of trust accelerates shared alignment. Transparency and clear engagement in the architecture decisioning process are key to establishing such a culture.

To scale shared decision making across an entire organization, it is necessary to have a very transparent decision-making process. That way, individuals who are impacted by the decision but were not a part of the initial decision-making process can review how the decision was made and feel comfortable with that decision. The level of comfort is dependent on the level of trust embedded into an organization's culture. If there is high trust in decision makers, then organizations generally find it easier to socialize and adhere to those decisions.

A Culture of Trust

Company culture is a powerful aid or detractor to the success of an effective enterprise architecture strategy. For enterprise architecture to thrive, there must be a foundational culture of trust to build upon. What does a culture of trust look like?

Trust is a loaded term. You may be thinking about relationships in your life when you read the word *trust*. In relationships where there is a high degree of trust, you have probably found smooth sailing, where it is easy to have conversations, even difficult ones. You can take comfort in being able to rely on a trusted relationship to come through for you. As you think about trust in your personal life, you can see how much trust can impact your professional life, at both the micro team level and the macro enterprise organization level. High-performing teams typically have a high degree of trust in one another. In a professional capacity, you may already have come across various trust models.

A culture of trust can be summarized into three key questions:

- Can you do it?
- Do you do it?
- Do you care about me?

The first question, can you do it, speaks to competency. *Competency* in this context means people are able to do the things that are expected of them—they have the skill set, the time, the ability, and the means to achieve the results. They have demonstrated behaviors in the past that allow for trusting that they can deliver in future. They set expectations and meet them.

The second question, do you do it, speaks to credibility. *Credibility* means believable, and this trait goes both ways, where employees see their leaders as credible decision makers and vice versa. Credibility means that people can be relied upon to achieve results consistently. Consistently is also key; it takes time to build trust through consistent successful results. Note, trust can be easily lost with one misstep. Credibility usually goes hand in hand with some degree of *autonomy* and *empowerment*, where employees have some degree of freedom to provide input into decisions and can make their own decisions.

The third question, do you care about me, speaks to *cooperative collaboration*. Employees feel respected by peers and management and therefore feel valued as individuals and as teams. There's no gossip, no underlying tensions or undermining actions. People are honest and both speak and act with integrity. They say what they do, and do as they say. Employees are incentivized to work together because they trust in collaboration and in teamwork. People willingly share knowledge and skills with others.

How does this apply to architecture? Here's an example. Imagine a scenario where a solution architect is tasked to deliver a capability target architecture. Without trust, many things can go wrong. If the solution architect is not trusted as competent and adding value in their subject matter area, the business and technology partners are not likely to engage and use the capability target architecture. If the organization does not view architecture as a value-added credible practice, again, it is difficult for the solution architect's recommendations to be taken seriously and make an impact. If the business or technology partner does not care about or value the architect's role and their contribution, it is nearly impossible for an individual architect to overcome this challenge to successfully deliver a capability target architecture in partnership with them.

There are some trust-inducing behaviors that a solution architect can exhibit regardless of company culture, such as active listening and keeping their word. Active listening allows the solution architect to understand the business and technology partners' needs, and build trust by providing solutions that meet those needs. Keeping their word around setting delivery expectations and doing as they say not only builds a personal brand around integrity but also builds trust through a consistent track record of results. While these behaviors are in an individual's control, ultimately the corporate culture is what dictates the value of and trust in the architect's role.

An effective enterprise architecture strategy must emphasize a culture of trust. It can instill mechanisms such as clarifying architecture roles and establishing standard architecture processes and engagement models that foster cooperation. Ultimately, it is the culture that will make or break an effective enterprise architecture practice.

KRs need to be measurable and should focus on the outcomes more so than defining a tactical to-do list. Hence, the specific set of KRs will vary by company. Here are some sample KRs for this first objective; see Chapter 3 for a framework to help you come up with your own:

- Increase culture of trust as measured by satisfaction surveys by 20%.
- Improve communication skills of architecture talent by 20%.
- Enable transparency of 100% of enterprise-impactful decisions.
- Decrease the number of decisions that are relitigated by 50%.

The outcome of the "create shared alignment" objective is that key stakeholders agree on an architecture decision. So what? What's the business benefit of this agreement?

The business benefits are that this preexisting agreement causes acceleration in delivery processes by precluding churn and also reduces duplication among the solutions being delivered.

With this in mind, here are some examples of leading KPIs focusing on the business benefits:

Duration of delivery process
    If this plateaus or seems high due to churn, that's an indication that there isn't enough shared alignment. Ideally, your trend line goes down over time, as illustrated in Figure 2-1.

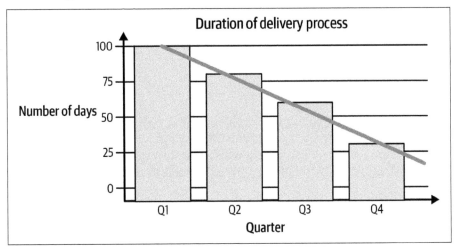

Figure 2-1. Example of a duration of delivery process KPI

Uniqueness
    Compares the number of unique solutions to duplicate solutions. If this decreases or plateaus, that's an indication that there isn't enough shared alignment to converge and deprecate. Ideally, your trend line shows an increase in unique solutions over time, as illustrated in Figure 2-2.

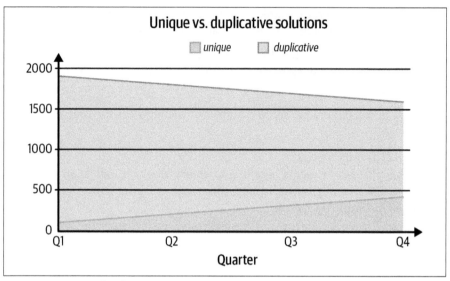

Figure 2-2. Example of a uniqueness KPI

Employee satisfaction

Tailored toward architecture practitioners and their partners, this can indicate a healthy culture or signs of an unhealthy one that impact the ability to make, align, and adhere with architecture decisions. Ideally, your satisfaction scores plateau at an acceptable threshold or trend upward, as shown in Figure 2-3.

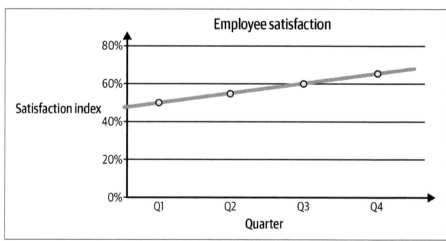

Figure 2-3. Example of an employee satisfaction KPI

Here's an example of a lagging KPI:

Number of decisions made that were revisited in a six-month span
> If this seems high, it indicates that too many decisions are being litigated too often, which could mean that the right stakeholders aren't involved and/or there is a lack of cultural trust.

To achieve the objective of creating shared alignment, let's turn our attention to principles that you can introduce or amplify in your company culture.

Principles to Create Shared Alignment

The degree of *shared* in shared alignment that is necessary for a given architecture decision depends in part on your organizational culture. Organizations that have a well-ingrained ability to *disagree and commit* and *command and control* may need less consensus than those that are focused on achieving *consensus*.

Disagree and Commit

Disagree and commit refers to the management principle that you can disagree with a decision yet stay committed to adhering to that decision. Diversity of thought is usually encouraged such that anyone can disagree with a proposal prior to that proposal being approved as a decision. Once approved as a decision, though, anyone who still disagrees with it needs to commit to following through with the decision. This process is illustrated in Figure 2-4.

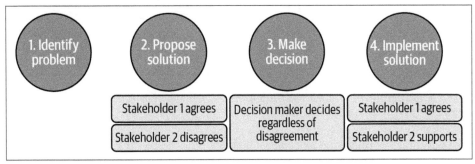

Figure 2-4. Disagree-and-commit management principle illustrated in making a decision

The advantage of the *disagree-and-commit* principle is that decisions can occur even with gridlock. The cycle time for decision making is sped up, because there is a clear decision maker that is empowered to make the decision without needing full consensus. Moreover, decisions are not revisited with endless churn, and therefore they are upheld efficiently. The disadvantage of this principle is that it is quite difficult in practice to execute correctly; it's really hard for people to support a decision enthusiastically that they may fundamentally disagree with.

That is why the first objective for an effective enterprise architecture strategy is to create shared alignment. Even when there is a disagreement of opinions or perspectives, it is essential that the culture allows for dissent and healthy debate and then promotes active united support to overcome the initial position. The *disagree-and-commit* principle can be very helpful to apply to architecture decision making since the more complex and nuanced a problem is, the more possible ways there are to solve that problem, and the more trade-offs there are to consider in the decision. It is highly likely that there will always be disagreeing opinions in such complex, contentious architecture decisions and so a disagree-and-commit approach can help to move decisions forward with the support necessary to implement them.

Next, let's look at the *command-and-control* principle.

Command and Control

Command and control refers to the management principle where a person with positional authority tells subordinates what to do, and they must obey. The leader with positional authority is given great power and responsibility to understand what needs to be done and to direct actions accordingly. Typically, the leader makes the decision themselves with little to no input. This process is illustrated in Figure 2-5.

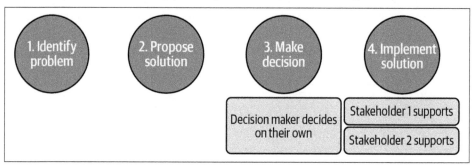

Figure 2-5. Command-and-control management principle illustrated in making a decision

The advantage of *command and control* is that it tends to be the most optimal in risky situations that require decisive action. It ensures consistent decision making and discipline to follow through on those decisions without any operational inefficiencies due to pushback. The disadvantages are that this style can miss opportunities to strengthen the solution and lead to miscommunication and feelings of disempowerment from employees.

This principle can be very helpful to apply in creating shared alignment as a result of an effective enterprise architecture practice because there are times when enterprise architecture needs to declare standards and/or apply constraints due to regulations. Protecting customer data and ensuring privacy regulations are met, for example, are paramount, and no discussion is entertained to fight that this is in fact a requirement for software delivery. Rather, the discussion can constructively be turned toward how best to meet these requirements.

Next, let's look at the *consensus-driven* and *consensus-seeking* principles.

Consensus-Driven and Consensus-Seeking

Consensus-driven refers to the management principle where all relevant stakeholders are solicited for input, and their agreement is necessary to move a decision forward. The goal is truly to have agreement and acceptance of the decision unanimously. Stakeholders are empowered to debate and engage in healthy dialogue until they come to an agreement. Figure 2-6 illustrates this process.

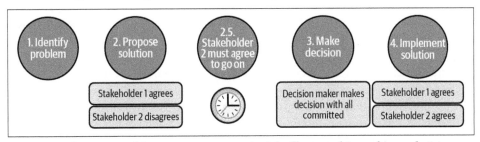

Figure 2-6. Consensus-driven management principle illustrated in making a decision

The advantages of the consensus-driven principle are that the act of building consensus increases cooperation, is very inclusive and empowers stakeholders to take ownership of the final decision, and overcomes differences to create better, stronger solutions. The disadvantages are that consensus building can take a lot of time and can seem endless if there is no common goal or purpose or clear arbiter or if there is lack of trust to make a decision. Also, there is a risk that decisions are reopened and relitigated when there is a change in stakeholders, because the new stakeholders also need to get to consensus.

To overcome these disadvantages, it is helpful to tailor the *consensus-driven* principle to the *consensus-seeking* principle. *Consensus-seeking* refers to the management principle where the wisdom of the crowd is sought to provide diverse perspectives into making a decision, but there is one clear arbiter that is empowered to make that decision and a simple majority suffices to represent consensus. Generally speaking, the US Congress is an example of where a simple majority is used to achieve consensus.

This *consensus-seeking* principle can be very helpful to apply to decision making in an effective enterprise architecture practice because there are so many opportunities to do creative problem-solving, where there are a number of stakeholders that need to come together and figure out the best path forward. For example, in the scenario where stakeholders need to lay aside differences to deprecate one solution and converge on another, it is very helpful for all stakeholders to agree to work together with trust that any advantages of the deprecated solution will be built into the converged solution.

So if we use these principles to achieve the first objective, to create shared alignment, then we have alignment to adhere to the architecture decisions that result from effective enterprise architecture practices. That is wonderful, but how do people actually make the decisions?

For that, we turn our attention to the next objective and associated KRs.

The Embedded and Accessible OKR

To support making great architecture decisions, it is necessary to empower architecture practitioners by providing architecture information at the right time, through the right process, and using the right tools. In other words, making architecture information embedded and accessible is key to effective usage of that information in architecture decision making. *Embedded* means that following an architecture standard or process, and using an architecture deliverable, is intrinsically part of normal software delivery processes used by the organization. They are not separate, distinct processes that require extra effort to find and follow. *Accessible* means that architecture information is easily intuitive, usable, and consumable by the desired audience—typically architects, engineers, and product leaders.

Specific KRs will vary based on your organization's maturity in processes and tools. Here are some sample ones around embedded and accessible architecture information:

- Integrate 100% architecture standards into software delivery processes.
- Increase library of architecture patterns by 20%.
- Ensure 100% of all architecture practitioners complete annual architecture training.
- Improve usability of architecture patterns and standards by 20% as measured by surveys.

The outcome of the embedded and accessible objective is that architecture information is readily available and consumable through software delivery processes. So what? What does this outcome really lead to?

The business benefit is that architecture decisions will be more consistent and sustainable, since the practitioners of architecture and their key partners are empowered by the architecture information to inform great architecture decisions.

With this in mind, here are some example leading indicators focusing on the business benefits:

Architecture knowledge gained
> This should increase over time as processes and training materials improve, as illustrated in Figure 2-7.

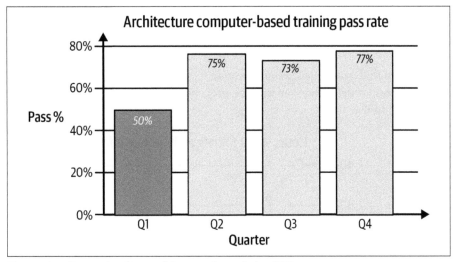

Figure 2-7. Example of an architecture knowledge KPI

Net promoter scores (NPS) of architecture tooling
> This should improve over time to indicate a high degree of usability and satisfaction, as illustrated in Figure 2-8.

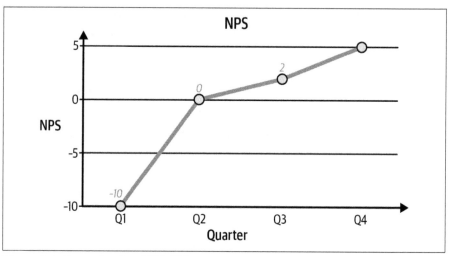

Figure 2-8. Example of an NPS KPI

Hours spent finding architecture information
    This should decrease over time as processes and training materials improve, as shown in Figure 2-9.

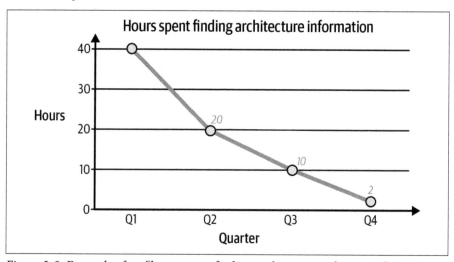

Figure 2-9. Example of an "hours spent finding architecture information" KPI

Here's an example lagging indicator:

Number of architecture decisions changed
    A high number or rate could indicate that the right information wasn't available, leading to a high degree of change.

Chapter 1 referred to architecture patterns as a typical architectural deliverable. In these sample KRs, I've also included a mention of architecture standards. That is just one more type of architecture information. The next section elaborates on architecture information.

What Is Architecture Information?

Architecture information refers to any type of architectural content that is used to inform an architecture decision. In addition to the architectural deliverables described in Chapter 1, which included architecture patterns, architecture decisions, capability target architectures, and application target architecture, architecture information is more generic and also typically includes principles, standards, frameworks, best practices, architecture diagrams, and metrics.

Architecture Principles

A principle is a rule or idea that guides you. An *architecture principle*, then, is simply the rules or ideas that guide consistent architecture decision making. The enterprise architecture strategy function should define architecture principles that are aligned with senior leadership's beliefs.

For example, an organization may define principles stemming from risk tolerance of vendor lock-in to make consistent build-versus-buy decisions when using cloud services. Some organizations may define cloud native as their principle, having decided that the benefits of using cloud native services outweigh the risks of lock-in. Others may define cloud agnostic as their principle, having decided that the benefits of being free from lock-in outweigh the risks of abstraction.

In this scenario, let's say an engineering team is trying to make an application architecture decision on whether or not to use a cloud native serverless functions service. In the organization that has the cloud native principle, they are likely to use it assuming the service meets all of their technical requirements. In the organization that has the cloud-agnostic principle, they are likely not to use it, and to stick with containerized services instead as the more portable option.

Either way, this principle will guide the organization's technical architecture decisions for its solutions, capabilities, and strategies—but only if the decision makers know about and understand what the principles are. Hence, the architecture principles must be transparently embedded and accessible to the decision makers.

Next, let's look at architecture standards.

Architecture Standards

An *architecture standard* defines the requirements that guide consistent architecture decision making to produce well-architected solutions and strategies. A *requirement* is something that must be true, and results in governance actions if violated. The enterprise architecture strategy function defines standards that the enterprise architecture enablement function empowers end users to meet, and that the enterprise architecture oversight function enforces is met.

Architecture standards can encompass any kind of technology requirement that an organization needs to support the business, and they are effective when that requirement can be both enabled and enforced. For example, an organization may define a standard as granular as what software languages are approved to build applications, or as broad as what makes an application modern. Enabling such standards is what the embedded and accessible objective helps with.

In addition to what must be true, architecture can also define what should be true. Let's first look at architecture frameworks as a type of architecture information that helps define what should be true.

Architecture Frameworks

Architecture frameworks define guidance—structure and methods—that can be used in architecture decision making. The enterprise architecture strategy function and all architecture roles can define reusable frameworks. It is usually not necessary to enforce the use of a specific framework, as they are usually meant to provide a baseline of helpful guidance.

For example, there are well-known enterprise architecture frameworks like TOGAF (*https://oreil.ly/8lsJb*). Many organizations also establish their own tailored architecture frameworks, such as a build-versus-buy assessment framework to guide architecture decisions around whether or not to develop or purchase software to fulfill a business need. In fact, this book is filled with frameworks in upcoming chapters for you to adapt and use as you see fit.

In addition to an architecture framework, the other kind of architecture information that helps define what should be true, and how it should be true, is architecture best practices. Let's look at them next.

Architecture Best Practices

A *best practice* in general is a proven way to do something better than alternative ways. An *architecture best practice* is a proven way to solve a problem that is usually defined in an architecture pattern. Best practices are typically not enforced with the same rigor as a requirement that is defined in an architecture standard.

An organization should define whatever architecture best practices are most relevant to the solutions it needs to deliver. For example, perhaps an organization is trying to modernize by using cloud technology. In that scenario, it would be beneficial to define best practices for migrating applications from on premises to the cloud, and for operating those applications in the cloud, rather than defining best practices for maintaining on-premises fleets. Again, these best practices only return the investment made in defining them when they are used—thus, making sure that these best practices are embedded and accessible to end users is essential.

Architecture Diagrams

An *architecture diagram* is a visualization that explains characteristics of a solution or process. The enterprise architecture strategy function should define standards around diagramming for consistency and easy understanding across multiple diagrams. These standards should include types of diagrams, any industry standards used to model the diagram, the tools used for the diagram, and the legend of colors, shapes, and lines used in the diagram.

Architecture diagrams can be very helpful visual aids to illustrate logical boundaries, concepts, workflows, and sequences, to name a few things. However, they risk becoming stale quickly, where the information is out of date. Thus, freshness and dynamism are important elements of embedded and accessible architecture diagrams. How do I keep an architecture diagram living? How do I codify an architecture diagram so that it is in code, generatable, and queryable rather than a static drawing? These are questions that you should answer as part of your KRs in the embedded and accessible objective.

Architecture Metrics

A *metric* is a quantifiable measurement or evaluation of something. An *architecture metric* is therefore a quantifiable measurement in the context of an architectural concern. If you recall, I started this chapter with an emphasis on measuring business outcomes as a result of architecture deliverables.

Architecture metrics are another architecture information type because they help inform architectural decisions. For example, metrics around total cost of ownership and return on investment can make a compelling business case for investing in one technology over another. As another example, metrics around enterprise architecture standard adoption and requirement adherence can tell a factual story around what is working well and what needs improvement in enabling and enforcing those standards.

Now that we've reviewed typical architecture information types that can inform architecture decisions, let's go into the relationship between them a bit more.

Architecture Information Powers Architecture Decisions

I mentioned earlier that architecture information needs to be embedded and accessible to inform architecture decisions. Figure 2-10 shows the relationship between architecture information content types and the architecture decisions that are strengthened by using them at a high level.

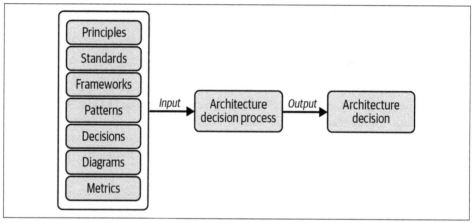

Figure 2-10. Architecture decisions powered by architecture information

For example, let's say an application architecture decision needs to be made around high availability design, where the business states they need high availability. The following inputs would apply to the decision makers:

Principles
Guidelines such as what constitutes a fault domain, cloud native versus not

Standards
Requirements such as recovery time objective and recovery point objective

Patterns
Best practices around highly available application architectures

Decisions
Previous decisions around scaling, monitoring and alerting, database type

Diagrams
Visualizations of the application's deployment architecture

Another example in the solution architecture space could be around an architecture decision for investing in a new capability. The following inputs would apply to the decision makers:

Principles

Principles such as modernization

Standards

Requirements such as technology standards for capabilities—is there already an existing technology solution that meets the new capability need?

Frameworks

Build versus buy, domain-driven design

Decisions

Previous decisions on related capabilities

Last but not least, an example in the enterprise architecture space could be around an architecture decision such as a new technology standard, like standardizing on a database type:

Principles

Principles such as vendor stickiness, modernization

Frameworks

Frameworks such as analysis of alternatives

Decisions

Previous decisions on related standards

Thus, you can see how there are various types of architecture information that need to be available to a given architecture role, and to all the partners that they have in making a decision, at the time that the decision needs to be made.

Chapter 4 discusses common mechanisms for making such information available.

 The more embedded, accessible, and just-in-time available architecture information is, the more reuse and efficiency you get from it being able to inform architecture decisions.

With this embedded and accessible objective and KRs, architecture information will be more effectively used in both making architecture decisions and adhering to architecture standards. Speaking of adhering to architecture standards, let's look at an objective that ensures they are effective.

The Enable and Enforce OKR

Architecture standards and their requirements can be much maligned if they are enforced with a heavy hand when teams are not enabled to easily adhere to them. By *enabled*, I mean that the process or activity to conform to the standard is well defined, highly automated, and limits necessary friction.

If the opposite is true, meaning the process or activity to conform to the standard is ill defined and highly manual, and it has undue friction, be prepared for negative feedback and the perception of architecture as a bottleneck. For example, let's say an enterprise architecture standard requires applications to log using a specific schema and sending those logs to a centralized log analysis tool. If applications are flagged as noncompliant because they did not log or logged incorrectly, yet there is no automation, documentation, or support on what to log, how to log, and how to use the log analysis tool, software releases will get bogged down while engineers deal with this issue, and there will be several complaints to deal with.

Similarly, if there is enablement without enforcement, then the organization carries the risk that the standard will not be met in full. In such an opt-in model, some teams will opt in, but enforcement is what verifies that all teams did. Let's go back to the logging example above. This time, let's say there is automation, documentation, and support available on what to log, how to log, and how to use that log analysis tool. However, in this example, there's no enforcement check, meaning applications do not get flagged as noncompliant. Because there is still a level of effort involved in adhering to the logging requirement, and getting the logs right, some teams end up skipping this requirement as a trade-off to release software ever faster. As a result, the risk that this requirement was trying to mitigate, pertaining to operational troubleshooting and mean time to repair for issues, is still a prevalent risk.

Thus, this objective is centered around both the enablement and enforcement of architecture standards. Chapter 5 discusses mechanisms and a framework to decide how to enable and enforce, and the trade-offs inherent in the degrees of enablement and enforcement.

Just enabling, or just enforcing, an architecture standard isn't enough. You need to do both to ensure the standard is effectively adopted.

Specific KRs will vary based on the sophistication of your organization's enablement and enforcement mechanisms. Here are some sample KRs:

- 100% of architecture standards are adopted by new technology development.
- Increased convergence to standard solutions by 20% (meaning alternatives are deprecated).
- Reduced level of effort by 20% to adhere to a given architecture standard.
- Improved satisfaction scores of architecture standards by 20%.
- Increased enablement automation of architecture standards by 20%.
- Increased enforcement automation of architecture standards by 20%.

The outcome of the enable and enforce objective is that the activity to adhere to an architecture standard or requirement is clear, well understood, and easily doable, and that the output of those activities is enforced in such a way to determine compliance. Again, so what? What is the business benefit of compliance?

Depending on the standard, the business benefit will differ. For example, a standard around highly resilient and reliable architecture would claim the business benefit of high availability, thereby helping maintain high customer satisfaction and protecting brand and reputation.

With this in mind, leading indicators should be framed around the business benefit of the standard and will vary based on the standard.

Examples of lagging indicators include the following:

Number or % of violations
    This should trend down lower over time, else it indicates a flawed enablement or standard.

Number or % of overrides
    This should trend down lower over time, else it indicates that perhaps the standard itself should be revisited.

Number or % of preventive controls
    This ideally trends higher over time, because preventing a compliance issue as early as possible is generally better.

Number or % of detective controls
> This ideally plateaus over time, as controls shift toward preventive.

Number or % of automated controls
> This ideally increases over time toward 100% coverage, since automation is generally more sustainable than manual enforcement.

Number or % of automated enablement activities
> This ideally increases over time toward 100% coverage, since automation is generally more scalable than manual.

While the enable and enforce objective has to do with architecture standards, it is also worth thinking through KPIs for the effectiveness of the architecture standards themselves.

Architecture Standard KPIs

The objective of an efficient set of architecture standards is that they create high-quality target architectures. This applies whether the scope of that architecture is a single component of an application, the application itself, a group of applications, or a group of capabilities.

What does *high-quality target architecture* mean to you? There are various ways to define *high quality*. What I recommend considering is that it results in well-architected applications that meet the following criteria:

Scalable
> The application can expand or compress based on demands in an automated manner.

Resilient
> The application is able to recover swiftly from failure, usually through automated means.

Reliable
> The application mitigated risks of critical failures caused by dependencies and its own deployment architecture such that it can withstand failures without loss of data or available critical transactions.

Cost-optimized
> The application has traded off on cost levers in its deployment architecture for a cost-optimal design.

Functional
> The application meets business requirements.

Future-proof
> The application has an optimized amount of technical debt, allowing it to easily adapt to changes.

Aligned
> The application has alignment across all of its impacted stakeholders to build or buy in accordance with the defined architecture.

Secure
> The application protects data and aligns with cybersecurity principles.

Modular
> The application is able to be independently deployed into an ecosystem and reused in that ecosystem without adverse impact to other solutions.

Extensible
> The application has well-defined interfaces, allowing for growth and interoperability.

Compliant
> The application is compliant or has approved exceptions to all policies, standards, and procedures that apply to it.

With this framing, leading indicators focused on high-quality application architecture include these examples:

Cost to deliver application
> If this is higher than expected, it may indicate that the application isn't cost optimized and can adversely impact net profits.

Incidents caused by application
> If this is higher than expected, it may indicate that the application isn't built to be scalable, resilient, and/or reliable and needs corrective action or it can adversely impact the company's brand and reputation.

Lagging indicators focused on high-quality application architecture include this example:

Number of approved architecture exceptions associated with application
> If this is higher than expected, it may indicate that a level of risk has been accepted for this application that can cause adverse impact in its compliance and operational postures.

To deliver the enable and enforce objective, let's review some principles that you can establish in your organization.

Principles for Enablement

The principles illustrated in Figure 2-11 help guide investment in the work necessary to enable software engineering teams to adopt and adhere to architecture standards.

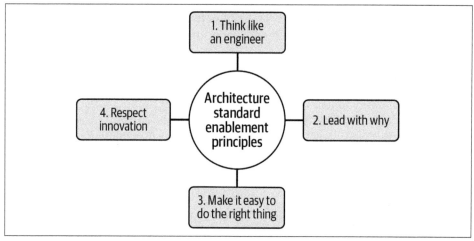

Figure 2-11. Architecture standard enablement principles

The first principle, *think like an engineer*, is first and foremost because the engineer role is, after all, the target audience of an architecture standard. They are the ones who need to understand the standard and be enabled to adopt it. What do they need to know about the standard? When do they need to know it? What is different for them now that they need to follow a standard? How are they going to use the provided tools and process in their day-to-day work? The more you think like an engineer when determining the best method of enablement, the more optimal your enablement solution will be.

The second principle, *lead with why*, builds on the same theme as mentioned earlier in the section "The Shared Alignment OKR" on page 32, which is that it is important to get human buy-in on a standard. Clearly and transparently communicating the context of the standard and requirement in terms of why it is a requirement, what risks it mitigates, and how to meet it, avoids confusion and increases the chances that the requirement will be adequately fulfilled. In addition, it is helpful to clarify roles and responsibilities for compliance—who does what, when, and how during the activities necessary to be compliant to the requirement. Last but not least, it is also helpful to be transparent about any constraints or known pain points to set expectations and reduce extemporaneous efforts. Excellent, well-maintained documentation is a helpful mechanism to provide such communication.

The third principle, *make it easy to do the right thing*, may appear self-explanatory. Software engineering teams have a lot of demands on their time. As a result, the simpler that you can make enablement, through reduced process and increased automation, the more you will incentivize the right behaviors for compliance. Also, make it easy for engineers to scale enabling automation with a contribution model and incorporate a feedback loop so that the enablement mechanism continuously improves and encourages more adoption. In addition, ensure that there are sufficient support and resources—both for training and for troubleshooting help.

The last principle, *respect innovation*, is something that I personally believe in strongly. While the premise of the *enable and enforce* objective is around supporting standards, enablement is generally about *how* to meet a requirement in a compliant way. Often, flexibility is needed given that there is generally more than one way to solve for a how. This principle speaks to understanding when to force uniformity and when to allow for deviations, as well as when to include a feedback loop in the enablement mechanism such that deviations can become new valid conformance options. This can manifest as decisions around when to abstract versus when to give choice, such as in a configuration option.

I've used these principles in real life to enable and enforce personal standards too. For example, one standard rule that we have in my household is to take off shoes and put them away when entering our home. Along with my children, I even had to change my behavior and build a better habit of putting away shoes (you see, I originally was in the habit of just kicking them off by the door). So we thought about the end user—in this case, the kids and me—to figure out what would be easiest for them, which turned out to be individualized shelves in a cubby. We lead with why by explaining and reiterating why we were a shoeless household, and why cluttering the front door was a bad idea. We made the right behavior easy by keeping the shoe cubby close to the door. We respected innovation by using the kids' suggestion to keep rain boots separate and my husband's suggestion to get shoe organizers to maximize the cubby space.

Now that we've looked at principles for enablement, let's elaborate on principles to guide enforcement of architecture standards.

Principles for Enforcement

The principles illustrated in Figure 2-12 help guide investment in the work necessary to enforce that software engineering teams adopt and adhere to architecture standards in a compliant manner.

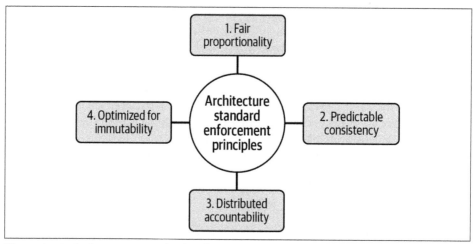

Figure 2-12. Architecture standard enforcement principles

The first principle, *fair proportionality*, refers to ensuring that the consequence of the compliance violation is reasonably commensurate with the risk or threat posed by that offense. If the risk or threat is considered to be critical, then and only then is the most severe consequence taken—for example, an alert that summons on-call support, or termination of the violating resources, or blocking the deployment of the noncompliant software. Whereas if the risk or threat is low, then a less severe consequence occurs, such as a notification with a time period in which to rectify the error. Instilling a fair and proportional system of enforcement will reduce backlash and drive human behavior to pay attention to the most risky violations, therefore optimizing the usage of human judgment and time to rectify the error.

The next principle, *predictable consistency*, complements the first one. It means that the software engineer can expect the same behavior for a pass or fail of an enforcement policy. It doesn't matter if the policy is run in different environments, or at different enforcement points; the same outcome occurs. Furthermore, when coupled with fair proportionality, the same type of consequences occur for similarly assessed risk violations. This consistency in defining the risk level of the requirement and consistency in resulting compliance actions allows for humans to learn the right behaviors more quickly than when faced with inconsistent enforcement.

For example, a simple schema that supports fair proportionality and predictable consistency to assess the risk of a standard requirement violation could be as follows:

Critical

Immediate corrective action needed. If enforced during deployment, deployment is blocked until the issue is corrected. If enforced post-deployment, then a high severity incident is created and incident management is used to correct the issue and/or resources are terminated/quarantined.

High

Near-term corrective action is needed, where "near term" is a specific consistent period of days. If not corrected within that near-term period, then the issue is escalated to critical. If enforced during deployment, deployment is blocked but allows for escalation approval to override blocking behavior. If enforced post-deployment, then a low severity incident is created and incident management is used to correct the issue.

Moderate

Mid-term corrective action is needed, where "mid term" is a specific consistent period of days. If not corrected within that mid-term period, then the issue is escalated to high. If enforced during deployment, deployment can proceed with a warning. If enforced post-deployment, an alert is generated.

Low

Long-term corrective action is needed, where "long term" is a specific consistent period of days. If not corrected within that long-term period, then the issue is escalated to moderate. If enforced during deployment, deployment can proceed with a warning. If enforced post-deployment, an alert is generated.

The third principle, *distributed accountability*, refers to that right behavior. This principle is all about ensuring that the software engineer understands and cares about what actions they are accountable for (and in many cases, also responsible for). Empathize with the plight of the software engineer and the demands of their time to drive automation as a high priority in enforcement. Automation should reduce the amount of human decision making and limit what requires human judgment, thereby saving the engineer time. Automation can encompass a range of things associated with enforcement, such as checking for the violation (the earlier the better), correcting the violation, and providing a self-service dashboard. Note, the engineer still needs to understand what the automation did and why to fully support their software application. While it is ideal to never have a compliance issue, if in fact there is one, it is best to allow for failing fast and failing early, to correct as early as possible and reduce duplicative issues or entirely deter future violations. It is also helpful to provide a feedback loop for the scenario in which the enforcement policy is incorrect or does not recognize a valid exclusion from the compliance requirement.

The fourth principle, *optimize for immutability*, recognizes that enforcement capabilities themselves require investment, especially given the ever-changing landscape of risks and threats as technology and standards rapidly evolve. To optimize this investment, it is best practice to enforce or check for a compliance violation only at the times or points of the software development lifecycle that it is possible to make a change that affects that compliance posture. Also, in the spirit of distributed accountability, it may be helpful to have a testing period or early warning period for new or changed enforcement policies to ensure they are working as expected prior to releasing them with full enforcement powers.

Applying these principles should help to provide a positive, scalable enforcement experience that aims for willing cooperation over compulsion yet verifies for assurance in a consistent, reasonable, and proportional way.

So far, you've learned about three OKRs: creating shared alignment, making architecture information embedded and accessible, and, most recently, enabling and enforcing standards. What's left? Glad you asked! Next up: the proactive and reactive OKR.

The Proactive and Reactive OKR

The nature of the decision itself is missing—is the architecture decision *proactive* or *reactive*? *Proactive* means trying to control the future situation, considerations, and trade-offs by predicting what the future holds. Proactive architecture decisions are strategic, and high-quality proactive architecture decisions are future-proofed and sustainable. *Reactive* means using already occurring information and considerations to make a more tactical decision. Reactive generally means that there is some sort of trigger, stimulus, or constraint causing a problem that needs to be solved.

If you think of a set of weighing scales measuring the number of proactive and reactive decisions, one extreme or the other is not where you see the most benefit. Proactive strategy without reactive tactics isn't helpful because then the strategy is rendered infeasible and therefore indefensible. Similarly, reactive tactics without proactive strategy isn't enough—it will ultimately take longer to get to where you want to go, since you're only ever solving the problems of today rather than the big picture problems of tomorrow.

Can you think of a real-life example where this applies? For me, my kids' wardrobe comes to mind. My children are still growing, and every year they need a different clothing size. If I am only reactive, then the day comes where they are dressed in too-small clothes, with no other recourse. If I am proactive, then I buy the next size up in advance so that on that day, they can change into the next size. I can't be overly enthusiastic in my proactiveness, though, and buy a whole set of clothes in the next size, because their tastes may change, or buy clothes two or three sizes up, because my storage is limited. So I balance the proactive and reactive decision making to future-proof their clothing enough that they will always have something that fits, and then react to the information that they need new clothes to buy more when needed.

Thus, the final objective of an effective enterprise architecture strategy is around promoting a balance of proactive and reactive architecture decisions. By being proactive and reactive to technology and business trends in the industry and within the organization, architecture can be more effective at defining the future direction. This future direction can then be based on a well-formed proactive strategy with well-defined reactive tactics to achieve it.

Specific KRs will vary based on your organization's tolerance for change. A sample KR would be a 20% increase in the number of approved architecture strategies.

The outcome of the proactive and reactive objective is that architecture decisions are made in anticipation of future problems and outcomes, and they also solve current relevant problems. The business benefit is that the architecture actually is defining strategic intent, that north star that we discussed in Chapter 1, in an aspirational yet achievable way.

An example of a lagging indicator could include the number of approved architecture strategies. Assuming these are good-quality strategies, the more strategy the more direction has been clarified.

Summary

To establish a strong, effective enterprise architecture practice, you need a strategy to guide and establish that effective enterprise architecture practice itself. This chapter covered key objectives in such a strategy aided by the OKR framework to define clear, measurable OKRs. Measurement is key, to tie architecture work to business outcomes. Outcome-based KRs are also known as *key performance indicators* (KPIs). KPIs are used to indicate progress toward an objective and to incentivize behavior.

The objectives include:

Shared alignment
> This relies heavily on a culture of trust throughout the organization to bring relevant stakeholders together and align on an architecture decision for implementation. This section covered management principles such as disagree and commit, command and control, and consensus based or consensus driven to achieve alignment.

Embedded and accessible
> This refers to ensuring that various types of architecture information, including but not limited to principles, standards, patterns, best practices, frameworks, and previous decisions, are embedded in everyday processes and tooling and accessible or usable by the end users that are meant to use the information in making architecture decisions.

Enable and enforce

This reviewed the need to both enable and enforce architecture standards, or rather the requirements associated with those standards. This section also covered relevant principles for guiding enablement activities as well as for guiding enforcement solutions.

Proactive and reactive

This discussed the need to both make and balance strategic and tactical architecture decisions.

Achieving these objectives should yield efficient architecture practices that create shared alignment, are embedded and accessible through familiar processes and tooling, are enabled and enforced transparently and intuitively, and support both proactive and reactive problem-solving.

The next four chapters dive deep into each objective so that you can tailor the OKRs and KPIs to what your organization needs to establish an effective enterprise architecture strategy.

CHAPTER 3

Shared Alignment

The heart of an effective enterprise architecture strategy is creating shared alignment for architecture decisions. In Chapter 2, you learned that creating shared alignment means that all impacted stakeholders are aligned to adhere with an architecture decision, even if they don't necessarily agree with that decision or would have preferred an alternative. You also learned that a culture of trust is foundational to achieve alignment. In this chapter, you'll go deeper to better understand mechanisms that you can use to create shared alignment and the culture of trust that is a prerequisite for it.

Did you know that enterprise architecture as a function is uniquely positioned to bring a group of individual stakeholders together with a common goal? It is unique because enterprise architecture is concerned with a holistic perspective and solving problems with the whole company in mind. This is different from organizational functions like engineering, business development, and cybersecurity. Whereas these functions do work toward the company's common goal, such as increasing business revenue, each function tends to focus on solving its own problems first. For example, cybersecurity may seek additional protections and risk mitigations, while engineering may seek to modernize, and business development may seek to penetrate new markets. Only enterprise architecture is positioned to look across all of these functional areas to define the north star as a modernization strategy with security built in to allow for new market growth.

To establish an effective enterprise architecture practice, you must transform teams of individuals to teams of a collective whole, and you need to do that at scale. While enterprise architecture as a function enables architect roles (enterprise, solution, and application) to chart paths into the unknown and define the north star of technology strategy and technology solutions, the paths need to be implemented by the efforts of partners such as engineering, product, and cybersecurity. This is necessary whether the north star guidance is as broad as an enterprise strategy or as narrow as a single application. At the broadest level the partners are at senior leadership level, whereas at the most granular level the partners are specific to a single application team.

A real-life example is the construction of a house. I'm sure you would agree that it does no good for an architect to create great blueprints if the construction manager can't find the building materials to build them or the electrician is nowhere to be found to do the wiring because they're too busy with other jobs and priorities. Whereas, if the architect, construction manager, and electrician worked together from the beginning, they could have come up with a feasible blueprint and aligned schedules to make the delivery work—for them, and for their customer.

Effective enterprise architecture as an organizational function can set the course for bringing stakeholders together to work collectively. The first step to creating shared alignment for an architecture decision begins with knowing who needs to align.

Align on Who

Knowing who needs to be engaged and aligning them on the problem statement along with, and prior to, aligning them on the solution, is essential to the success of architecture work. If the wrong stakeholders are included, then the credibility of the decision is likely to be undermined, the decision is likely to be ignored and not get implemented, and the decision is likely to be relitigated once the right stakeholders get involved.

Have you ever gone through a long, arduous collaboration process to get to a decision only to find out, after the decision was approved, that some key stakeholders had been missed in the impact analysis or that you had the wrong approver? I have, and it is exceedingly frustrating to be in this circumstance. It took me some time to understand that it didn't matter how good of a job I did in thinking through my analysis and recommendations if I didn't bring the right stakeholders along with me on that decision-making journey.

Fortunately for me, I have the benefit of project management and consulting experience to draw from, and I learned several techniques around stakeholder management that I can now share with you to help prevent such frustrating scenarios from occurring.

So, what exactly do I mean by a stakeholder? Let's find out.

What Is a Stakeholder?

A *stakeholder* refers to a person or group that is *impacted* by the decision, has *authority* over the decision, and/or is a *subject matter expert* in the decision's problem space.

Impact refers to any positive or adverse change that occurs as a result of implementing the decision's solution. Going back to my real-life house example, the homeowner is positively impacted, and the neighbors are also impacted, potentially in an adverse way during construction.

Authority refers to positional or designated ability to approve changes recommended by the decision. In the real-life house example, the construction manager has approval authority over his team to oversee the implementation work. It may also be necessary to attain a permit to do the construction work. The permit approver has authority over issuing that permit.

Subject matter expert (SME) refers to having the expertise necessary to vet the decision in terms of completeness, feasibility, and/or impact. For example, when considering a house, a housing inspector is the SME on housing regulations and can tell whether or not the house is compliant.

Now, when you think about all of the stakeholders that meet one or more of these criteria for your architecture decision, you may end up with a very long list. To filter or prioritize this list, you also need to consider the *influence* level of the stakeholder and the *importance* of the decision to that stakeholder.

Influence refers to the ability of the stakeholder to impact the outcome of the decision itself. High influence means that their dissent is a roadblock or impediment. For example, let's say a decision requires implementing a change to query logic of a reporting dashboard. The engineering and product owners of that reporting dashboard would be highly influential in that decision.

Importance means that the stakeholder has an internal or external motivation to be engaged in the decision-making process. An example of internal motivation is when the decision impacts an area that aligns with their interest or passion, and therefore they consider it important. Personally, my love for cloud technology drives my willingness to participate in strategic cloud-related decisions. An example of an external motivation is an organizational incentive; perhaps there's a reward or recognition for someone to be involved or the decision is important because it impacts the success of an initiative or solution that they own or the decision-making process requires their approval.

Figure 3-1 illustrates the dimensions of influence and importance in a quadrant chart.

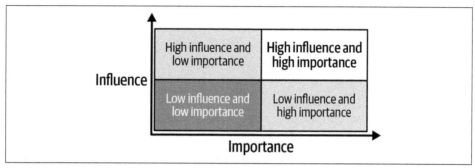

Figure 3-1. Stakeholder mapping to influence versus importance

The top right quadrant contains your key target stakeholders, those with high influence and high importance. These are the ones that need regular engagement in your decision-making process and need to be kept mollified. They should be engaged from the very beginning and throughout the decision-making process, and their engagement is quite active. For instance, they are invited to meetings, they review documentation, they are provided frequent updates, and they can provide comments. In the real-life house example, the homeowner and the construction manager are stakeholders in this quadrant.

The top left quadrant of stakeholders is important to consider and keep aligned because of the high influence that they wield. However, because they would consider this decision to be less important and therefore of less relevance to them, you likely only need to monitor them and reach out sporadically. For example, you could set up infrequent check-ins to ascertain their needs and provide briefings, or disseminate documentation as milestones in the decision making process are hit. Note, you may even need to convince them that they are key stakeholders by making a case for why this decision should be important to them. In the real-life house example, the permit approver is in this quadrant because construction cannot proceed without them yet they don't have a specific tie to any given construction project.

Stakeholders in the bottom right quadrant, low influence and high importance, are likely to be noisy if not engaged in some fashion, so it is best to keep them informed and abreast of updates, even if they are not actively part of the decision-making process. For example, let's say there is a decision that changes a key reporting metric and there are some power users that heavily use the metric in multiple downstream reports. The change is of high importance to the power users, but they could be deemed as low influence in that the change has to happen with or without their support. As it is usually better to have support, it would be good to give them a chance to be informed and react to the change early and provide feedback, even if they can't actually change the outcome of the decision. In the real-life house example, the neighbors fit this criteria.

The bottom left quadrant, low influence and low importance, means that these stakeholders are not needed in the decision-making process. Only if the decision actually impacts them would there need to be an effort to communicate essential relevant information once the decision is finalized. For instance, taking the same example above, of a decision that changes a key reporting metric, let's say this time there are only end users that sometimes use that metric. They would need to be notified to understand the change, but they would not necessarily be included in the decision-making process of the details of the change if they are mapped as low influence and low importance. In the real-life house example, the housing inspector fits in this quadrant; they need to know the house was built to do the inspection, but they are not directly involved in the decisions made to build the house.

To perform a stakeholder mapping, first brainstorm all the possible stakeholders against the criteria and then map them against the quadrant chart. You could use a table format like Table 3-1.

Table 3-1. Stakeholder mapping template

Name	Impact	Authority	SME	Influence	Importance
Person/Group	Yes/No	Yes/No	Yes/No	High/Low	High/Low

Table 3-2 shows using this mapping for the real-life example of the house.

Table 3-2. Stakeholder mapping example for building a house

Name	Impact	Authority	SME	Influence	Importance
Homeowner	Yes	Yes	No	High	High
Construction manager	Yes	Yes	Yes	High	High
Permit Approver	Yes	Yes	No	High	Low
Neighbors	No	No	No	Low	High
Housing Inspector	Yes	Yes	Yes	Low	Low

Your stakeholder mapping for a given architecture decision will tell you who needs to be *engaged* in making that architecture decision. But what exactly does engaged mean? The next section explains.

What Is Stakeholder Engagement?

Stakeholder engagement defines how to include a stakeholder and for what activity. *Engaged* means that a stakeholder is one or more of the following:

Responsible (R)
> This stakeholder ensures that all necessary decision-making process steps are followed, and they may also need to implement next steps.

Accountable (A)

This stakeholder ensures that the outcome of the architecture decision is realized.

Consulted (C)

This stakeholder provides inputs that help shape and strengthen the architecture decision.

Informed (I)

This stakeholder needs to be told about the decision, typically with respect to the result of the decision and transparency into who made the decision and with what considerations.

A common depiction of engagement is a RACI chart as shown in Table 3-3.

Table 3-3. RACI chart template

	Stakeholder 1	Stakeholder 2	Stakeholder 3	Stakeholder 4
Activity	A	R	C	I

There must only be one accountable stakeholder for each defined activity. Shared accountability doesn't work very well in practice since it diffuses and weakens accountable authority. That's very different from responsibility. While there must be at least one responsible stakeholder to ensure that someone does the activity, there can be more than one. The accountable stakeholder can also be responsible, though does not have to be. Overall, for an architecture decision-making process, for every activity, you need one accountable and at least one responsible stakeholder. Depending on the specific architecture decision, there may be none, one, or multiple consulted or informed stakeholders.

Table 3-4 provides an example RACI chart filled out for an architecture decision.

Table 3-4. Generic example of RACI chart applied to an architecture decision

	Architect	Engineering lead	Product lead	SME
Conduct analysis of alternatives	A/R	C	C	C
Complete proof of concept	A	I	I	R
Approve decision from business perspective	I	I	A/R	C/I
Approve decision from engineering perspective	I	A/R	I	C/I

In this example, the architect role is accountable and responsible for providing the analysis that goes into the decision. They actively collaborate with other stakeholders to vet and document the architecture decision. They also work with an SME to perform a proof of concept to validate their recommendation. (Note: as this is a generic decision, I've used the generic architect role rather than the more specific application architect, solution architect, or enterprise architect role. The type of architect, and seniority of architect, vary based on the scope of decision.)

The engineering lead is accountable and takes responsibility for the results of the decision from a technology perspective. They actively review and approve the decision from an engineering implementation perspective. The seniority of the engineering lead varies based on the scope of the decision and organizational structure.

Similarly, the product lead is accountable and takes responsibility for the results of the decision from a product perspective. They actively review and approve the decision from a product need and prioritization perspective. The seniority of the product lead varies based on the scope of the decision and organizational structure.

The SME is consulted to provide input and vet the alternatives and analysis conducted in the decision. They bring relevant subject matter expertise in the business and/or technology referenced by the decision to strengthen the decision.

Your RACI should be a transparent artifact that sets the expectations of the stakeholders that you engage with. That transparency up front also allows them the ability to confirm whether or not they are in fact the right stakeholder for that specific level of involvement. For instance, you may end up with an accountable stakeholder providing you with delegates that are responsible, such that the responsible stakeholders are engaged in day-to-day collaboration and the accountable stakeholder just needs to be debriefed periodically. You may find out that you need a higher level of seniority to be your accountable lead.

It is very important to complete this confirmation step as part of your stakeholder mapping process. Otherwise, you may risk making false assumptions of who is your stakeholder, and how they should be engaged.

What if your stakeholder map ends up with an unmanageable number of stakeholders with whom to engage? For that, let's look at scaling stakeholder engagement.

How Do You Scale Stakeholder Engagement?

Especially for transformational decisions that impact the entire enterprise or organizational units, it is impossible to directly include every stakeholder that will be impacted by that decision. Rather, the organization should have a culture of trust such that there is a trusted individual that can serve as the authoritative representative of a group, an organizational unit, or a functional area in the enterprise and can voice the larger group's opinion.

In an organization in which consensus is deeply rooted, it may be beneficial to include a *request for comment* (RFC) period as part of the transparent decision-making process. RFC allows for a large group to be invited to consult on the proposal beyond the SMEs that are directly involved in collaborative meetings. It can also be helpful to timebox a decision, meaning give a deadline. That way, there is a finite time period in which to debate and then come to a conclusion, rather than perpetually bring in more and more stakeholders for input and/or drag on the discussions.

In addition, for all types of organizations, the decision-making process should be very transparent and well documented. That way, the reasoning for the decision, the alternatives considered, the implications identified—all of that is available for people who were not directly involved in making the decision to better understand the decision. This transparency is also helpful if you need to include new stakeholders along the way because of organizational changes or because new impacts are identified as part of the decision-making process.

How Does "Align on Who" Relate to Your Effective Enterprise Architecture Strategy?

Knowing who to include, and how exactly to engage them, is essential to creating shared alignment. How does knowing this help you in your organization? Well, as part of establishing the objective of creating shared alignment, consider the maturity of your organization. Are there processes or organizational elements that need to be improved to do the following?

Clarify stakeholder role definitions
Do definitions exist? Are people aligned with them? Is there training to confirm that understanding?

Clarify stakeholder engagement for activities relating to architecture decisions
Do RACI charts exist? Do people understand them? Do people use them? Is there an authorization hierarchy that is well understood?

Provide mechanisms for stakeholder mapping
Are templates available? Do architects understand how to do a stakeholder mapping? Is there a baseline defined for the enterprise that enterprise leadership aligns to, which can be tailored as needed for a given architecture decision? Are stakeholders included consistently in decision-making workflows?

Increase trust between stakeholders
Are stakeholders incentivized to work as a team? Is leadership advocating for collective goals?

Increase transparency in architecture decision-making process
Does such a process exist? Does tooling exist to support that process? Is it easy to find decision documentation? Is an RFC process needed, and if so, is it operational? Is there consistent execution of these processes?

Any gaps or improvement opportunities become inputs into your specific key results (KR) for this strategic objective. For example, maybe your organization doesn't have shared alignment on architecture roles and how to engage them. In that situation, that could be the first KR that your enterprise architecture strategy function goes after, to define a baseline stakeholder role definition and stakeholder engagement RACI that your senior leadership agrees with. Maybe the enterprise architecture enablement function provides templates and tooling. Perhaps the enterprise architecture enforcement function comes up with requirements around engagement at key points of the software delivery lifecycle. The details of the KRs will vary by organization, but if you assess your organization and figure out where the highest-leverage opportunities are, you can turn those opportunities into specific KRs that are relevant to your organization.

To identify who is engaged in an architecture decision, I mentioned earlier that you'll want to consider who is impacted by the decision. To understand who is impacted, it is necessary to have a well-grounded understanding of the decision's problem statement to identify those impacts. Let's look at this in detail in the next section.

Align on the Why

If the stakeholder doesn't care about the problem, understand the benefit of solving that problem, and/or understand the need to solve it now, then there is very little prospect that they will engage in problem-solving in the desired timeline and align with the recommended solution that is documented in an architecture decision.

The first act of engaging the stakeholder is to review the problem statement and ensure that you and the stakeholder are interpreting the problem statement the same way. It is very easy to assume that stakeholders understand the problem, but I found from my experience that people often talk past each other instead of to each other to define a shared understanding.

So, methodically state the problem statement, but do so in a way that sells its value and makes it clear that solving the problem will provide a collective gain.

Sell the Why

When defining a problem statement, ensure that you *sell the why*, which means that you are able to clarify the following to avoid conflicting goals:

- Why this problem? What is the context for it?
- Why now? Why not later?
- What's the impact in business terms of this problem?

The mistake that I have made and often see is stopping with stating what the problem is, rather than emphasizing why that problem is impactful.

To make this less abstract, here are two real-life problems that I experienced while writing this paragraph today:

1. My car doesn't have enough gas to get very far.
2. We are missing a main ingredient for our dinner.

Which of these problems do I tackle first? Do I get gas or go grocery shopping?

To answer that, I need to first understand the impact. Problem number 2 is impactful because without that main ingredient, we will have no dinner, and we need to eat. It definitely needs to be solved. Problem number 1 is only impactful if I need to use my car to drive somewhere. Thus, most likely I will table problem number 1 until I need to drive, and solve problem number 2 by walking to the grocery store. On the other hand, if I was dealing with time pressure, I would get gas on the way to the grocery store, thereby solving both problems together. There's no right or wrong answer here; it's more that thinking through impact is more helpful for problem-solving than just stating what the problem is.

Along with articulating impact, you also need to state the *benefits* of solving the problem. By *benefits*, I am referring to tangible, positive business outcomes that help attain business objectives. The reason I stress business outcomes here is because effective architecture marries the usage of technology to business needs; it is only in delivering business value that the architecture work delivers value. Ask yourself these questions:

- What business objective is achieved or what progress is made toward that objective?
- Who benefits if the problem is solved?
- Are there ways to expand the benefits, either to more stakeholders or to more reuse?

Business benefits are often stated in terms of the following:

Financial benefits
 Include cost reduction, increased cost efficiency, improved return on investment, avoidance of future costs, and increased profits or revenue

Risk benefits
 Include risk reduction or mitigation

Productivity benefits
 Include reducing level of effort, increasing human productivity rates, faster time to market, improved employee satisfaction, increased employee retention, and increased operational efficiency

Branding or reputation benefits
Include increased quality of service, reliability of service, improved customer satisfaction, and increased loyalty

I highly recommend quantifying as much as you can. It is much more compelling to have quantitative data for the problem statement's impact and benefits than it is to have qualitative assertions. For example, a 20% productivity improvement is more compelling and easier to understand than stating that solving the problem would help increase productivity. Be sure to ground your qualitative output in a credible basis, such as historical precedent, assumptions, and/or anecdotal evidence that is then extrapolated.

 Get into the habit of sizing the problem, sizing its impacts, and sizing its benefits.

Let's review an example:

Attempt #1: "This problem causes challenges for our developers."

This problem statement is very weak. So what if it causes challenges? Developers face tons of challenges.

Attempt #2: "This problem causes challenges that waste developers' time."

Better, but still not getting a sense of scale. Is this a papercut or a true blocker?

Attempt #3: "This problem causes challenges that waste 20% of the average developer's capacity every release cycle. Fixing this problem will enable 1.5x new business features to be developed every quarter."

If I'm a business stakeholder, I now care. I want more features! If I'm a technology stakeholder, I care. I want to free up my most precious resource, human developers! If I'm a cybersecurity stakeholder, I don't care yet.

Attempt #4: "This problem causes challenges that waste 20% of the average developer's capacity every release cycle. Fixing this problem while incorporating security controls will enable 1.5x new business features to be developed every quarter safely."

Boom! Now, as a cybersecurity stakeholder, I can tell that my expertise will be needed in a consultative manner. As a business and technology stakeholder, I know that I will be accountable and responsible for this decision for my particular areas of responsibility. As a developer, I am excited to see this decision get made, because it benefits me.

 Always ask yourself "So what?" when you review a problem statement, to help you define the *why*.

Now that you have a compelling problem statement that clearly articulates impact and benefit, you are one step further on your journey to get shared alignment. However, sometimes, you may find that even with the best-written problem statement, your stakeholders still don't agree that the problem has to be solved right now. What happened? Most likely, a priority mismatch.

Align on Priority

I've been in situations where stakeholders agree that there is a problem, and that it would in fact be good to solve it, but, because there were higher-priority fires burning that absolutely had to be solved right now, that this one would have to wait. The capacity of human resources, after all, is a finite resource.

What's a passionate architect to do in this situation?

1. Get really frustrated and quit.
2. Try again to build a more compelling business case.
3. Disagree and commit to helping with the burning fire, so that you can come back to the problem that you really care about later.

If I thought I had misunderstood the importance factor and did not make the argument as relevant or compelling as it could have been based on the stakeholder's motivations, I would probably put some effort into number 2. If I thought that the return on investment (ROI) really wasn't there for the problem as compared with others, then I would likely do number 3, but I would still get commitment from the stakeholders that they would revisit and evaluate at a later time.

To prevent getting to this frustrating point, get familiar with that stakeholder's prioritization framework. This would be the criteria that they use to prioritize what work must be done versus what work should be done versus what work needs to wait or not be done. Common criteria include impact and benefits, which were discussed earlier in this chapter. The others tend to be effort, investment, and risk. *Effort* refers to level of effort, or human labor. How many stakeholders need to be involved and for how long? What kind of capacity is required? *Investment* refers to a material stake; for example, will a proof of concept be needed that requires infrastructure or third-party resources? *Risk* refers to all types of risk—technology, cybersecurity, business—is any new risk incurred by deviating resources to work on this?

Ultimately, you're trying to make the business case that there is more value to be gained than there is effort needed, whether you're trying to get alignment just to execute the decision-making process or you're trying to get alignment to execute on implementation after an approved decision.

How Does "Align on the Why" Relate to Your Effective Enterprise Architecture Strategy?

Knowing how to align stakeholders on the problem statement, and why it is important to solve that problem now, is essential to creating shared alignment. How does knowing this help you in your organization? As part of establishing the objective of creating shared alignment, assess if there are processes or organizational elements that need to be improved for the following:

Clear strategic business objectives
Are there high-level enterprise objectives that new work can be aligned against?

Problem statement communication
Does your organization run on slideware? Whitepapers? Something else? Whatever it is, is there a template available for architects to use in this style to explain problem statements with quantitative benefits? Are there forums where leaders can be engaged to discuss problems and priorities?

Prioritization framework
Is there a consistent prioritization framework across the organization? Or at least within organizational units? Do those prioritization frameworks include referencing architecture decisions?

Now that the stakeholders have been identified and aligned with the why, it's time to discuss how to get alignment on the decision itself.

Align on the Decision

To gain shared alignment from your various stakeholders on the decision itself, you need to become adept at conflict resolution. Conflict during the decision-making process can actually be very positive, as this allows for diverse perspectives to be considered. Concerns can be transparently aired and addressed to strengthen the solution recommendation in the final decision.

There are many methods for conflict resolution. What follows is what I have seen work well from experience. The first part of my conflict resolution approach is to consider different perspectives.

Consider Differing Perspectives

Put yourself in a stakeholder's position. What are their motivations based on their role and responsibilities, historical record of actions, and goals? What concerns could they raise? What are they worried about, and what is their most pressing priority? How much context do they already have, and what information do they need? See Figure 3-2 for visualization.

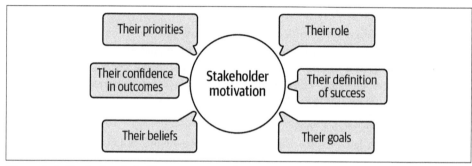

Figure 3-2. Typical stakeholder motivation drivers

You've actually done some amount of motivational analysis previously in your stakeholder mapping, when you determined how important the problem statement and solving it are to the stakeholder. If you have direct access to a stakeholder, a preexisting relationship, and/or experience with them, it is of course much easier to ascertain their motives. If you do not, though, which very well may be the case if you're working in a new area or if you are at a more junior level than the stakeholders that you need buy-in from, then you may need to do some detective work via networking first. Find peers who can get you information about their organizational purpose, and about them. Find a manager who might have better access than you do to make some introductions to people who can get you the insight that you seek.

To preclude relationship-based conflict where people don't get along, it is very important not to judge motivations and the concerns that stem from them. Rather, it is much more beneficial to review concerns with curiosity to truly understand them. This can be difficult, since people typically have predefined beliefs, biases, and assumptions that color concerns. Sometimes, emotions get involved, too. Even still, it is better to really listen to the stakeholder rather than to try and validate your own assumptions of how the stakeholder should be thinking.

For example, there were times in my career where I thought that a particular architecture decision was a no-brainer. The solution was based on thorough analysis, and it seemed to be a no-regrets move to go forward with it. However, sometimes I would get surprised when a stakeholder in a different area, like legal or cybersecurity, would balk at the solution. In those situations, I needed to take a step back and get rid of my preconceived notions to ask them what they were concerned about and why.

 Seek to understand other points of view with curiosity rather than defending your position. Invest in listening.

Getting concerns aired transparently is key to identifying the source of conflict. Your conversation skills can help do this, and that brings me to the second part of my conflict resolution approach, which is to foster positive conflict in conversation.

Foster Positive Conflict in Conversation

In conversations where the goal is to align stakeholders, I recommend the following:

Demeanor
> Be positive, open, approachable, and engaged. Be clear and concise. Acknowledge concerns and varying perspectives, even if you don't agree with them. Everyone wants to be respected, heard, and understood.

Be factual
> Separate facts from fiction. Sometimes people have firm beliefs that are not actually true.

Neutralize
> Beware of emotions. Diffusing tense situations typically requires a person to control their own emotions before they can diffuse others'.

Be humble
> Doing the right thing is more important than being right. And that could mean compromising, admitting when you were wrong, and/or changing your point of view of the right path forward.

Be confident
> Add value to the conversation by offering your point of view and your opinions.

Table 3-5 provides some prompts and revisions that you could use to help listen and align the stakeholder's views.

Table 3-5. Communication optimizations

Instead of...	Try to...
Being open-ended to solicit input, with statements such as "What do you think?"	Be more specific. For example, "What concerns do you have about this solution?"
Saying only "Great, thanks" to show you appreciate their input.	Play back what you heard: "Thanks! It sounds like...about..." Example: "Thanks! It sounds like you're concerned about introducing new risks with this solution." If you don't understand enough of what they said to play back, ask: "Thanks for sharing. Please tell me more. When you say new risk, what do you mean?"
Providing your point of view without acknowledging theirs, by saying, "I think this solution works well because..."	Share your point of view while acknowledging that you understand theirs: "I understand that this solution introduces a new risk, and here's my point of view on how we can mitigate that." Include them in problem-solving if you don't have an answer: "I understand how important it is to address new risks. What are some mitigation measures that we could take?"
Closing the conversation without gratitude. For example, "OK, we'll get back to you."	Manners and gratitude go a long way. Human connection is an essential basis of establishing trust. Remind the stakeholder that this is an "us" issue for the greater good: "I appreciate you sharing your concerns openly; thanks for taking the time to work through them together."

With these communication aids, your positive conflict conversations should be productive in that they raise the true concerns. Next, you have to deal with them productively. That brings me to the third and final part of my conflict resolution approach, which is to resolve the positive conflict.

Resolve the Positive Conflict

Document concerns as part of the trade-off analysis of the architecture decision to (a) show that you listened and (b) provide a tangible artifact for them to review and validate that you heard correctly. This is especially necessary if the concern needs to be accepted as a risk and cannot be ameliorated by changing the decision.

Speaking of documentation, make sure you also get alignment documented, in the form of concurrence or formal approval, either in meeting minutes or as part of the decision record. This documentation for posterity can be very helpful to avoid future rehashes of the same topic, and it also shows that the stakeholders really were on the same page and not just assumed to have been aligned.

Remember that you can *timebox* if you need to curtail chatter and bring about a resolution—whether that is a consensus-based resolution or a disagree-and-commit resolution. Timebox means putting a timeline against how long a decision will be debated before it is finalized.

Escalation is another mechanism, but it should be used sparingly. Escalation means going to someone with higher authority than the stakeholder expressing concerns to see if they can bring about alignment using their positional authority. Escalation is usually only necessary if the stakeholder refuses to disagree and commit, but it can also backfire if the root cause of the concern is not actually addressed, since the escalation authority may in fact have the same issue.

Get Commitment as a Result of Alignment

Just agreeing with a decision isn't enough. You also need commitment from stakeholders that the decision will be implemented. Commitment means that the stakeholders also feel that they have an obligation to ensure that the outcomes sought by the decision are actually achieved. The stakeholder clearly understands what part they play, and what value they bring, in getting to the overall collective goal.

Commitment means that there is follow-through on an implementation plan relating to the decision. The work required to implement the decision should be formally tracked and absorbed into however work is managed at your organization. It's a good idea to revisit the decision and celebrate joint successes when the outcome is achieved, or if the decision is for something complicated and long-lived, for the milestones as well. Also, if the people in a stakeholder's role change over time, then also make sure that they know about the previous commitments to be able to honor them.

Now that we've covered conflict resolution and commitment, let's see how they relate to your effective enterprise architecture strategy.

How Does "Align on the Decision" Relate to Your Effective Enterprise Architecture Strategy?

Knowing how to align stakeholders on the decision itself is essential to creating shared alignment. How does knowing this help you in your organization? As part of establishing the objective of creating shared alignment, assess if there are processes or organizational elements that need to be improved in the following areas:

Communication skills
    Is there training available for your talent? Are there preferred communication styles?

Cultural values
    Is positive conflict part of the cultural mindset? Is positive conflict embraced as part of collaboration, or is there conflict avoidance?

Accountability
    Do stakeholders understand accountability? Is there a culture of holding each other accountable for commitments?

With this basis of aligning on who, aligning them on the why, and aligning them on the decision, you should be in good shape to create shared alignment to a greater degree than what exists today.

Case Studies

Let's review a few case studies related to creating shared alignment and examine some thematic dos and don'ts that they reveal. Let's pretend that we're reviewing a software company called EA Example Company.

Let's look at the first scenario, *the mandate*.

The Mandate

EA Example Company had a problem. Software release after software release went to production rife with bugs and issues. Engineering teams were constantly in the mode of fixing incidents caused by changes. New features were being delayed.

The senior engineering executive—let's call him Tom—needed to solve this problem. He turned to his enterprise architecture team for help. The enterprise architecture team reviewed recent incident history and talked with some of the engineering teams involved in those incidents. They quickly determined that the root cause of this vicious cycle of bugs and issues was a lack of effective testing. If there was good-quality testing, then the bug or issue would have been caught earlier in the software delivery lifecycle, prior to the production release. The engineering team would still have to fix the bug or issue, but much earlier and under much less time pressure than when the issue became an incident. Further, if the testing was automated, then the volume of tests could scale more quickly to match the pace of desired releases.

Tom was excited to get this insight. He promptly issued a mandate that no code was to go to production without automated unit testing coverage of 90%.

Tom's engineering teams grumbled a bit, but because they were under a mandate, and that mandate was enforced by their deployment tooling, they complied. They spent side of desk time learning how to automate unit tests. They spent time developing unit tests, and changes that went to production did pass those unit tests.

However, EA Example Company noticed that there was still a trend of production incidents caused by changes, particularly those dealing with dependencies or integrations with other systems. In addition, employee satisfaction was declining.

What happened here? Let's take it point by point.

The enterprise architecture team engaged stakeholders—the engineering teams—to figure out the root cause of the problem. But they did not dig hard enough. Why was there a lack of testing efforts? Was testing incentivized by the organization? There are multiple types of testing; why focus only on the bare minimum of unit testing? Automated testing is easier said than done; where was the feasibility analysis for enablement?

The leadership gave a mandate to solve what they thought was the problem, but it wasn't quite the right problem, and there was a lack of stakeholder buy-in and enablement to conform to that mandate. There was no explanation provided to the engineering teams having to do the work. The engineering teams didn't have proper tools and processes to be successful. There was no priority trade-off allowing engineering teams to upskill in the automated testing needs. There was no trusted representative of the engineering teams to engage in the decision-making process.

So, to summarize, key takeaways from this tale are as follows.

Do:

- Engage stakeholders to validate assumptions and come up with a recommendation.
- Use mandates to enforce requirements if needed, but provide transparency into the mandate's rationale and benefits.

Don't:

- Blindly mandate metrics. Metrics drive behavior. In this case, the mandate incentivized greater unit testing code coverage without emphasizing the quality of the tests. Therefore, the outcome of improving incidents was not realized.
- Issue mandates without an explanation or without an understanding of the feasibility of adhering to that mandate.
- Ignore impacted stakeholders as part of the decision-making process.

Let's now take a look at another scenario, *the relitigation.*

The Relitigation

Jane spends a lot of time making architecture decisions. She does a stakeholder analysis and includes the right stakeholders to be accountable, responsible, consulted, and informed. She makes sure to document the decision, along with the decision's approval.

Over time, there are changes at EA Example Company, and as a result, there are new people in the roles of the former approvers. The new people aren't aware of the previous decisions, and they start directing contradictory work. Jane finds out and reviews the decisions with them. They decide that the decisions made by their predecessors are invalid, and therefore, new decisions need to be made. The decision-making process starts all over again.

What happened here?

Jane did all the right things in getting alignment to the original decision, but the decision was not lasting due to factors outside of her control. Apparently, there's an underlying issue of a lack of trust between the new set of stakeholders and the original set, and/or the stakeholders thought their way was better than the old way.

Key takeaways from this tale are summarized below.

Do:

- Consider the right stakeholders and follow a transparent decision-making process.
- Establish a culture of trust in the organization. It is always possible that decisions need to be refined if there is new information that changes an assumption or constraint that was considered in making the decision, but changing people should not invalidate a former decision.
- Define principles for consistent decision making.

Don't:

- Assume that new leaders understand why and how a previous decision was made. Recommunicate as needed, and keep documentation records.

Next, let's look at a scenario called *the silo*.

The Silo

EA Example Company needed to solve problems with data management and data privacy. The data management team included their solution architect, product lead, and engineering lead to come up with an architecture and solution for registering data and managing data lineage. Similarly, the data privacy team included their solution architect, product lead, and engineering lead to come up with a great architecture and solution for classifying data and filtering data access based on privacy rules. However, neither solution worked well with each other. Thus, engineering teams had to provide data classification information as part of the data management solution and as part of the data privacy solution. There were no cross-checks between them to gather insights into the data or scale the efforts around the data.

What happened here?

While each decision at a local level seemed like the right decision, when looked at together, it is clear that they were made in silo. Either the data management and data privacy architects should have engaged one another, or an overarching enterprise data architect should have been engaged to bring their efforts together. The stakeholder analysis was not done or missed the fact that the data management and data privacy solutions would impact one another.

Let's summarize the key takeaways from this tale.

Do:

- Ensure that all impacted stakeholders are identified and included.
- Share decisions.
- Promote collaboration between silos.

Don't:

- Assume limited impact from a given decision.

Now, let's look at another situation, called *the never-ending debate.*

The Never-Ending Debate

EA Example Company once experienced a conflict between two application architects, Jane and John. The compute layer of an application was already containerized but was running on a self-managed compute service that came with an infrastructure management tail. Tom, the engineering manager, thought it would be good to get out of the infrastructure management overhead, and he asked them for a decision on what cloud service technology to use for the compute layer of their application.

Jane had good experience with serverless compute and thought that was best. John, however, was adamant that containers were already a great compute option and they should just stick with that, but in a managed container service form. They both stuck to their convictions and could not come to an agreement. As a result, the engineering team did neither and stuck with their self-managed option.

What happened here?

It doesn't matter if Jane was right or if John was right. Because they could not agree on a direction, the engineering team ended up not doing anything differently and therefore did not get any benefit. Tom's problem was not solved, and he probably lost some trust in the role of application architects.

Ideally, either Jane or John could have taken the lead on conflict resolution. They could have set aside their differences to learn from one another on why they had such firm convictions on their solution outcome. They could have taken a step back to factually review the needs of the compute layer and compare that with the service capabilities to figure out the best option. They could have timeboxed their debate time, and, if all else failed, agreed to disagree and commit, to make progress. Any decision is usually better than no decision, assuming that the culture is OK with taking some amount of risk. Last but not least, they could have invested in taking some time to connect with one another to strengthen their own relationship.

Key takeaways from this tale are summarized below.

Do:

- Timebox decisions.
- Promote a culture of collective gain.
- Invest in relationships and human connection.

Don't:

- Refuse to compromise.

Summary

To achieve the shared alignment objective and tailor KRs for your own organization, consider any weak points in your organizational structure and/or processes that may hinder creating shared alignment across varied stakeholders. What can you strengthen to support stakeholder management?

First, you need to institute the mechanisms necessary to clearly identify who needs to be engaged in making the architecture decision and how they should be engaged:

- Are there techniques for stakeholder mapping, to identify who is impacted by this architecture decision, who wields the right level of influence, and who considers the impact important to them?
- Are there mechanisms for defining stakeholder engagement plans, where it is clear who needs to be accountable, who is responsible, who needs to be consulted, and who needs to be informed for all relevant activities?

Second, you need to establish mechanisms that allow for gaining alignment on the problem statement, and the priority of that problem statement:

- Is there any methodology, frameworks, or templates available to support defining problem statements in terms of impacts and business benefits, in quantifiable terms?

Third, you need a foundation to get alignment and commitment on the decisions themselves:

- What are the challenges that the organization faces in creating shared alignment? Are there cultural issues, such as a lack of trust? Are there pace issues, such as mismatched priorities? Are there talent issues, such as a lack of skill to provide the level of conversation needed to agree?
- Is there transparency in the architecture decision-making process? At every level of the organization? Are decisions well understood? By leadership? By teams?

Use this framework to diagnose weaknesses in your organization that you can strengthen through your enterprise architecture strategy objective and KRs for creating shared alignment. Next up, we'll go in detail on embedded and accessible architecture information.

CHAPTER 4

Embedded and Accessible

Chapter 2 shared that the second key strategic objective for an effective enterprise architecture strategy is to make architecture information embedded and accessible to all practitioners of architecture and their partners. It's important to be deliberate and thoughtful on what architecture information needs to exist, and how to make it easy for end users to understand and use it.

Have you ever felt overwhelmed with the amount of information that you're expected to consume and act on in a single day? Between emails, messaging applications, and websites, just a few ways that you see digital information on a daily basis, it is difficult to know what information to retain and when to use it. Do this, do that, know this, look up that, remember to tell that person something…the digital age of information is relentless.

Thus, when it comes to enabling great architecture decisions, it is necessary to be very deliberate in figuring out how to make architecture information available to all those involved in making an architecture decision. Solving this problem brings best practices together from *knowledge management* and *user interface* (UI)/*user experience* (UX) design.

This chapter reviews these concepts and also dives into common mechanisms, principles, and a framework that you can use to define key results (KRs) for the objective of making architecture information embedded and accessible.

Knowledge Management in Embedded and Accessible Architecture

Knowledge management is the processes and tooling around creating and using knowledge across an organization. An enterprise architecture organization is well positioned to establish knowledge management processes and tools around architecture information.

What Is the Goal of Knowledge Management?

The goal of knowledge management in an architecture context is to teach the users of the architecture information—architects, product managers, engineers—how to *apply* the knowledge gained from architecture information to solve similar or new problems. For example, it should be possible to understand a pattern about event-driven architecture and another pattern about extract, transform, and load (ETL) processes to apply them together in an application to process real-time data events.

It probably comes as no surprise to learn that I am a big believer and advocate of education and the power of knowledge. The reason that the second objective of an effective enterprise architecture strategy centers around making architecture information embedded and accessible is that it puts the power of architecture knowledge into the hands of those who most need to learn that knowledge to apply it to solving problems. And solving problems effectively and consistently needs to be done at scale—by all architects.

Chapter 3 established a culture of trust as a prerequisite for creating shared alignment. A culture of trust also applies to this objective. Only a culture that promotes knowledge sharing and the value of learning can support establishing an effective enterprise architecture strategy. The opposite of this culture is a competitive culture that actively inhibits transparency, openness, and sharing. Of course, a culture of trust doesn't mean ignoring data protections—confidential and sensitive data should not be as open as other kinds of information.

A culture of trust—with values of transparency, openness, and knowledge sharing—is a prerequisite to making architecture information embedded and accessible.

Now, that doesn't mean that there aren't differing levels of knowledge and expertise. Such differentiation may be necessary to consider in managing the architecture information. For a real-life example, take mathematics. To do calculus, you first need to learn precalculus, which in turn requires trigonometry, and so on and so forth, as illustrated by Figure 4-1.

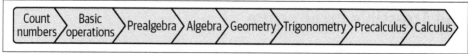

Figure 4-1. Example of knowledge progression using mathematics

Generally speaking, more people will need to know the simpler knowledge on the left than the more complex knowledge on the right. Similarly, with architecture information, everyone may need to understand architecture principles to apply them to decision making, but fewer people may need to understand complex architecture patterns like solving for eventual consistency in a multiregion system.

Although architecture information comes in different types, and has variances in the levels of comprehension needed, there is a common need to establish a knowledge management lifecycle to create, disseminate, and maintain that information.

What Is the Knowledge Management Lifecycle?

The enterprise architecture strategy function would define lifecycle management stages as shown in Figure 4-2 in detail for each architecture information type.

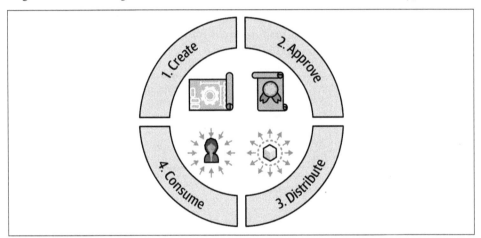

Figure 4-2. Knowledge management lifecycle applied to architecture information

Create refers to the initial stage of ideation and drafting the architecture information content. Consider who should create what architecture information type, how they should collaborate, and how to incentivize them to contribute information. There should always be an owner of architecture information that takes accountability and responsibility to keep the information fresh and accurate.

After the creation stage, it is possible to have an approval stage. Not *all* architecture information types need approval—only those that need to be curated, like standards. The desired level of veracity and quality of the architecture information type dictates the amount of rigor and layers of approval. For instance, more review and approval may be needed for a new architecture standard than for a new architecture pattern. As a result, you could end up with tailored approval workflows such as the example illustrated in Figure 4-3.

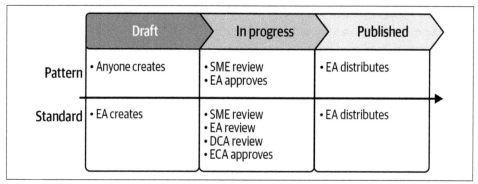

Figure 4-3. Example approval workflows demonstrating differentiation in approval layers

The *distribute* stage refers to disseminating the information out to the end users. The most common mechanisms for making architecture information available in this stage are *push* and *pull*, as described in Figure 4-4.

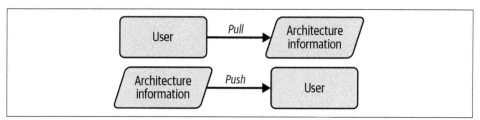

Figure 4-4. Pull versus push mechanism

Push means that the source of the information provides the information to the human user. This is generally a passive way for the human user to consume information. For example, an organization may use email newsletters to publish information. The email may be full of good information, but the human user may not remember to use the information when it becomes relevant to an architecture decision or may not even read it to absorb the information. I know that as a human user I am not alone in skimming my emails.

Pull means that the user triggers the action of receiving the information, and is therefore typically motivated to consume the information. An example of a pull mechanism is self-service search. The effectiveness of search varies depending on the user's ability to understand and describe what they are looking for, as well as the richness of the metadata provided with the information being searched. Ever do a keyword search or converse with an artificially intelligent chatbot? If so, you know exactly what I am talking about.

Table 4-1 compares push and pull.

Table 4-1. Comparing push and pull

Mechanism	Pros	Cons
Push	Scales to large audiences of consumers easily.	Does not ensure active engagement by the human user. If the time at which the information is consumed is disconnected from the time that it is needed to make an architecture decision, there is a risk of lacking effectiveness.
Pull	Ensures active engagement by the human user.	The effectiveness of targeted results depends on the information architecture, coverage, and experience available for the information.

All of the architecture information types defined in Chapter 2 (for example, architecture principles, standards, frameworks, patterns, best practices, diagrams, and decisions) can be provided with either a push mechanism, a pull mechanism, or both. However, given the trade-offs explained in Table 4-1, it is of the utmost importance to consider usability and effectiveness.

For example, providing a common documentation knowledge management repository is a fairly straightforward and common way to provide architecture information. However, just having a repository that stores information isn't enough. Even enabling a robust taxonomy and search pull mechanism isn't enough. Coupling this repository with push mechanisms to pick up specific, relevant bits of information can work very well, particularly when that push mechanism is embedded into a process.

It is more effective to build push and pull mechanisms into the processes, tools, and experiences that result in architecture decisions, rather than siloing architecture information into an independent standalone solution.

Finally, the *consume* stage refers to the act of end users using the information to gain knowledge and to potentially improve it. It's important to consider continuous improvement as part of this knowledge management lifecycle.

Knowledge that is gained comes in different forms, as described in the next subsection.

What Are the Types of Knowledge Relative to Architecture Information?

Knowledge gained from architecture information is both concrete and abstract. Concrete knowledge is predominantly *topical* and *explicit,* whereas abstract knowledge is *implicit* and absorbed through *experience.* Figure 4-5 illustrates these concepts further, to show at a high level how concrete knowledge is used to clarify what needs to be known while abstract knowledge guides how and why people use knowledge a certain way. Concrete knowledge is what you see, and it is proportionally less in volume than the abstract knowledge that you cannot see, yet the usage of the concrete knowledge heavily depends on the abstract knowledge.

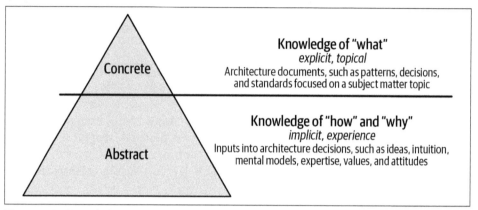

Figure 4-5. Knowledge management types

Topical refers to knowledge specific to a subject matter area. For architecture, this relates to information types like best practices, patterns, principles, and standards associated with a specific business area or technology domain. Chapter 1 discussed specializations within the architecture field, like security or cloud, which are examples of topical areas.

Explicit refers to knowledge that can be clearly stated and is easy to document and share. In architecture, all information types need to be explicit to be shared, from architecture diagrams and decisions to patterns and standards.

Implicit refers to knowledge that is the opposite of explicit; it is knowledge that is not clearly stated or easy to document and share. For example, unwritten rules, ways to navigate in an organization, understanding motivations, intuition-based decisions, undocumented historical knowledge, anecdotal experiences—all of these can be valuable when shared to support more effective architecture decision making. However, implicit knowledge is typically shared organically through conversations rather than with deliberate strategic intent. An enterprise architecture organization could consider what implicit knowledge should become explicit and provide the mechanisms necessary to do so—for instance, mining existing solutions for patterns through a *community of practice*, which is a group of like-minded people exchanging ideas. (See Chapter 5 for more in-depth discussion of the community of practice.)

Experience refers to knowledge gained from personal experience. The adage that experience is the best teacher comes to mind. From an architecture perspective, this applies to learning by doing and is inclusive of learning from mistakes. You have to prove architecture theory through implementation experience. This could mean that if you are the architect, you implement the proposed solution yourself or by influencing an engineering team to do the implementation for you. You observe what works well and what doesn't and apply those lessons learned to the next problem. You could then share those lessons learned and how the proposed solution works in the form of an architecture pattern. If you are in the enterprise architecture organization, this experience principle could translate into not approving an architecture pattern for reuse until the pattern has been proven by at least one implementation.

I'm reminded of a simple real-life example to describe this point. When my kids were little, they didn't like to wear hats and gloves. Although I could tell them to do so when the weather was cold and hope that they learned from listening, or I could lead by example and hope they learned from observing, neither of these mechanisms were effective. What actually sustained their learning was having them go outside, experience being cold, and realize that they preferred to be warm through the use of hats and gloves.

There Is No Shortcut for Experience

When it comes to developing the skills, talent, and knowledge necessary to be a successful architect, there really is no shortcut for experience. People in architecture roles tend to be seasoned technology leaders. As leaders, they are visionaries who are able to clearly communicate their vision and collaborate with others to both create and implement that vision. They tend to have years of experience in solving problems with an architectural mindset.

An architectural mindset consists of having a holistic, objective, big-picture perspective. It considers not just how to solve a problem to fulfill a given requirement, but also the holistic view of how the solution fits into the business and technology ecosystem, how it will be robust, scalable, and sustainable, and how it will meet nonfunctional requirements (see Chapter 5 for more in-depth discussion of nonfunctional requirements). The focus on longevity and sustainability allows for identifying and mitigating potential design risks and requires deep technical expertise with the technologies being considered in the solution. It is this holistic perspective, this big-picture thinking, this deep understanding of both technology and business, that separates the architect from other roles.

Developing such a holistic, objective, big-picture perspective, along with leadership and communication skills, as well as technical expertise, takes time and experience in working with technology and other people to solve business and technical problems. It's a progression of learning how to design solutions, as shown in Figure 4-6, where each experience to solve a larger problem relies on the ability to solve the problems of smaller scope.

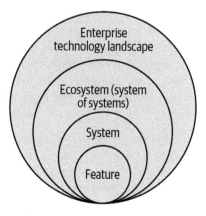

Figure 4-6. Progression of problem-solving spheres

My own career follows this example. From each experience, I learned something. My earliest software engineering experiences gave me a deep appreciation of what it means to code and deliver software, and what it takes to maintain operational production systems. I solved little problems first, like a script to deliver a feature that automated a single business process step. From that small solution, I learned about behavior-driven development, automated testing, and logging. That helped me years later when I was the architect for a logging solution, where I could better advise on logging format, logging collection and analysis, and logging at scale. Similarly, my consulting and management experience strengthened my communication and empathy skills, both of which were essential to being able to influence change at scale.

In summary, be open to new experiences, and gain knowledge through experience.

By strategically supporting knowledge management of architecture information as part of the objective to make architecture information embedded and accessible, the enterprise architecture strategy should result in several benefits described in the next subsection.

Summarizing the Benefits of Knowledge Management

Ever hear the saying, "If a tree falls in a forest with no one to hear it, does it make a sound?" Similarly, if architecture information is produced with no one to reuse it, does it add value?

If you do knowledge management in the context of architecture information right, you can get the right information to the right users at the right time to solve their problems. This requires both an optimized knowledge management lifecycle and the ability to extract implicit and experience-based knowledge to make it shareable and explicit. This is usually a significant optimization because it does the following:

Prevents duplication
It leverages lessons learned from previous mistakes to allow learning from failures without having to repeat those mistakes.

Enables reuse
It reduces time to market by enabling reuse of knowledge and solutions.

Increases productivity
It avoids knowledge hoarding, silos, and bottlenecks where knowledge is trapped only in the heads of a few people. It empowers the masses by sharing that knowledge freely and making it available and retainable for everyone who needs to know it.

Increases efficiency
Better communication, transparency, and quick access ensure that users always have the latest and greatest information and are never operating with stale information.

Ultimately, you will avoid frustration and increase human satisfaction by enabling users to be successful with the right knowledge at the right time. Speaking of humans, in addition to knowledge management, it is also useful to be familiar with UI/UX design, the topic of the next section.

UI/UX Design in Embedded and Accessible Architecture

Given that humans are the key recipients of gaining architecture information knowledge, it is necessary to consider human needs in the forefront of the embedded and accessible architecture information objective. That is what UI and UX design helps with.

What Is UI and UX Design?

UI design emphasizes look and feel to interfaces or access points used by humans. Good UI design seeks to create easy-to-use, satisfying, and delightful interfaces. These interfaces include graphical user interfaces (GUI), like web or mobile where users interact with graphical elements, and voice-controlled interfaces (VCI), like smart assistants where users interact through voice commands. For example, the knowledge repository website that human users interact with to find architecture information is a GUI.

Chapter 1 stated that an effective enterprise architecture practice overcomes siloed decision making; *UX design* breaks down silos in the human experience. It is more holistic than UI design in that it considers the entire user experience across a spectrum of interfaces and beyond.

The use of architecture information is necessary in a variety of experiences that require outputting architecture decisions. For example, perhaps one experience is around understanding what solutions already exist to provide a capability before building or buying a new one. Another experience could be around designing a software application prior to building out its code, and deciding on key architectural elements, like what technologies it uses, how to deploy it, and how to make it highly available. It is highly probable that each of these experiences leverages multiple UIs that need to work together to construct a seamless experience.

The enterprise architecture enablement function should partner with whomever is necessary in the organization to ensure that architecture information is leveraged as part of software delivery experiences. It should be a natural consequence of building software to use embedded and accessible architecture information, rather than a one-off, siloed experience to have to go and find it, as shown in Figure 4-7.

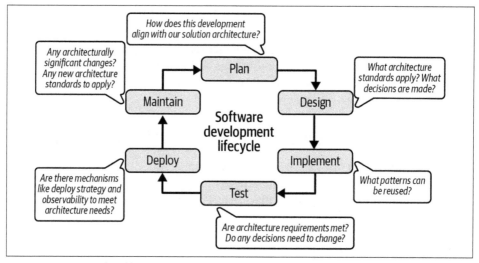

Figure 4-7. Example of how to think about answering questions that apply during the software development lifecycle (SDLC) with embedded and accessible architecture information

As you can see in Figure 4-7, many questions can and should be asked by a software delivery team that pertain to architecture during software development.

For instance, while planning new software investment, it is necessary to be deliberately aligned with the solution architecture work conducted to define a capability target architecture. If this new work is not aligned with that capability target architecture, why not? Does that capability architecture need to be updated? Or is this new work in fact duplicative or not needed from a business perspective? The architecture information that needs to be presented here to inform this decision is associated with the capability target architecture and what capability this new planned investment provides. The ability to compare and contrast is also helpful.

UX would consider the plan experience to figure out the most optimum way to present this information. UI would consider the interfaces themselves; perhaps there is a catalog that indexes existing capabilities and solutions, and perhaps there is a GUI that shows approved capability target architectures that are easily understandable.

Thus, both UI and UX focus on keeping the human user's needs and goals in mind, to create products that are simple and enjoyable to use. UX solves for the overall human user experience, and UI solves for the interactive elements that the human user uses inside that experience. Together, these provide benefits as shared in the next subsection.

Summarizing Benefits of UI and UX

While there are many benefits of a high-quality UI and UX design, I emphasize the top three benefits when it comes to using UI and UX with architecture information:

Promotes optimal usage and satisfaction
> Humans are the consumer of architecture information, and as such, they must be able to optimally use the information. UI/UX design emphasizes this and designs for usability first, avoiding costly rework later.

Reduces support needs
> As a consequence of optimal design, humans can be self-serviced with fresh, accurate, and easily understandable architecture information. This reduces churn, questions, and the need for a handful of experts to be available to explain the architecture information, which in turn also reduces bottlenecks in the overall UX process.

Promotes brand
> I mentioned earlier how important it is for architecture to be seen as an enabler, as part of building software as one team. UI/UX design can help promote this brand identity by ensuring that architecture information is easy to use and embedded and accessible directly within the software development process and tools.

The enterprise architecture enablement function is best positioned to figure out what the experiences are and to advise the strategy and governance functions on how to best simplify and deliver delightful experiences. It can do so by applying a number of principles that stem from knowledge management and UI/UX design. Let's look at these principles next.

Knowledge Management and UI/UX Principles

Knowledge management and UI/UX design together provide a core set of principles with which to guide achieving your embedded and accessible architecture information objective. These are principles that you can work to establish for your organization when operationalizing the roles, processes, and tools for creating, organizing, and using architecture information.

This section covers principles to apply throughout the knowledge management lifecycle stages:

Create
Champion knowledge sharing.

Approve
Many over few.

Distribute
Just in time, transparent to find, single source of truth.

Consume
Easy and enjoyable, flag it or fix it, measure to improve.

Let's start with championing knowledge sharing.

Create: Champion Knowledge Sharing

This principle is helpful to instill a culture of trust around knowledge management. The act of sharing knowledge should be recognized and rewarded, preferably publicly. There should be incentives, such as public praise, gamification rewards, and/or performance management acknowledgement.

Applying this principle could lead to a culture where the following occurs:

Leaders lead by example
Leaders explain how knowledge management of architecture information is a part of everyone's role and responsibilities. They partner with the enterprise architecture enablement function to establish the mechanisms used to create, update, and disseminate architecture information. They publicly recognize and reward behaviors around architecture information knowledge sharing and encourage reuse.

Knowledge champions exist
Perhaps there is a role called *knowledge champion*, whose duties are to encourage people to follow all of the knowledge management practices and contribute their architecture information knowledge. Sometimes the knowledge champions take

ownership of certain topical areas. Other times, they primarily collaborate with other people to encourage them to contribute and use architecture information.

The champion knowledge sharing principle helps create a culture that promotes knowledge sharing. How do you then encourage and scale knowledge contribution? The next principle, many over few, helps do that.

Approve: Many Over Few

Another key principle to enable accessibility of embedded architecture information is *many over few*. This means that the knowledge of many is often better than the curated knowledge from the few. In other words, architecture information should be provided by the audiences that are meant to use them, not just curated by a select few trusted sources.

A wiki is a good example where information is managed by many people, for many people to easily consume. The great thing about wikis is that information evolves quickly and grows based on what information is perceived to be most useful. On the other hand, the information is not always trusted or accurate.

The encyclopedia is a good example of a source of truth that is curated by a few experts, for many people to consume. The great thing here is that the information is definitely trusted and accurate. However, it takes more time to scale and grow the information, and it is not always focused on what people most need to consume.

Architecture information is typically somewhere in between the wiki and the encyclopedia approach. For example, many people in many roles should consume and contribute to architecture patterns. It may still be necessary to have a lightweight governance process to ensure the accuracy and integrity of an architecture pattern, but there is no need to restrict contribution to a few trusted sources.

So, with the first two principles of champion knowledge sharing and many over few, you have a culture that both promotes knowledge sharing and is inclusive of a large audience to engage in knowledge sharing. Now, you need to make sure that the architecture information that is created from these efforts gets to the right users at the right time.

Distribute: Just in Time

To embed architecture information into the processes, tools, and experiences that result in architecture decisions, a key principle is *just in time*. Just in time in this context refers to having the architecture information needed to inform the architecture decision at the time that the decision is being made.

A real-life example that occurs frequently for me is getting dressed. The getting dressed decision is informed by a number of factors:

Principles

For instance, wearing clean clothes is a good thing.

Standards

For example, there is a dress code for professional attire.

Patterns

Patterns can include how the clothes coordinate with each other in terms of colors, shapes, and types.

Situational factors

Includes the weather and the destination.

It is therefore helpful for me, when I am getting dressed, to know just in time what the weather is like today and what clean clothing is available that meets the standards for where I am going. I use pull mechanisms to check my weather app for today's weather, and my closet for clean clothes. I use a push mechanism to then broadcast the weather to my kids so that they can also dress accordingly.

Going back to Figure 4-7, let's look at that planning decision again. Is it more helpful to have capability information available when I need to decide on investing in new technology or when I'm already building new software? According to the figure, it's better to have that information available just in time when I am about to make that decision. So, you would need to determine what process and tooling humans are using when they make that decision, and how you can make this information available there, at that exact point. Is it as simple as a deep link to your capability target architectures and capability catalogs? Or is it more sophisticated, with machine learning prompts that bring similar capabilities to the human user's attention? Or maybe something in between?

With just in time, architecture information is available at exactly the right time. The next principle complements just in time to make sure that the information is transparent and available at any time.

Distribute: Transparent to Find

Recall that transparency is key to building trust, especially in an architecture decision process. Knowledge in general should be easy to create, find, and search, which means that architecture information by extension should be easy to create, find, and search. It should be very transparent and ideally intuitive to human users on how to create, and where to find, architecture information. If someone has to go hunting for a bit of architecture information, that's a tell-tale sign that the information is not transparent enough.

I once had a chief architect tell me that my application target architecture didn't exist if it wasn't linked correctly in the configuration management database that cataloged applications. It didn't matter that I'd produced the deliverable in collaboration with the engineering team and could produce a link when asked. It needed to be transparent for anyone to find it where they would be looking for it. I've taken that feedback to heart ever since, to ensure that my architectural outputs are transparent and easy to find.

Both just in time and transparent to find allude to an authoritative source of information. The next principle, single source of truth, covers that notion explicitly.

Distribute: Single Source of Truth

The *single source of truth* principle ensures that there is only one authoritative source to find a particular bit of architecture information. This principle avoids proliferation, or having multiple places to find the same information, which can cause confusion and increase maintenance headaches around maintaining duplicative information.

Based on the preceding transparency principle, it should be very clear what the source of truth for the architecture information is. For example, if someone writes a blog post that includes an architecture pattern, that should not be trusted with the same level of authority as the architecture pattern catalog that acts as the source of truth for approved architecture patterns in the organization. The author of the blog post should be commended for taking the time to share their knowledge and encouraged to contribute their pattern to the official source of truth and link to it for broader impact and wider reuse.

We've now looked at principles that can be applied for architecture information to be created, approved, and distributed. Next up, and just as important, are principles around using that architecture information, starting with easy and enjoyable.

Consume: Easy and Enjoyable

Earlier, I alluded to easy understanding. This is the last key principle—architecture information needs to be *usable*, meaning easily understood by its intended audience. The information should be very simple to understand, very clear in its main points, and very relevant to the audience. *Simple* often means short—clear and concise. These concepts apply to both visual types of architecture information, like diagrams, and written types, like documents.

Brevity and simplicity are key to usability.

In UI/UX, there is a concept of invisibility and intuitiveness. This means that humans don't care about the design per se, they care about getting their job done, and therefore the design should strive to be invisible and intuitive such that users can do the right thing without much effort. I emphasize this for architecture information. End users don't care about the beauty and elegance of a pattern or diagram so much as they care about whether or not that artifact applies to the problem that they are trying to solve.

Also in UI/UX, there is an emphasis on enjoyment and delight, or evoking good feelings through good design. This is important because humans are the end users, and it is human feelings that get associated with the brand they are using, which leads to their satisfaction to make them want to come back and helps them retain the information and gain knowledge. Delight can be attained by anticipating what humans might do with the information and ensuring that the design helps them do it as frictionlessly as possible, with reduced cognitive load. This could entail ensuring *familiarity*, meaning understanding what humans already expect when they see an element or hear a term. This also could encompass consistent and predictable elements like fonts, colors, and icons, which in turn promotes brand.

 In architecture, speaking in universal terms is very important. Don't redefine well-known industry terms for your own purposes.

The easy and enjoyable principle also includes efficiency. *Efficiency* in this context refers to understanding that new users may need more guidance, whereas experienced users may bypass certain workflows to speed up their experience. Similarly, efficiency relates to flexibility, which allows users to customize their experiences as needed.

Last but certainly not least, this principle always includes accessibility, meaning the information can be available to any user, including those with disabilities. See Section 508 (*https://www.section508.gov*) for US federal government guidelines on accessibility.

So now architecture information has been created and distributed and is easy and enjoyable to use. That's great, but it needs to be sustainable as information changes. How to keep information up to date? The next principle, flag it or fix it, addresses this question.

Consume: Flag It or Fix It

Flag it or fix it is a mechanism that complements the principle of *many over few*. For instance, if an architecture pattern is out of date, it is good for a consumer of that information to be able to fix that information or, if unable to directly fix it, to flag it to the author for review to fix.

Enabling consumers to fix it inspires contribution. Being able to flag it allows for proactive continuous improvement. Maintaining the freshness and accuracy of architecture information in the face of change—changing requirements, changing organizations, changing technology—is a daunting challenge to overcome. Putting the power of identifying changes and updating information accordingly in the hands of the users is a scalable mechanism to provide such assurance.

Feedback is an intrinsic part of both knowledge management and UI/UX. Flag it or fix it is a great way to get feedback directly from human users. Another way to get feedback is to measure to improve.

Consume: Measure to Improve

As with any architecture standard, you will want to understand the efficacy of your architecture information. What is being used? What is not? More to the point, what is *effectively* being used? What is not?

To answer these questions, it is necessary to figure out how to measure what is working and what isn't. Is there a way to understand how often architecture information is being read and how often it is being used in the software delivery process? Are there too many clicks to find architecture information? These are some examples of questions you can ask to figure out what to measure, how to measure, and what to do with the metrics that you attain.

The principle here is to make architecture information creation and usage measurable, so that you have data points to base improvement on.

How do you use all of these principles as part of your effective enterprise architecture strategy? The next section puts them into a framework that you can use to assess your organization and identify opportunities for your KRs that support the objective of making architecture information embedded and accessible.

Embedded and Accessible Architecture Information Framework

The embedded and accessible architecture information framework focuses on usability rather than on any one specific architecture information type. Working backward from the outcome of easy and enjoyable usability, the framework follows the sequence of *define, do,* and *dare* in a continuous feedback loop across both the product management lifecycle (PMLC) and software development lifecycle (SDLC), as illustrated in Figure 4-8.

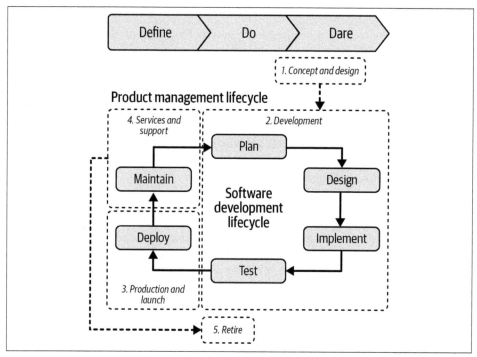

Figure 4-8. Define, do, dare framework overlaid on PMLC and SDLC

The reason that the PMLC is included is because architecture starts with business intent. Long before a technology is ever chosen, or the software created, there is first an architecture decision as part of the initial product concept and design phase that determines whether investment in a new capability is even needed as part of a capability target architecture. The next three phases of the PMLC overlap with the SDLC. Finally, there's a retire stage when the solution providing the capability is no longer needed, either because an alternative replaces it or the capability itself is deprecated.

The define, do, dare framework covers making architecture information embedded and accessible at all architecture decision points throughout this PMLC and SDLC. Let's start with the first stage, define.

Define

The first stage, *define*, establishes specific details of what architecture information is used by whom during specific interactions in those lifecycles, as shown in Figure 4-9.

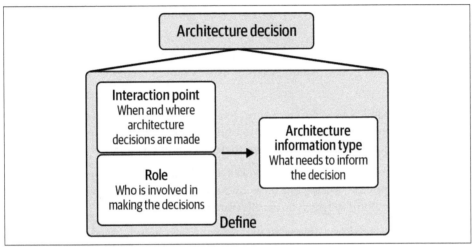

Figure 4-9. Embedded and accessible framework, define step

The define stage is predicated on first defining what the interaction points are. At what points in the product lifecycle and software lifecycle are architecture decisions needed? A few examples are listed by lifecycle stage as follows:

Concept and design
 Evaluate new product intent and determine the strategic technology direction to fulfill that intent.

Development-plan
 Confirm the bounded context of the new software solution and ensure that the new software fulfills a unique business need and that it should be built or bought. Confirm alignment such that the new software aligns with the capability target architecture for the architectural domain that the new software supports.

Development-design
 Provide a high-level application architecture design that decides on technology choices, pattern choices, interactions between this new application and existing ones in the technology landscape, and any related architectural decisions based on application characteristics like data protection or availability needs.

Development-implement

Decide the details of tuning implementation patterns and determine whether any learnings require revisiting application architecture decisions.

Development-test

Evaluate whether or not architectural requirements were met.

Production and launch-deploy

Make architecture decisions with regard to deploy considerations such as deployment strategy, resiliency, reliability, and observability.

Services and support-maintain

Review any change that impacts the application architecture, whether that change is instigated by new capability needs or by new requirements.

Retire

Update capability target architectures to reflect the retirement of an existing software solution. Determine whether to transfer assets owned by this software solution to an active software solution or to deprecate them entirely.

In what processes are these points hit? What tools are humans working with when they hit these points? Answering these questions will round out your definition of each interaction point in which an architecture decision is made.

In addition, you need to define what user persona or role is engaged in each interaction point. For each interaction point, who are the personas or roles that need to interact with architecture information? Let's review the examples again, this time with example roles added:

Concept and design

Solution architect partners with product lead to evaluate new intent.

Development-plan

Application architect confirms bounded context, unique capability, and build versus buy decision in partnership with product and engineering leads. Solution architect confirms capability target architecture alignment.

Development-design

Application architect provides high-level application architecture design and patterns in partnership with product and engineering leads.

Development-implement

Application architect in partnership with engineering lead reviews implementation.

Development-test

Engineering lead consults with application architect on remediation.

Production and launch-deploy

Application architect in partnership with engineering lead determines deployment architecture.

Services and support-maintain

Application architect partners with product lead on new intents and with engineering lead on new requirements.

Retire

Solution architect updates capability target architectures after consulting with product and engineering lead. Application architect may be engaged around transfer or deprecation decisions of assets, as those decisions may affect the bounded context of existing software solutions.

By methodically defining each architecture decision's interaction point and the roles involved, you will determine what architecture information types are necessary to support that interaction point. Here are the examples one more time with the architecture information types:

Concept and design

Capability target architectures, architecture principles

Development-plan

Existing capabilities and the solutions that provide them, capability target architectures, architectural domain mapping, build versus buy assessment framework

Development-design

Application architecture templates, architecture principles, architecture standards, requirements, patterns and best practices, relevant decisions

Development-implement

Architecture patterns and best practices, relevant decisions

Development-test

Architecture standards and requirements, and associated patterns

Production and launch-deploy

Architecture standards, requirements, patterns and best practices

Services and support-maintain

Capability target architectures, architecture standards and requirements

Retire

Capability target architectures

Now that you know what architecture information types are necessary for each interaction point, it's time to figure out how that information will be used by the roles involved. The next stage, called *do*, goes into this step in depth.

Do

The second stage, *do*, determines how the architecture information type will be used in each interaction point by each role.

How should consumption occur by the specified role in the interaction point? Should the information be passively consumed, where the onus is on the end user to apply choice, or dynamically consumed via a guided experience?

For instance, let's look into the details of making an application architecture design decision around high availability in the development-design stage. If there is a process to draft and review application design, and tooling to support that process, then a guided experience could inform the product and business leads of any relevant standards, intake their availability requirements, and pass that context along with relevant principles, standards, patterns, diagrams, and decisions that apply for this specific application to the application's engineers, developers, and architects.

If there is no such tooling, then manual steps can be taken to guide users to the same outcomes; for example, establishing templates for this kind of decision that links out to the relevant architecture information material. Or using a push mechanism from the process to alert the end user to pay attention to a specific piece of architecture information.

The exact details and possibilities will differ based on the maturity of your organization's processes and toolings. By the end of this stage, though, you will have determined the best consumption mechanisms and any changes needed to get to that end state for each interaction point that supports making an architecture decision in the PMLC and SDLC. But you're not done yet! The last stage of the framework, dare, explains why.

Dare

The last stage of the embedded and accessible information framework is *dare*. Dare to challenge to ensure that the architecture information is truly effective—effectively created, effectively distributed, effectively consumed. Continuous learning and improvement are how you make things better and more optimal.

Use the *flag it or fix it* and *measure to improve* principles to ensure that a usability feedback loop is built into the interaction such that you can measure effectiveness; for example, user satisfaction, number of clicks, or duration on a page.

Similar to the do stage, the exact details of feedback loops and measurement will differ based on your organization's tooling and processes.

Case Studies

Let's review a few case studies and examine some thematic dos and don'ts that they reveal, using the EA Example Company. The first scenario is the *new enterprise architecture standard*.

New Enterprise Architecture Standard

EA Example Company's enterprise architecture team diligently followed the company's processes to define a new standard around software languages, to narrow what software languages were approved for usage. This standard impacted all software engineers. In accordance with their processes, the enterprise architecture team socialized the standard to subject matter experts and senior leadership with direct briefings. They also published the standard on their website and announced the new standard in a newsletter that reached senior engineering leadership.

Software engineer Sasha stumbled onto the standard when she came across the enterprise architecture website, while searching for a different piece of information. Sasha told her teammates and was sure to use an approved language for the next piece of software they developed.

Software engineer Tony learned about the standard when his manager forwarded the newsletter to him. Tony realized that his application was written in a language that was not on the approved software list. He alerted his manager, and his manager, Tom, said that there was no sense in refactoring to convert to the approved software language. So, Tony continued development with his original software language.

Software engineer Mike didn't get the newsletter, or see the website. He used an approved software language purely by coincidence.

Software engineer Gina started a new job with EA Example Company and did not know about the standard; she recommended using a software language that she was familiar with to her team that was not actually on the approved software list.

Over time, the enterprise architecture team realized that their standard was not particularly effective.

What happened here?

A one-time push campaign was used, which was not a sustainable mechanism to ensure that the roles that needed to know about the standard were educated about the standard and could abide by that standard. In addition to the communication mechanisms employed, there should also have been effort around training, perhaps in software engineer onboarding, and/or just-in-time information about standards in software development processes. There should have been an enforcement mechanism as well in the software development processes to check that an approved software language was being used.

Key takeaways from this tale are summarized below.

Do:

- Follow established processes to define and approve new standards.
- Embark on communication campaigns.

Don't:

- Assume that one-time campaigns are enough.
- Stop at educating the current user base; be mindful that users change.
- Stop at simply publishing a standard and assume that users will seek it out; instead, work to incorporate the standard into the process and controls that the user will execute.

The next scenario is called the *best practices*.

Best Practices

EA Example Company's senior engineering leader, Tom, noticed that his software engineers were spending a lot of time duplicating work in solving the same or similar problems such as application logging. They tended to rely on searching the internet and asking each other for clarifications and answers.

Tom asked his enterprise architecture team for guidance. The enterprise architects decided that if they defined best practices in architecture patterns, they could share knowledge and have all software engineers reuse that knowledge. They set up a knowledge base and published several documents about best practices that they reviewed among themselves. They linked this knowledge base from the company's internal engineering portal.

Tom was happy to see the knowledge base form. However, as time passed, his software engineers still spent time duplicating problem-solving and still preferred to use the internet and each other rather than the knowledge base.

What happened here?

Patterns were documented, intended for reuse, but were not effectively reused. The knowledge portal was set up with good intent, but it didn't adhere to the principles mined from knowledge management and UI/UX design that specifically target reuse and many over few. Since the information was not as consumable or as usable as it could have been, the behavior of the software engineers did not change.

In summary, the following are the key takeaways.

Do:

- Define architecture patterns tailored for your company.
- Incentivize patterns contribution and reuse as part of engineering excellence, for example through gamification and/or as part of performance management.
- Make patterns relevant by including them in the processes and tooling that engineers use for solving specific architecture decisions.

Don't:

- Duplicate information widely available in other sources.
- Assume the audience knows when or how to use your pattern.
- Keep patterns in the curated hands of the few.

The last scenario to examine is called *the static artifact*.

The Static Artifact

EA Example Company's enterprise architecture standard required an application architecture artifact that described how that application interacted with other applications as part of approving that application to launch into production.

Application architect Annie wanted to be a good citizen and comply with this requirement. She asked for a template but did not receive one. She then asked for examples, and received some, but they were quite inconsistent with one another. So she documented a static diagram to fulfill the requirement based on her own experience. The application was approved for launch in production.

Over time, as the application ran in production, there were incidents, and new members of the application team wanted to understand how the application was architected. However, Annie had no reason to update the diagram, having fulfilled the initial requirement.

What happened here?

The architecture artifact was documented as required for the initial system launch, but it was not kept up to date since there was no refresh requirement and it was a highly manual effort to keep up with changes. Also, there was no template with prescribed guidance for consistency across applications.

Do:

- Use diagrams to describe systems.

- Use standards to keep diagrams consistent. For example, ArchiMate is available for enterprise architecture modeling, C4 model is available for software architecture modeling, and Unified Modeling Language (UML) is available for general modeling.

Don't:

- Make diagrams as static, one-time diagrams:
  - Think of diagrams as living documents that are updated frequently as part of change management. Ideally, updates can even be prompted by automated events.
  - Think of ways to make diagrams queryable. If architecture intent is queryable, then it can be compared with reality to diagnose gaps in implementation and can also have rules run against the queryable diagrams to forecast compliance to requirements.

- Make diagrams convoluted. Simple diagrams with clean lines, a clear legend, and bounded context are most easily understood.

Summary

To achieve the embedded and accessible objective and tailor KRs for your own organization, consider any weak points in your organizational structure and/or processes that may hinder creating usable, effective architecture information across various stakeholders.

Does your culture support knowledge sharing? Leverage knowledge management and UI/UX principles in this quest to make architecture information effectively created, distributed, and consumed across PMLC and SDLC.

Use the *define, do, dare* framework to uncover opportunities for your organization to make architecture information embedded and accessible during architecture decision making. These opportunities become your specific KRs for the embedded and accessible objective. The framework is summarized as follows:

1. For each type of architecture decision, first define when the decision is made, in what process and tools, by whom, and what architecture information they need to know as inputs to make a great architecture decision. This part of the framework yields a consistent understanding of interaction points, roles, and the architecture information types needed for each interaction point.

2. Do the hard work of figuring out how exactly that architecture information is consumed at that interaction point. What is the best way to embed that information and make it accessible, just in time, at that interaction point?

3. Dare to continuously improve. As architecture information is made available, is it achieving its purpose? What feedback loop and what measurements can you make that provide indications of effectiveness? How can you use this data point to refine your approach?

In the next chapter, we'll deep dive into the next objective: enable and enforce.

CHAPTER 5

Enable and Enforce

Chapter 2 shared that the third key strategic objective for an effective enterprise architecture strategy is to enable and enforce architecture standards.

What first comes to mind, when you think about standards? Chances are, you think about standards that are rules, such as laws and regulations, that must be followed or else there are consequences. Love them or hate them, speed limits are one such example; drivers who speed past traffic cameras get fined indiscriminately.

Look around and you'll see evidence of standards all around you. That door nearby? It was built to building code specifications. The stop sign or traffic light on the street that you cross every day? It is part of a standardized system designed to instruct drivers and pedestrians.

So far, I've talked about standards that tell you what to do. What about *how* to do it effectively? That is typically what best practices define.

Best practices are proven ways to achieve a standard. Violations of best practices still carry consequences, but potentially not as immediate or severe as violating a legal rule does. For example, paying off credit cards monthly is a best practice to manage finances. If a month's payment is missed, nothing dire may happen immediately, but after a while, credit card debt can affect the ability to make major financial transactions.

Similarly, look at the example of brushing teeth. It's a standard rule in my household that you have to brush your teeth twice a day. We've also been instructed by our dentist on the best way to brush teeth—brushing with circular motions rather than up and down, taking adequate time to brush rather than rushing, and brushing after meals instead of before. These techniques are best practices that help meet the standard for brushing teeth.

We're surrounded by standards. But why? What's the benefit?

The benefits of standards tend to fall into three categories:

Operational efficiency

This involves optimized processes and efforts to reduce costs and increase productivity—particularly when it comes to making informed decisions that align with your organization's business needs, and with regard to simplifying complex technology landscapes by reducing duplicative solutions.

Risk management

Risk management serves to mitigate the chances and/or impact of issues as related to operational risk, security risk, and data management risks.

Innovation

Chapter 1 discussed how a key benefit of effective enterprise architecture is to break down silos. Enterprise architecture standards are a great way to promote interoperability among systems, thereby allowing for innovative solutions using new technologies that can still work together and be compatible with one another. Such interoperability also allows for being resilient to change.

Formats are a great example of a standard that aims for operational efficiency through reuse and interoperability. Standardization of plugs and voltages allows for a common way to provide electricity to devices. Manufacturers don't have to worry about creating custom solutions for how devices draw power from the grid, allowing them to focus on innovating more value-added business choices. Standards can have limits, though. For example, the standard voltage and plugs differ across regions, such as between the United States and Europe, and adaptors are necessary to work across them.

Another example that outputs operational efficiency is *common terminology*. For example, there is a common symbology used to inform pedestrians of when to cross streets. It doesn't matter if that street is in Washington, D.C., where I live, or in New York, where I grew up; the red hand and the white person outline both mean the same thing. Thus, pedestrians experience reduced cognitive load and a streamlined approach to manage traffic.

Pharmaceutical quality standards are a good example of a standard that aims to mitigate risk. My parents worked in the pharmaceutical industry, where they managed quality for medicines. It was essential that every dose of medicine met the high-quality standards that prescribed every detail including strength, formulation, shape, and size to avoid adverse effects.

Now that we have a common understanding of what standards are and how they are used in general, let's apply this knowledge to architectural standards and learn why it's so important to enable and enforce them.

What Is an Enterprise Architecture Standard?

As you may have guessed, an *enterprise architecture standard* is a standard that defines the requirements for, and applies to, the architecture of a technology solution. These requirements are typically codified in approved corporate governance documents, as illustrated in Figure 5-1.

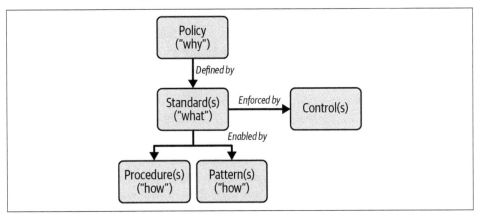

Figure 5-1. Typical governance document ontology

An enterprise architecture policy document defines the *why* behind needing enterprise architecture standards. It covers the overall business objectives and risks that are mitigated by the standards, and it defines key roles and their accountabilities and responsibilities, such as an enterprise chief architect.

An enterprise architecture procedure document is essentially a standard operating procedure (SOP) that details the process that needs to be executed to adhere to the standard's requirements. Enterprise architecture patterns, as detailed in Chapter 1, define best practices and elaborate on proven ways to solve problems in adherence to the requirements defined by the standard.

An enterprise architecture standard document defines requirements that support and guide decision making to acquire, create, deploy, and manage technology solutions in alignment to business objectives.

The next several subsections talk about the first major type of architecture standards, which are those that span several architectural concerns known as nonfunctional requirements (NFRs). A *nonfunctional requirement* defines what must be true for a specific solution quality.

Stability NFRs

The risk of technology failing is a prevailing concern with regard to business continuity and disaster recovery. Enterprise architecture can help mitigate the risk of experiencing adverse impacts from failures by defining standards that guide decision making to make sure that the technology works as intended and consistently, even in the face of failures. Note that the objective here isn't to prevent all failures, because that is an impossible feat, and failures will occur. The objective is to respond swiftly and mitigate the impact of any given failure. The following set of NFRs are defined to do just that:

Resiliency

Resiliency is the ability to tolerate failure, where failure is caused by a change to the technology solution or to its surrounding environment. *Tolerate* means that there may be acceptable degradation or, even more ideally, the failure is detected and resolved before escalating into adverse impacts. A typical resiliency measurement is *mean time to repair* (MTTR), which is the average time to resolve a failure and return to normal operations. The lower MTTR is, the better your system's resilience.

Recoverability

Recoverability is the ability to recover capabilities upon a failure. This is necessary to support resilience since this is what allows for tolerating failure. Recoverability is typically measured by *recovery time objective* (RTO) and *recovery point objective* (RPO). RTO is the amount of time that a system takes to restore capabilities after experiencing a failure. RPO is the maximum amount of data measured in time that can be lost without unacceptable adverse impacts upon experiencing a failure. For example, a 10-minute RPO means that the system can withstand up to 10 minutes of data loss in the event of a failure. Systems that automate their recovery capabilities are often called self-healing. *Self-healing* means that they do not require any outside intervention, let alone manual intervention, to recover from a failure.

Availability

Availability is the ability to provide expected transactions or capabilities with expected level of service. Availability is typically measured as the ratio of available time to total operational time, and provided as *service-level agreements* (SLAs) to end users by contract or *service-level objectives* (SLOs) to end users without a contract. Fault tolerance builds on availability to ensure zero downtime, meaning that RTO and RPO are zero.

Reliability

Reliability is the ability to provide consistent levels of quality service. A highly resilient application is not by itself reliable; for example, if it fails and recovers within a 10-minute RTO, that's great resiliency. But if it fails every day for 10 minutes, that's poor reliability. Reliability is typically measured with SLOs.

Durability

Durability is the ability to protect data from loss or corruption.

Observability

Observability is the ability to provide transparency and visibility into a system's behavior in support of troubleshooting and root cause detection. Related capabilities include logging, monitoring, and alerting on the system's performance. Observability supports *mean time to detect* (MTTD), which is the average amount of time that it takes to identify the root cause of a failure. To achieve minimal RTOs and swift MTTR, MTTD needs to be as small as possible.

Let's look at an example illustrated by Figures 5-2 and 5-3 of how applying these NFRs to a simple application changes the architecture of that application.

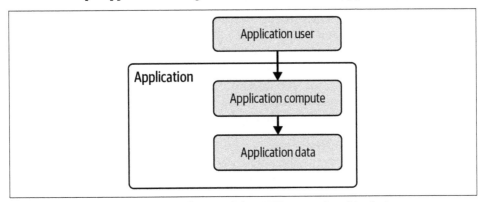

Figure 5-2. Simple application without stability NFRs considered in design

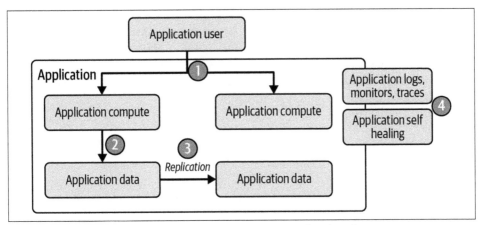

Figure 5-3. Simple application with stability NFRs considered in design

As Figures 5-2 and 5-3 illustrate, designing and building an application with stability NFRs in mind leads to making key application architecture decisions:

1. Routing

With needing to build for redundancy, if user driven, what kind of traffic routing policy makes the most sense—geographically pinned, latency-based, weighted policy? Does load balancing apply based on the selection of compute service? Do scaling groups apply, and if so, with what kind of scaling policy? Is redundancy employed in an active/active, active/passive, or active/standby manner? Does the redundancy support the ability to failover, such that you can reroute traffic to an operational stack (compute plus data) in the event of failure detected in one stack instantiation? How long do you keep this redundant stack around for, to support the ability to failover? Has capacity planning occurred to rightsize the redundant instances from a cost-efficiency perspective? What is the fault domain that determines the level of redundancy? Meaning, if the fault domain is a single availability zone, then you would employ redundancy across multiple zones. If the fault domain is a single region, then you would employ redundancy across multiple regions. In either case, you also introduce affinity concerns with the trade-off of performance and latency for any transaction that crosses zones or especially regions. How does the application deal with these concerns?

2. Compute to data interaction

Is the interaction from the compute layer to the data layer active/active, active/passive, or active/standby? What kind of consistency is necessary for the data, strong or immediate or eventual? Do consistency requirements differ based on data writes or data reads? Is a data caching layer required to buffer demands?

3. Data management

What kind of replication is needed to meet the consistency and availability requirements? How many replicas are needed; is a quorum needed? How about backups: what are the durability requirements? How often are backups needed, and are they full backups or incremental? Do you need backups or snapshots or both? Do you have to support point-in-time restore?

4. Observability

What kind of monitors, logs, traces, and alerts are needed to support observability? Are thresholds tuned based on testing? Do alerts trigger self-healing automation? What kind of failures can be self-healed?

Although not visualized, another key decision is dependency management:

Dependencies

What is the application dependent on, both inside the application and beyond the application, to provide design-time and runtime capabilities? *Design time* refers to building and deploying the application. *Runtime* refers to when the

---

application is operating. Out of these, what are critical dependencies, where *critical* means that if the dependency goes down, this application will also go down? A *failure mode effects analysis* (FMEA) is a helpful mechanism to identify and diagnose critical dependencies, thereby allowing for decisions to be made on how to mitigate the risk of a critical dependency failing (see Table 5-1).

Table 5-1. FMEA example template

Cause of failure	Probability	Impact	Criticality	Mitigation
Root cause	A number on a 1 to 5 scale, where 1 means failure is unlikely to occur, and 5 means failure will definitely occur.	A number on a 1 to 5 scale, where 1 means minimal impact due to failure, and 5 means severe impact due to failure.	Multiply probability by impact. The higher the number, the more critical the failure.	Method to reduce the criticality of failure

Keeping applications up and stable is a key benefit of defining architecture standards for stability NFRs. The next subsection shifts focus to optimally building, testing, and deploying applications, still with intertwined stability concerns.

Release NFRs

A typical business objective is to release new capabilities often. That is often accelerated by the ability to continuously build, test, and deploy software releases:

Testability
The ability to be testable, preferably in an automated way, to ensure output of code execution matches intent. There are many kinds of testing. Figure 5-4 shows my take on what kinds of tests to consider for a testability NFR.

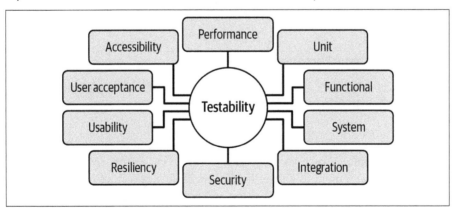

Figure 5-4. Example testing NFR areas

Deployability

The ability to build and deploy software to output a usable customer product. There are many deployment strategies to consider. Figure 5-5 shows a few examples, where *all in one* refers to immediately shifting all traffic to a new version, *blue/green* refers to deploying a blue stack for the original version and a green stack for the new version and only switching to the green stack after testing it, and *canary* is similar to blue/green in that it has two stacks, but traffic is shifted to the new stack over predefined intervals of time. The example shows three, but this can be as many or as few as you want to get to 100%. The idea is that you test with increased load to find adverse impacts prior to the full load experiencing an issue. The all-in-one deploy window is shortest and only requires the duration of deploying the change. Blue/green is next longest as it requires testing time. Canary can be the same or longer than blue/green depending upon the periodic interval of time chosen to complete the testing.

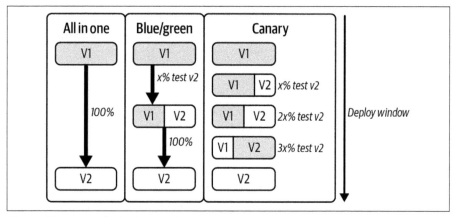

Figure 5-5. Example deployment strategies

Agility

The ability to make changes frequently.

Designing and building an application with release NFRs in mind leads to making key application architecture decisions:

Testing

The degree of modularity and composability of the application affects its testability. In addition, you may decide to do behavior-driven development and test-driven development to ensure testability. Resiliency testing might require you to get familiar with chaos engineering and run experiments to tune monitors, logs, and alerts.

Deployment strategy

Using strategies like blue/green and canary allow you to test before fully committing to the change. They also imply running more than one version of software at a time in production, which means backward-compatible changes. How will you get feedback that your new version is performing adequately? Do you have the right monitors and alerts in place? You'll also need to decide on whether you do a rollback or a rollforward strategy in the case an issue is detected. In blue/green or canary, you have the original stack available until the traffic is fully switched to the new stack, but do you need to keep it around even longer to have something to roll back to? Or do you rely on roll forward once the deployment is completed?

Quantum of deployment

In relation to agility, the unit of change is your quantum of deployment. Is your change a simple and small change, easy to deploy, troubleshoot, and roll back? Or is your change a larger, more complex, bundled change? Is there a lot of overhead to manage for changes, and how does that factor into your change size?

Keeping applications agile and able to release high-quality code frequently is an output of the release NFRs. The next subsection looks into another aspect of high quality: building highly performant and efficient software applications.

Operational Efficiency NFRs

Characteristics of well-architected applications include being able to use resources efficiently—both in terms of performance and cost—even when demands change. The qualities that operational efficiency NFRs aim to output include the following:

Performance

The ability to respond to a demand. Typically measured by latency and throughput. The lower the latency and the higher the throughput, the more performant the application is and the better the end-user experience.

Scalability

The ability to increase in performance and capacity as demands increase. Figure 5-6 shows typical scaling strategies. Scale up or vertical scaling strategy means to increase capacity by adding more resources such as memory or processing power to existing compute instances to handle increased demand. Scale out or horizontal scaling strategy means to add more identical compute instances to increase overall capacity; this strategy relies on the ability to load balance to distribute demand among the instances.

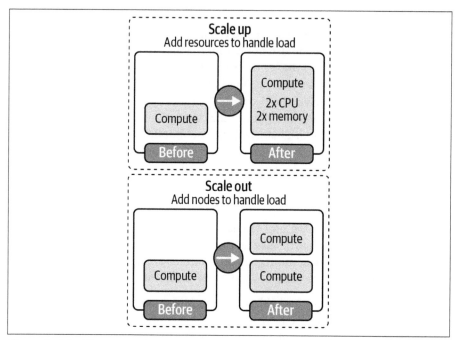

Figure 5-6. Scaling strategies

Elasticity
> The ability to automatically increase or decrease capacity as demands fluctuate. Can complement the use of automation with a scaling strategy.

Flexibility
> The ability to accommodate changes over time.

Simplicity
> The ability to be uncomplicated and easy to understand and maintain.

Practicality
> The ability to be sensibly implemented.

Cost efficiency
> The ability to optimize total cost of labor to build and operate the solution. Total cost of labor includes not only infrastructure cost but also the cost to operate and maintain the infrastructure and application.

Feasibility
> The ability to be implemented within the operating constraints.

Usability
> The ability to be used by end users easily and delightfully.

Designing and building an application with operational efficiency NFRs in mind leads to making key application architecture decisions:

Resource utilization
> What are choices that reflect in your memory, disk I/O, storage, and CPU usages and selections? How about container image dependencies, software dependencies, the size of your binaries? Do you use asynchronous or synchronous interactions, and what is your tolerance for latency? What choice of compute and storage meets your performance requirements?

Capacity
> Do you reserve capacity and pre-allocate capacity to handle your peak demand, thereby trading off cost for the assurance of availability? Or do you invest in elasticity and automate scaling, assuming the time it takes to scale is tolerable? Can you scale out horizontally, and if so, what would your minimum and maximum number of scaled units be, and your load-balancing strategy?

Management
> From a total cost of ownership and feasibility perspective, is there more benefit to going with a serverless offering or a managed service offering over self-managed? Or how about a vendor software as a service offering?

Cost levers
> Are you monitoring spend? Is your spend efficient? Are your workloads sized and utilized effectively? Is your traffic bursty or steady, and are you using cost-effective compute and databases based on those access patterns?

Making applications highly performant, able to respond to changes, and cost-effective is a result of the operational efficiency NFRs. The next subsection looks into another set of NFRs for a key architectural consideration essential to breaking down silos.

Interoperability NFRs

An essential architectural ingredient in optimizing systems for local purposes while enabling the integration necessary to compose seamless experiences is *interoperability*. These NFRs help to mitigate the risk of silos, promote innovation, and use proper levels of abstraction:

Extensibility
> The ability to easily add new capabilities.

Interoperability
> The ability to work with other systems.

Portability
> The ability to transfer capability from one system to another.

Reusability

> The ability to be used again in another system.

Adaptability

> The ability to be future-proofed and withstand changes without major rework.

Designing and building an application with interoperability NFRs in mind leads to making key application architecture decisions:

Interfaces

> What are the interfaces such as APIs through which this application will exchange information with other applications? What are the standardized contracts for this exchange? Will the information exchange be real time or batch?

Modularity

> What is the modular structure of the application? How are components defined, and specifically how are their boundaries defined to specify interfaces to exchange data across them?

Making applications interoperable allows for a high degree of loose coupling, which enables agility and adaptability and mitigates dependency risk, as shown in Figure 5-7, since each application can independently change from one another and communicate through well-defined and well-managed interfaces.

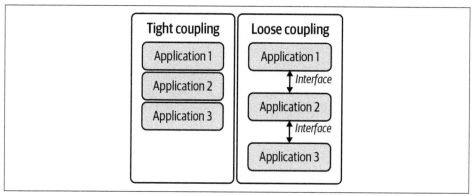

Figure 5-7. Comparison of tight versus loose coupling

Last but not least, let's wrap up our discussion of NFRs with a quick look at security.

Security NFRs

An essential characteristic of a modern application is its security posture, the ability to protect data. At the highest level, there are at minimum these NFRs:

Security

> Protect applications, data, and infrastructure from threats and attacks.

Verifiability
  Inspect that what was intended in the architecture is implemented.

Designing and building an application with security NFRs in mind leads to making key application architecture decisions:

Data protection
  What kind of data is being processed and stored, and what is necessary to protect it, such as encryption at rest, encryption in transit, at field level, or overall? Are the right kinds of keys being used? The right certificates? Is data isolated appropriately?

Access
  Are there appropriate authentication and authorization mechanisms? How does least-privileged access affect the design of the application? Are both human and system access well controlled? Is every transaction authorized? Is the identity boundary well defined? Is the network boundary well defined? Is network segmentation adhered to appropriately?

Audit
  Are logs available to support security analysis in the event of a security issue? Is history available and are actions repeatable?

As you can see, architecture standards in terms of NFRs encompass a great number of areas across application design.

Summarizing NFRs

We just reviewed a lot of words ending in *ity*. Check out the ISO 25000 (*https://oreil.ly/dDYkK*) software and data quality standards for more. Each organization's enterprise architecture enforcement function should define the NFRs that matter the most to their business needs. To define an NFR, consider what must be true for each quality. Using availability as an example, an organization may choose to define an NFR that all of their applications must be available 99.99% of the time.

Since each NFR also acts as a constraint on solution design, it's important to understand the prioritized trade-offs between them. In the preceding example, if 99.99% is so highly prioritized, then the inherent redundancy required to support that NFR becomes part of cost efficiency.

Architecture patterns are typically used to describe how to implement a design or solution that will meet certain NFRs. Patterns, generally speaking, are best practices. Only if there is truly one way to solve a problem, to answer the question *how*, should a pattern itself be a rule/requirement. This scenario is somewhat rare.

While NFRs are a large portion of enterprise architecture standards, they are not the only ones. The next subsection talks about another type of enterprise architecture standard, which I call architecture technology standards.

Architecture Technology Standards

Sometimes called a *technology reference model* (TRM), *architecture technology standards* define what is an approved technology service, product, or software for the organization. For example, take software languages. Perhaps one organization is a Java shop, and another is all about Rust. The enterprise architecture strategy function should define principles that help guide decisioning in this space.

Also, I recommend instituting a champion/challenger model to prevent approved standards from getting stale and missing out on using advances in technology. *Champion/challenger* refers to having an approved standard as the champion but enabling challengers to that approved standard to be raised and evaluated as potential replacements of that standard, based upon whatever criteria was decided upon as the basis for the standard.

So far, we've looked at two kinds of architecture standards: NFRs that serve as the requirements and constraints guiding an application's design, and architecture technology standards that serve to streamline the technology choices made to implement the application. The next subsection looks at the type of standard that answers the question: "What is an application anyway?"

Architecture Metamodel Standard

The enterprise architecture strategy function should define the *enterprise architecture metamodel*, which is intrinsically intertwined with everything that any team does to deliver technology solutions. The reason that the architecture metamodel is so essential is because it does the following:

Common definitions
    The metamodel defines terms to provide a common lexicon with which to converse and collaborate. Words like *solution, product, service, capability, process, component, application, platform*—what do they mean in your organization's context?

Common structure
    The metamodel defines the foundational underlying structure for your technology landscape—from each type of component and application and asset, to the relationships among them, to the attributes that describe them.

The metamodel must strive to achieve these outputs in an easily understandable way, without oversimplifying so much that business questions cannot be answered. A good metamodel will clearly organize all of the necessary components relating to people, processes, and technology into an efficient end-to-end picture that shows how they are interrelated. Figure 5-8 is a very simple generic example.

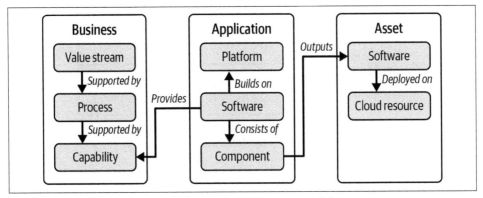

Figure 5-8. Illustrative example of an architecture metamodel

While not shown in Figure 5-8, you can extend the metamodel to define the attributes or metadata for each box. This is key because it anchors governance processes. For example, there are many reasons why you need to know who owns an application, such as understanding who is paying for it, who is building it, who is accountable for its compliance, and who can fix any issues with it. Being clear with the definition of such an attribute—the purpose of how it will be used, the lifecycle of how its value will be managed, the data quality rules with which it will be governed— will be very helpful to streamline operational efficiency of the processes that use this metadata while increasing risk assurance of comprehensive and accurate metadata. In other words, if you are looking for an owner to fix a high-priority compliance issue, it doesn't help if the value is out of date!

The metamodel must be tailored for your organization to add business value. It is helpful to consider what questions need to be answered. For instance, in my recent experience, I was trying to answer questions such as "What is a platform? What is the tenant boundary within a platform?" This helped me figure out what information I needed to capture in my metamodel.

Now that you know what the different types of enterprise architecture standards are, it's time to look at when you need them.

When Should a Standard Be Declared?

Now, before we get too excited about standards and declare a standard for everything, remember that standards also act as constraints. Having so much prescription that human ingenuity is stifled is probably not going to be in an organization's best interests. Rather, look for the high-leverage opportunities to standardize, where the benefits of reuse, operational efficiency, and risk reduction outweigh the need for developers and engineers to make their own choices. See Figure 5-9 for a visualization of this trade-off.

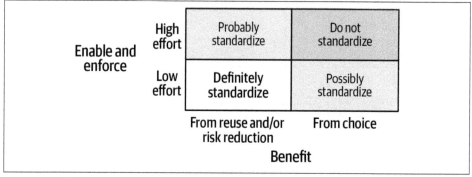

Figure 5-9. Quadrant chart of standardization

The difference between *probably* and *possibly* in this chart is that *probably* means that standardization is likely worth it in terms of benefit outweighing investment to standardize, and *possibly* means that there may be low-hanging fruit to standardize but the return on investment may not be compelling.

 Architecture standards still need to promote creative freedom and innovation.

Recall that standards typically mitigate a risk of some kind. Yet, when risk is not perceived as a threat, standards are likely to be flouted. For example, consider a rolling stop at a stop sign. If the risk of noncompliance is not perceived as a true threat, it is easy to overlook the standard, and the standard is rendered ineffective.

But should we only ever operate under the weight of a threat? Do what you're supposed to do or bad things happen? While fear can be a powerful motivator, I find it to be an utterly exhausting one.

If architecture standards are only viewed as a *have to do it* as a compliance activity—a check-in-the-box bottleneck to move past to get real work done—then architecture as a function has failed. It's too easy to dismiss architecture as a bureaucratic nightmare in this perception.

 If it's too hard to adhere to a standard, then people are less motivated to follow the standard, let alone to follow it well.

And that brings me to my main point of the third objective of our enterprise architecture strategy: you need to both *enable* and *enforce* architecture standards to realize their benefits.

What Is Enable?

To *enable* means to make it easy for developers and engineers to follow the standard, with training, processes, and tools.

Training material can be delivered in a variety of ways:

Computer-based training (CBT)
Self-service, self-paced training using a computer, whose completion is measured and recorded.

Classes
Instructor-led training.

Just-in-time process
An informal method, where the material is offered directly in the process that the user is following just in time. See Chapter 4 for more.

In addition, another mechanism that serves to promote training and knowledge sharing is centers of excellence or communities of practice. A *center of excellence* (CoE) is a formal group with an established charter, mission, and set of stakeholders—typically funded. The CoE is seen as a beacon of knowledge for a particular subject matter area, and it provides both deliverables and support for other teams to gain knowledge. A *community of practice* (CoP) is a more informal structure. CoPs bring together groups of people interested in the same topic, typically unfunded and held on a voluntary basis. A CoP can also grow knowledge by sharing lessons learned and creating informational materials but does not typically have the consulting arm that a CoE has to support outreach to other teams. Table 5-2 highlights the key differentiators between a CoE and a CoP.

Table 5-2. Key differences between a CoE and a CoP

	CoE	CoP
Organization	Formal, funded	Self-organized, voluntary
Outputs	Defined deliverables, supports the deployment of technology in the subject matter area with migration and consulting support	Self-defined, supports improvements in the use of the technology in the subject matter area

The enterprise architecture organization may sponsor one or more CoEs and CoPs based on the technology subject matter areas that are new to help bridge skill gaps in an organization's talent.

Processes and tools are also key for enablement. Chapter 4, for instance, covered making architecture information embedded and accessible, which is a form of enablement. Chapter 2 covered general principles to use and apply in making enablement possible. To further help to decide how to use training, processes, and tools in enablement, the next subsection discusses recommended principles.

Principles of Enablement Mechanisms

The following principles can be used to guide decisions around making enablement possible:

Be specific
> Be as specific and explicit as possible in the intent or purpose of enablement and about who needs to be enabled. For example, if your architecture technology standard includes containers, it's helpful to be specific on standards for building containers such as hardening and logging configuration that can be enabled.

Automate
> Automating enablement processes and tools helps to scale to all of the developers and engineers who need to adhere to the standard. For example, an automated container build process could readily take care of the hardening and logging configuration specified in the previous principle.

Shift left
> Focus enablement efforts as early in the software development lifecycle as possible to avoid rework later. For example, the container build process from the previous principle could result in golden images that are used as the basis of all container development, thereby shifting the specific standard as far left as possible.

These principles are applied in the enablement framework, elaborated in the next section.

The Enablement Framework

The *enablement framework* can be used to assess your current state and identify opportunities to make adhering to the standard so simple and so easy that it is effortless. The framework is illustrated in Figure 5-10.

The first step of the enablement framework is *specify*. In this stage, you identify all of the activities that are necessary to perform to adhere to the standard. For each activity, you also determine when they need to be done and whether any of them repeat. You also enumerate the options that may exist to complete them.

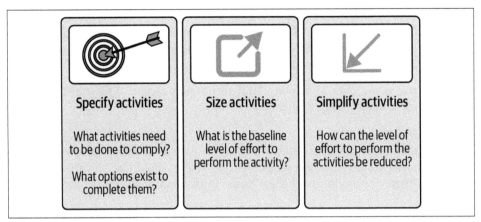

Specify activities	Size activities	Simplify activities
What activities need to be done to comply? What options exist to complete them?	What is the baseline level of effort to perform the activity?	How can the level of effort to perform the activities be reduced?

Figure 5-10. Enablement framework

The next step is the *size* of each of the required activities. In the size stage, you will estimate how long and how much effort it takes to complete the activity. These estimates should be grounded in data gleaned from performing these activities. This is also a good way to figure out what the bottlenecks are—what specific actions in each activity take the longest and/or the most amount of effort.

The final step is to *simplify* and determine the best way to make these activities frictionless and efficient. How do you alleviate the bottlenecks? The solution's approach may require several aspects, from better process to better tooling and automation, and it involves analyzing trade-offs. The trade-off of making enablement frictionless is that doing so requires investment in establishing and maintaining the enablement processes and tools.

As a real-life example, let's look at my coffee routine. Coffee, for me, is a necessity to go about my day. To make coffee, I need to have coffee beans available, a functional grinder, clean water, and an operational coffee maker. Further, I can either make it myself, wait for my husband to make it since he's up before me, or use a timer and load the coffee maker the night before. This example illustrates the degrees of enablement:

None (make yourself)
    The onus is on the developer or engineer to make decisions, problem-solve, and figure out how to adhere to the standard.

Partial (reuse husband's coffee)
    Some information and/or tooling is provided, most often in a self-service way, for the developer or engineer to reuse a solution that will adhere to the standard.

Automated (using a timer)

The cognitive load on the developer or engineer is fully reduced such that they don't need to expend any effort to figure out how to adhere to the standard; a guided experience or automated process/tool does it for them.

Let's go back to the high availability NFR mentioned earlier. What can be done to enable teams to achieve high availability?

Specify activities

One activity would be around designing a high availability architecture. The application architect should do this activity, and it should be a one-time activity unless there are significant changes to the application architecture.

Size activities

If the application architect has to design the architecture from scratch, this may take a significant amount of time to work through details such as load balancing, scaling strategies, and traffic routing, not to mention all the data layer concerns around trade-offs among availability, consistency, and performance.

Simplify activities

The application architect's job could be eased if design patterns around high availability architectures are easily available. This could be further streamlined if in addition to being available as a documented blueprint or reference architecture, it was also available as a running reference implementation and/or an infrastructure as code template for a starter application.

Now that we've reviewed enable, let's move on to enforce.

What Is Enforce?

To *enforce* means to ensure that the standard has been effectively adopted or adhered to. Mechanisms include *preventive* controls and *detective* controls, as shown in Figure 5-11. These control points are often delivered via policy enforcement points integrated into processes and/or tools. *Preventive* means that the enforcement point is constructed in such a way that a noncompliant result can never occur. For example, a standard continuous delivery (CD) pipeline could act as a preventive control by preventing deployment of software that doesn't pass required checks. *Detective* means that there is a risk of noncompliance, but if it does occur, it can be detected and then remediated. Reporting is a common mechanism for detective controls.

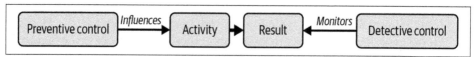

Figure 5-11. Preventive versus detective controls

To construct specific enforcement points, the next subsection describes principles that will help. These are different from and additional to the high-level principles described in Chapter 2 around determining your approach to enforcement.

Principles of Enforcement Mechanisms

The following principles can be used to guide decisions around making enforcement possible:

Reuse
> Centralize enforcement as much as possible rather than redoing the compliance choice at the local team level. For example, centralizing checks into standard CI/CD pipelines rather than every team redoing a check in their own pipeline.

Automate
> Automating enforcement processes and tools is the best way to reduce level of effort and improve assurance. For example, automating a check for hardening configuration in a standard CI build process rather than expecting teams to review hardening as part of code reviews.

Prevent
> Focusing enforcement efforts as early in the software development lifecycle as possible to avoid noncompliance results in significant savings. For example, automating network security checks like using private endpoints to run against infrastructure as code rather than waiting to inspect after deploying resources whenever possible.

These principles are applied in the enforcement framework discussed in the next section.

The Enforcement Framework

The north star of enforcement is to prevent the wrong result, rather than only detecting and reacting to it with corrective action. For example, preventing the association of a public IP address to a cloud compute instance through automated checks of infrastructure as code is better to prevent risk than monitoring and notifying for corrective action after that public IP address is already associated.

To achieve this north star, the first step is to figure out where all the policy enforcement points are in which enablement activities occur and their outcome can be measured for compliance. The second step is to deduplicate enforcement points to determine which ones to use and how often enforcement should take place. The last step is to educate, because empowering developers and engineers with knowledge of compliance allows them to succeed. Figure 5-12 illustrates this enforcement framework.

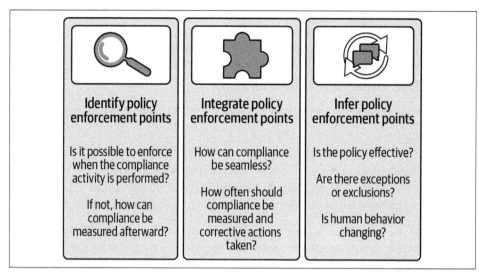

Identify policy enforcement points	Integrate policy enforcement points	Infer policy enforcement points
Is it possible to enforce when the compliance activity is performed? If not, how can compliance be measured afterward?	How can compliance be seamless? How often should compliance be measured and corrective actions taken?	Is the policy effective? Are there exceptions or exclusions? Is human behavior changing?

Figure 5-12. Enforcement framework

The first step of this enforcement framework is *identify*, which means to review the compliance activities output from the enablement framework and determine if compliance can be embedded directly into that activity. For example, let's say you had a security requirement to keep your network traffic private. When deploying cloud-hosted resources, there are configuration settings that support private networking. The compliance activity associated with this requirement is to apply that configuration setting. The preventive control for this activity would be to ensure only the right configuration is possible by controlling the infrastructure as code used. The detective control for this activity would be to monitor the configuration setting after the resource is deployed and to prompt corrective action if the setting was incorrect.

The next step of the enforcement framework is *integrate*, which means to incorporate the compliance controls as seamlessly as possible into the developer's workflow. In the same example of private networking, let's say you decide to go with preventive control. In that scenario, there are several options to make that work, including the following:

1. You could provide a template with the right configuration setting and expect the developer to use that as a starting point and, further, not override that setting.

2. You could provide a custom resource definition that the developer is required to import and cannot override for this particular configuration setting.

3. You could provide a separate compliance test process that they can run their infrastructure as code files through.

There are probably other options available, too, but just looking at these three, what is the least disruptive option to the developer's workflow? What is the most natural action for them to take? What makes it easy for them to adopt? Out of these three options, I'd recommend option 2.

The last step is to *infer*, meaning to monitor the enforcement mechanism or control and understand if any refinement needs to occur to make it more effective.

Here's a real-life example with a stop sign. I've observed that on certain streets in my neighborhood, where there are stop signs on every block, drivers tend to do the rolling stop. However, if that intersection is coupled with a school sign, and it is during school hours, drivers tend to make a full stop. Or, if there is a pedestrian or cyclist at the intersection, drivers tend to stop and make way for them. Moreover, if there is also a crossing guard or cop at a school intersection, drivers not only make a full stop, they also pay attention and wait to cross the intersection when directed. This example illustrates the degrees of enforcement:

Opt in
>   No mechanism of enforcement, just knowledge of the rule. Some people will follow the standard, some will not.

Encourage
>   A mechanism that prefers enforcement. More people will follow the standard.

Mandate
>   A mechanism that requires enforcement. All will follow the standard.

Refer to Chapter 2 for related discussion of consistent severity schema to apply to taking corrective actions.

 Use data from monitoring the control in the infer stage to understand whether you have the optimal degree of enforcement or if you need to make changes.

Now that you know more about architecture standards and frameworks to enable and enforce them, let's review some case studies and study the lessons learned.

Case Studies

Let's review a few case studies and examine some thematic dos and don'ts that they reveal.

The first scenario is *the free-for-all*.

The Free-for-All

EA Example Company wanted to attract top software engineering talent. To do so, one of the things their recruiters touted was technical growth in software languages. Over time, the organization ended up with hundreds of applications built with dozens of different languages such as Java, Ruby, Python, Go, Rust, JavaScript, Scala, Elm, R, and C#.

Initially, software engineers appreciated the variety and the flexibility to work with a language of their choosing. Over time, though, they started to hit roadblocks. Sometimes they spent time developing only to find that they couldn't release what they had developed to production because cybersecurity couldn't actually scan their software, and scanning was a non-negotiable requirement. Cybersecurity had a terribly difficult time keeping up with the different languages to ensure they were scannable and that vulnerabilities could be found and managed.

Sometimes they found that they could not easily get the software libraries that they needed in their software language. Multiple methods of building and deploying software artifacts and binaries for each language had to be supported and maintained, and the central tooling teams could not keep up with the variety of demand.

Sometimes, some software engineers wanted to change teams to grow with new opportunities. However, they faced an uphill knowledge curve when trying to take advantage of organizational mobility due to having to learn whole new languages to support the software. The organization's business leadership was displeased to learn that features were delayed because software engineers had to first spend time learning the software languages of that particular product.

What happened here?

EA Example Company had good intent, but without standards on software languages, they created an environment of chaos as first mentioned by Chapter 1. EA Example Company did not consider the operational and cybersecurity maintenance needs, nor the fungibility inhibitors, of supporting disparate software languages.

In summary, *do*:

- Carefully consider the cost versus benefit of a given developer or engineering choice in the context of the business need or outcome.

Don't:

- Go to the extreme of chaos without any guidance whatsoever.

The next scenario is called *the suffocation*.

The Suffocation

EA Example Company wanted to focus software engineering on business logic only. As a result, they decided to get rid of the need to expend engineering labor on other parts of the software application. To do that, they prescribed and dictated every detail of the technology stack that the engineers worked with, from infrastructure to the application itself, encompassing both requirements and best practices. Now the engineers didn't have to make so many choices and could presumably focus on business logic.

Indeed, this strategy helped with fungibility of talent and streamlining of cybersecurity and operational processes and tooling to support this technology stack. However, over time, the technology stack became outdated. Engineers pointed out that new technology was emerging that could not be used. Talent attrition started to occur, in part because software engineers felt that the technology was antiquated and that there was no path to evolve, so they could learn more elsewhere.

In addition, the prescribed technology stack did not foresee every possible use case, every possible permutation of business need. Thus, it did not work cleanly for every use case. Engineers with more complex use cases that didn't fit cleanly still expended a significant amount of effort either trying to conform without avail or trying to explain their noncompliance to the enforcement processes. Both of these paths were unduly frustrating, and engineers began to leave to seek greener pastures elsewhere, with less bureaucracy.

What happened here?

EA Example Company mistakenly viewed standardization as a one-time activity and resisted updating the standard because the standard was working to streamline operations, and migrating to new standards was hard. Thus, while they did benefit in the near term from their standardization, in the long term, their method of standardization proved to be brittle.

Moreover, by attempting to overprescribe every detail, they did not allow for any flexibility or innovation. This was a mistake because it is impossible to foresee everything, and by dictating best practices in addition to requirements, they essentially closed the door to discovering more best practices and enabling more use cases. Innovation itself was slowly suffocated over time.

The takeaway here is that you *do*:

- Declare standards where appropriate.

Don't:

- Forget to include an approach to evolving standards as part of declaring standards. For example, the champion/challenger model where a challenger is incubated and evaluated to take over a champion.
- Overprescribe, especially when it comes to best practices.

The last scenario is called *the reporter*.

The Reporter

EA Example Company mandated certain standards. In trying to figure out how to ensure that those standards were met, they found that the easiest compliance mechanism was a reporting solution. At first, this reporting solution was highly manual and prone to human error. So they invested in measuring compliance against those standards with a robust automated reporting solution. This reporting solution could detect noncompliance and trigger a corrective action process to remediate the noncompliance at scale. This remediation process did serve to correct the noncompliance issues, but was still costly and disruptive to teams trying to develop new features. Over time, EA Example Company noticed a sustained pattern of detection and remediation, sometimes multiple times within the same team and same product.

What happened here?

EA Example Company emphasized detective enforcement, without any consideration given to preventive enforcement. Although they did try to improve the solution through automation, and the automation allowed measurement to scale, the reliance on detective enforcement caused issues to be caught very late in the development cycle, which caused more rework to fix. Additionally, teams did not learn how to prevent issues; instead, their learned behavior was to get caught and fix after the fact. They were essentially not enabled to be successful.

To summarize, *do*:

- Automate enforcement.
- Provide a feedback loop via enforcement that educates developers and engineers on how to comply in the first place.

Don't:

- Overlook preventive enforcement.
- Overlook the value of enablement.

Summary

To achieve the enable and enforce objective and tailor key results for your own orga-nization, consider balancing risk mitigation and operational efficiency benefits with the creative freedom needed to inspire innovation. Declare standards where there is the most to gain and the constraints are acceptable friction for teams to adhere against. Typical enterprise architecture standards include NFRs spanning areas such as stability, release, operational efficiency, interoperability, security, technology stand-ards, and the metamodel.

For every standard, be sure to enable and enforce that standard. Use the enablement-and-enforcement frameworks to figure out your specific enablement-and-enforcement mechanisms.

With the enablement framework, you can:

- *Specify* the activities that engineering teams need to perform to comply with a standard.
- *Size* these activities in terms of level of effort.
- *Simplify* these activities to reduce that level of effort and make it easy to comply.

With the enforcement framework, you can:

- *Identify* the possible policy enforcement points for controls to ensure that the compliance activities output by the enablement framework do in fact comply with the standard.
- *Integrate* the policy enforcement points as seamlessly as possible into the software delivery processes and tools.
- *Infer* the behavior of humans and efficacy of the policy enforcement points over time to see if any improvements are needed.

Use these frameworks to diagnose weaknesses that you can strengthen through your enterprise architecture strategy objectives and key results centered on standards.

CHAPTER 6

Proactive and Reactive

You've now learned the three main objectives of an effective enterprise architecture strategy in considerable depth. You know more about creating shared alignment across all stakeholders and making architecture information embedded and accessible to all roles that need it to make a decision. And you've seen the importance of both enabling and enforcing architecture standards. Putting that all together, you have a foundation for defining objectives that result in architecture decisions that will have alignment and be well informed, and architecture standards that will be thoughtful and well adopted.

You can do all that, though, and discover that it's still not enough. You may learn that those architecture decisions weren't quite the right kind of decisions. Maybe they weren't proactive or aspirational enough, or they didn't lead the way enough. The decisions were solving the problems of today, perhaps, which is good and necessary, but that's not where architecture shines, and it's not where architecture is uniquely positioned to add value.

Architecture shines in making great decisions where, if the decision is changed, the change causes a significant amount of rework. I've heard these called *one-way door* decisions, because there's a finality about them. You only want to go one way. Whereas *two-way door* decisions have more flexibility. You still want to put in a good effort, but there is not as much of a consequence in getting it wrong or having to adjust.

For example, take cloud account design decisions' impact of where to place workloads in the cloud. If, for some reason, there's a significant change to that cloud account design, whereas the implementation of the change to the cloud accounts themselves might be fairly minor, the impact to the workloads will be enormous, because it will require a full migration from one account to another. Cloud account design is therefore ideally a one-way door decision. By contrast, the design decision to use a managed container service or a serverless managed container service is a two-way decision. Yes, there may be some rework if you have to change your deploy target, but it is less significant compared with one-way door decisions.

Given that architectural capacity is a finite resource, it makes sense to prioritize one-way door decisions highly, and to address these proactively. *Proactive* means to address something before it happens. Proactive architecture is about defining and addressing a target state vision, which is the picture of the destination—the future.

The opposite of proactive is reactive. *Reactive* means to address something after it has already occurred. Reactive architecture is about solving a problem, or making a decision, after a stimulus has already occurred. Examples of stimuli include a new or changed requirement, a new or changed intent, or an incident.

Speaking of incidents, let's look into that example a little more closely. Proactive architects will define a target state vision to be where customers do not experience adverse impacts due to an application or infrastructure failure. To achieve this target state vision, proactive architects will conduct failure mode analysis and design the solution to mitigate failures and self-heal when failures do occur, such that an incident is prevented.

Reactive architects, when an incident does occur, will jump in to help the engineering team diagnose the root cause and recover operations. In the heat of the moment of reacting to an incident, reactive architecture is helpful. But isn't it better to be proactive architecturally and prevent the incident in the first place?

If you answered yes, I'm inclined to agree with you. On the other hand, it is also quite reasonable to expect that you may not be able to predict every possible potential situation. For example, maybe you made what seemed like a perfectly valid assumption on how your system would behave under a stress condition. You might be constrained by timeline pressures to have to accept that risk and wait and see what happens. If you are unconstrained, though, you could instead be proactive to perform testing to output predictable system behavior.

This balancing of aspiration (for example, preventing incidents) with constraints (such as limited time and/or ability to test) is essential to effective architecture. Developing effective vision and strategy, where *vision* is your destination and *strategy* is your plan to get to that destination, requires getting very good at this balancing act. You need to be proactive to anticipate and aspire, yet you also need to be reactive to respond to all the stimuli that impact feasibility.

Proactive architecture strategy is not simply about optimizing the present. It's about imagining and exploring *what could be*, being aspirational rather than just optimal. This aspiration must be grounded in customer needs. You don't want to be aspirational in terms of random proclamations. Rather, you want to start with your customers and focus on business needs. Customers and the business ecosystem in which your technology solutions operate are challenging and complex to understand; but the proactive architect will identify patterns that determine the basis of a strategy. It is important to distinguish the ability to identify these patterns from simply extrapolating the past into the future in a linear fashion to optimize. The reason this is such a pitfall is because the future is decidedly not linear. Optimizations can be somewhat beneficial, but customer-centric aspirations can be revolutionary.

Effective strategists understand that the future is shaped by aspirational disruption that relates to customer needs.

To deliver proactive architecture strategy, you need to become a strategic thinker if you aren't already. The rest of the chapter will dive into principles and a framework to support the strategic thinking necessary to output an architecture vision that is achievable through a strategy outlined in proactive and reactive architecture decisions.

Principles of Strategic Thinking

Strategic thinking means being able to predict and plan for the future. How do you become adept at predicting the future, when the future is filled with unknowns and uncertainty?

While there's no guaranteed way to predict the future accurately, I've found several principles, shared in the next few subsections, to be helpful.

Understand the Right Problem

Understanding the right problem is what defines the strategic purpose of a vision. The right problem must be clearly associated with business outcomes and with customer needs. Otherwise, you are at risk of providing a proactive architecture vision, strategy, and decisions that don't add business value.

Here's a quick checklist:

- Did you spend enough time to deeply understand customer needs?
- Is your understanding of customer needs indicative of a pattern?
- Can you quantify or size the problem statement in a way that illustrates the business impact of solving the problem?
- Can you trace the problem to business outcomes?

A *no* response to any of these questions means you need to spend some more time understanding the right problem.

For example, let's say your organization has a strategy to migrate workloads to the cloud. What was the customer need that that strategy is based on? It is doubtful that customers asked for the cloud. Rather, it is more probable that customers asked for greater agility, more features, lower cost, more self-service, more great experiences, or perhaps all of the above. Being grounded in customer needs will help shape that cloud strategy to deliver business outcomes around better, faster, and cheaper services. Otherwise, the cloud strategy is at risk of using cloud technology *lift and shift* style only, without customer-focused goals. Lift and shift refers to moving a workload as is, without refactoring.

Initiate Innovation

Initiating innovation is all about employing a combination of critical thinking, logical thinking, and creative thinking skills to generate a strategic vision:

Logical thinking
  The ability to reason about a problem and come up with possible answers. Logical thinkers use reason to analyze a situation. *Reason* is often categorized as either inductive or deductive. *Inductive* reasoning, as shown in Figure 6-1, is about forming a general conclusion from a specific premise or observation. *Deductive* reasoning, as shown in Figure 6-2, is about forming a specific conclusion from general premises or observations.

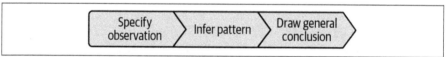

Figure 6-1. Inductive reasoning as part of logical thinking

Figure 6-2. Deductive reasoning as part of logical thinking

Critical thinking
  Often used with logical thinking, critical thinking is the ability to analyze data, facts, and connections across multiple areas with an objective point of view to infer or formulate a clear conclusion. Critical thinkers are adept at analysis and can glean insights that are beyond the obvious. They don't blindly accept other people's opinions; instead, they question them and align with them after using their own judgment.

Creative thinking

Creative thinking is the ability to brainstorm new and unique ideas. Creative thinkers are able to look at things through different perspectives to figure out new ways of doing things or unique ways of solving problems.

Let's take a hypothetical situation where the problem is that the operating costs of running applications in the cloud are too high. A logical thinker with inductive reasoning may do the following:

1. Make a specific observation that a mission-critical application spends a lot of money on redundant cloud infrastructure.

2. Extrapolate this observation into a *pattern* that all mission-critical applications have several degrees of redundancy built in.

3. As a result, form a *general conclusion* that all mission-critical applications incur cost due to redundant infrastructure.

A logical thinker with deductive reasoning may think about the problem as follows:

1. Start with the *general theory* that redundant infrastructure adds cost.

2. Make a *hypothesis* that redundant infrastructure is a key characteristic of highly available architectures.

3. Test that hypothesis by evaluating mission-critical applications to determine the *specific conclusion* that mission-critical applications have more redundancy than less critical applications, and therefore incur more cost.

If you stopped here, you might have a knee-jerk reaction that you simply need to reduce redundancy of these applications to reduce cost. However, a critical thinker would use logical thinking to ascertain that redundancy adds cost and would also realize that redundancy is necessary in highly available architectures. The critical thinker would go a step farther than the logical thinker and ask when the redundancy is most effective; is it necessary to be fully redundant at all times or is it possible to operate with less redundancy at some times? Such critical reasoning would give rise to the notion of *spend* efficiency, which in this context would optimize redundancy against cost.

A creative thinker would then brainstorm ways to achieve spend efficiency. They would brainstorm capacity planning and scaling strategies that could be used to optimize redundancy against cost and performance.

Rather than simply reacting to high cost to shut down redundancy, thereby incurring operational risk, in this scenario the combination of logical, critical, and creative thinking allowed for initiating innovation around spend efficiency, which made acceptable trade-offs between cost and availability.

Be a Change Agent

The future is different from the past. As a result—and this may seem obvious—changes are needed to achieve the future. That is why effective strategists are also effective *change agents*, leaders who are able to lead humans through change.

 Architecture strategies aren't successful simply because they can output new or modified technology and/or processes. They are successful because they can get people in the organization to embrace the changes necessary to achieve the target vision.

You may have come across the change curve in a leadership course, which starts with the natural reaction of *shock or denial* when a person is faced with a change. Then people move to *anger or fear*, an escalation of the previous shock or denial to confront the change. If a change gets stuck here, it will be hard-pressed to be successful. The leader has to be able to move people along to the next stage, *acceptance*, where people finally stop resenting the change and come to accept it. The final stage is *commitment*, where people embrace the change and are willing to adhere to the change as their new normal.

Communicating changes with empathy and providing the knowledge, skills, and training necessary for people to manage the change successfully go a long way to accelerating the change curve to acceptance and commitment. In fact, getting alignment along the way while forming the strategy is even better than having to sell the strategy at the end to get that buy-in.

For example, let's look at a hypothetical organization in the throes of a migration from data center to the public cloud. The network engineers who operate the data center could very well feel shock or denial that their entire scope of work is changing. They might swiftly fear for their job security and be angry that they had no choice in this change. Over time, if leaders are empathetic and provide them a clear path for reskilling as cloud network engineers, these engineers may find themselves more accepting of the change, and eventually they will be committed to being excellent cloud network engineers.

To help you and your organization get better at strategic thinking to define an architecture vision and the strategy to achieve it, the next section lays out a framework that applies these principles.

The 4 Cs Framework

As illustrated by Figure 6-3, the 4 Cs framework is about establishing proactive strategic architecture visions and decisions through the stages of curiosity, challenge, credibility, and communication.

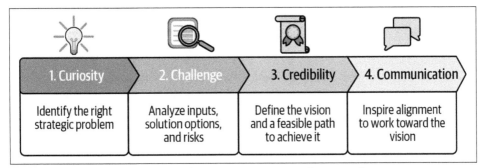

1. Curiosity	2. Challenge	3. Credibility	4. Communication
Identify the right strategic problem	Analyze inputs, solution options, and risks	Define the vision and a feasible path to achieve it	Inspire alignment to work toward the vision

Figure 6-3. The 4 Cs framework of proactive strategic architecture decisioning

The next few subsections dive into each stage of this framework.

Curiosity

The first part of this 4 Cs framework promotes your *curiosity*. The outcome of the curiosity stage applies the first principle of strategic thinking—to understand the right problem.

Curiosity is essential in identifying the right problem to solve as the foundational strategic purpose that is clearly associated with a business outcome. This requires asking strategic questions to better understand the big picture problem, desired business outcomes, and any potential solutions. *Big picture* is another important concept. Zoom out from the day-to-day issues that you face to figure out the bigger, impactful issues. Remember, a great strategy doesn't merely optimize the present day; it calls for a disruptive change to rewrite the future.

Being curious is what enables you to ask questions that uncover big-picture concerns. Asking a diverse population of stakeholders will get you different perspectives.

Examples of strategic questions for an organization's stakeholders include the following:

- What are the major technology trends for software development, and how is the organization positioned to take advantage of them?
- What is the competition doing better or differently, and how should we respond?
- Where will growth originate in the next five years, and how will technology support that?
- What are the high-leverage pain points across the enterprise organization that are inhibiting business development?

And make certain that you get the customer perspective, too. Review any assumptions critically and try to get below the surface. Strategic questions could include these:

- What do you wish could go better with the current solution? Why is it a problem?

- What feelings come to mind when you use the current solution? What would it take to bring about feelings of delight?

- What takes the most time for you to complete when using the current solution?

- What is stopping you from doing what you want to do with the current solution? Why?

For instance, take a real-world situation where a company attempts to gain market share with their software. This software is built on cloud technology and is optimized for the mobile space, but it is prone to bugs, which is garnering it negative customer feedback. Without curiosity to fully understand the right problem, it is possible that a strategy would be formed that tries to prevent bugs through better testing and/or resolve bugs through better detection.

While such a strategy could help, being curious with the above questions could solicit insights like the following:

- Major technology trends include GitOps workflows and integrated artificial intelligence (AI) for guided experiences.

- High-leverage pain points include too many shortcuts taken to develop software, leading to risk and poor quality, because cycle time is the main measure of success.

- Current software is optimized for mobile experiences, but many users are using laptops.

Together, these insights may form a strategy that emphasizes parity across digital channels, as well as GitOps workflows to provide the guardrails necessary to improve software releases, an update to metrics to include quality measures, and even some strategic research and development on incorporating AI. The guardrails could still include the testing improvements from the earlier strategic conclusion, but the strategy stemming from curiosity is now more holistic.

Being curious and inquisitive with an open mind and truly listening will help you detect big-picture customer concerns directly associated with business outcomes.

On Deep Listening

I recall being amazed when I learned that there was more than one way to listen, though I knew that listening was an essential skill of communication. I learned that there are multiple types of listening:

Discriminative listening

This uses other aspects of communication rather than words, such as tone, verbal cues, and nonverbal cues. It is helpful to use this type of listening to understand body language. For example, if you're looking for alignment, and you ask someone if they are aligned and they say yes but their body language makes it seem like they are not fully behind that answer, you can dig deeper and make sure they are truly comfortable and aligned.

Informational listening

This requires a high level of engagement to absorb information. For example, if you're taking training or listening to a lecture, you would use informational listening when you focus on what you're hearing to absorb the content. If you are the presenter of such material, take a moment to make sure your audience is actually engaged.

Selective listening

This is when all the words are heard, but only a select few are paid attention to and recalled. For example, let's say you're giving a briefing on an architecture decision, and your audience is fixated on one detail. You're not going to be able to effectively deliver your message until they are ready to listen to the whole story.

Sympathetic listening

This is when you make the effort to focus on the emotions of the speaker, and you validate their feelings first in your response. For example, let's say someone is vehemently arguing with you to make their point because they feel trapped. You could diffuse the tension by sympathizing with their emotion of feeling trapped, before trying to progress the conversation.

Empathetic listening

This is when you try to relate to someone, which is different from sympathetic listening. Using the preceding example, if someone is vehemently arguing, you could diffuse the tension by imagining yourself in their shoes and validating that they are coming from a place of passion and good intent. So instead of getting upset in return, you respond from a place of calmness and empathy.

Comprehensive listening

This is what usually comes to mind when the word *listen* is used; it is the ability to understand what you're listening to.

Critical listening

This is similar to critical thinking in that you listen to what is being said but also use your own judgment and experience to evaluate what is being said. For example, let's say a team presents an architecture decision to you. Instead of taking it at face value, you can question some of the assumptions they made and ensure that they considered a variety of factors to make that decision.

Successfully completing the curious stage requires using all forms of listening. Avoid distractions, interruptions, and talking too much.

Challenge

Based on the strategic purpose and problem statement defined in the previous part of the framework, the next part of this framework relies on your critical thinking skills. Applying the principle to initiate innovation requires analyzing various inputs, brainstorming possible solutions, considering challenges, and predicting what could go wrong if potential solutions were realized.

Inputs include market research to validate assumptions and to identify and understand trends. Market research could include interviewing customers; using conferences, news articles, and technology research services; and/or reviewing public literature from competition. Review historical trends related to your problem area to identify patterns of what worked well and what did not. This type of insight, coupled with market research insights, is what allows you to anticipate future trends and challenges.

To strengthen your proactive strategic architecture vision and decisions such that they can stay the course in the face of changes and challenges, consider contrary ideas and naysayer points of view from other people. Poke holes in the problem statement and the solution options. Be aware of and challenge any assumptions. Consider what could go wrong in implementing the solution. This due diligence will enable you to bolster your strategic recommendation such that it can withstand these challenges. This challenge process is essential to navigating the unknown future effectively.

Here are some examples of questions that you can use to challenge assumptions and the proposed solution options:

- Why do I expect this to work?
- Is there anything else that could be true?
- How could this go wrong?
- Where can I find evidence to support this conclusion?

For example, there's that quote from the movie *Field of Dreams*: "If you build it, they will come." But why? This assumes that just because you build something, customers will flock to it. What if they don't? What if it doesn't solve something that they actually need or want?

 It may be uncomfortable to contemplate failure and to probe solutions to see where there are risks. It is, however, extremely important to do a risk assessment to evaluate the probability and impact of possible risks that, if materialized into issues, can cause failure. Challenging your initial thinking allows you to formulate better conclusions overall.

Let's review the previous example about a company attempting to gain market share from their software. The strategy included using GitOps workflows to incorporate guardrails to improve quality and reduce risk of buggy software. The key assumption to challenge here is that GitOps workflow alone is what will improve quality. Examining this assumption, particularly around what else could be true and what could go wrong, would also add additional context such as:

- The mechanisms that need to be strengthened to ensure that all development follows the workflow and that the workflow cannot be bypassed
- The talent gaps that need to be overcome when it comes to automated testing to ensure that skill sets are able to pass the checks included in the workflow

Credibility

This part of the framework focuses on defining a credible strategy, which is the approach to achieve the proposed target state vision.

It is in this stage that you will make one or more reactive architecture decisions in collaboration with stakeholders to drive progress toward your strategic vision. These reactive decisions respond to current constraints and gaps and are guided by your architecture principles, organizational priorities, and constraints (as shown in Figure 6-4) to determine the best path forward. This is the part of the framework that turns the aspirational strategic vision into a feasible, achievable, and measurable series of decisions to get there.

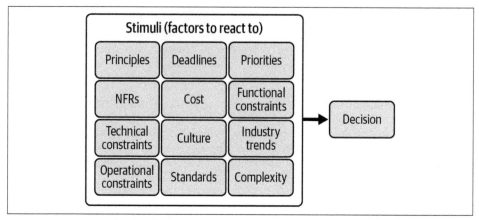

Figure 6-4. Various factors that a reactive architecture decision reacts to

For each milestone that your strategy defines, be sure to define a measurable incremental value that is achieved by that milestone. That will help buffer the propensity to change course by helping stakeholders see demonstrable progress and the value of the original strategic direction.

It is also helpful in general to be able to show a series of *quick wins* when undergoing a significant change for a long-term outcome. It can be very difficult for people to make the leap into a long-term change; a series of "quick win" milestones builds credibility and trust to make the long term eventually achievable.

> Proactive, strategic architecture decisions are at risk of being perceived as too aspirational and therefore unattainable. Be sure to define a credible approach using reactive architecture decisions to demonstrate a series of quick wins that allow you to pursue the long-term strategic intent.

One mechanism that you can use in the credibility stage is a feasibility study. This is a method of detailed analysis that determines the probability of success by considering the practicality of implementation aspects, including the following ones:

Technical
Evaluation of both the technologies required and the expertise or skills of available talent to implement those technologies.

Financial
Evaluation of the total cost needed to invest in the solution against projected returns or savings. This is often referred to as a *cost/benefit analysis*.

Operational

Readiness determination of the organizational structure and operating model to handle and support the changes described by the strategy. This part also reviews the proposed timeline and roadmap for critical path dependencies to determine viability.

Market

Evaluation of the competitive marketplace for the strategic solution's impact.

Regulatory

This depends on the industry, but some industries have regulatory requirements that need to be assessed for adherence in the proposed strategy.

For example, let's say you are championing a serverless strategy for your organization because your customers need more business logic, and one constraint inhibiting the release of more business logic is infrastructure maintenance. A feasibility study could provide an analysis and emphasize the need for training to upskill your talent and the need to update cybersecurity tooling to work with serverless technologies, while assuaging any doubts on financial return, market trend, and regulatory concerns.

The feasibility study goes hand in hand with the risk assessment that was conducted in the previous challenge stage. By the end of the credibility stage, you will know whether or not you have the people, processes, and tools necessary to create and/or use technology to achieve your strategic aim. You will also know whether your strategy is positioned to get you the return on investment (ROI) that is expected when the problem is solved.

Communication

The ability to communicate is essential to success. Being able to make people care about a vision and be motivated to achieve it is powerful. Being able to distill a strategy from complex ideas into simple terms that resonate with an audience, and getting them to understand and buy into the journey that arrived at the conclusion, are critically important to getting the strategy agreed upon and implemented. You can use simple, written materials as an aid to your speaking style. Expect to do several revisions before you complete your simplification efforts.

 Don't underestimate the amount of time and thought that it takes to simplify a message.

Here are some tips to provide simple, written materials:

- Identify the outcome you're seeking, and understand your audience in terms of how they communicate and what they care about. Use that to focus your communication.

- Simplify language to use plain terms that everyone can understand. I try to pretend that I know nothing about the topic, so that I can explain it in the most basic terms and avoid jargon.

- When discussing abstract ideas, use commonplace examples, analogies, and/or metaphors to make them relevant.

- Get to the main point as quickly as possible, both when using words and when using visuals.

- If using slides, stick to only one point per slide, with as few words as possible.

Storytelling is a popular way to communicate a message. Rather than relying only on logic and facts to make a compelling argument, storytelling couples that with compelling conflicts and solutions to make an emotional connection with the audience.

For example, let's say you have a system that is experiencing some availability issues, and you've developed an architecture decision that recommends resolving the root cause. A factual, conventional way to present this architecture decision might be something like this:

Problem statement
Systems are unavailable x% of time.

Solution approach
We will improve the system availability while keeping in mind our SLAs and balancing cost.

Solution options
We explored different ways to improve, and here are the pros and cons of each.

Solution recommendation
Based on our analysis, we recommend this particular option.

Next steps
We need your approval to implement this option.

A storytelling way might be something like this:

Conflict
Our customers weren't able to do what we promised they could do because our system was not available x% of time.

Journey to resolution

We care about our customers and understand there are requirements and constraints to trade off against. We thought through three options.

Solution

We recommend this option as the best path forward and need your help to implement it.

Which version do you think will get a better response in your organization?

Improving Communication

Communication is a competency and skill set that can always be improved further. My background in history gave me a great foundation of written skills, and my professional consulting background gave me a great foundation of verbal skills. Yet still, year after year, I have worked on refining these skills further.

I have often been asked for advice in my mentoring and coaching relationships on communication. Here is what I have shared:

Become a good listener.

Think of communication as a two-way interaction that yields a connection, not just the dissemination of a point. Thus, you have to listen first, and truly understand your audience to connect with them.

Keep it simple.

It doesn't matter how much you know if others don't understand you. Simplification is hard work, but it's worth it to bring others along.

Practice makes you better.

I don't like to say *practice makes perfect*, because that is an unrealistic expectation. Practice does, however, help refine technique, calm nerves, and help you learn from experience. It can be helpful to have allies in a room who observe you and give you feedback on your communication, so you can learn from constructive criticism.

Take your time.

Sometimes people feel the need to speak and come across as dominating or incoherent or generate some other negative perception. I've found that this often happens when people are insecure in their standing and feel that they need to say something to be considered an active participant. Or they may feel rushed and compelled to say something without fully thinking through their points. Try not to rush. Take your time. And if you are facilitating the discussion, create ground rules and a culture that allows people to take their time and that is considerate of hearing each person's point of view.

> *Use emotion wisely.*
>
> Passion, excitement, caring, kindness—all of these emotions can positively impact communication. To wield them wisely such that they add to your message and do not detract from your overall point, you need to first become self-aware enough that you understand and acknowledge that you are in fact feeling an emotion. For example, I have gotten better at recognizing when something frustrates me in a conversation. I do not allow that frustration to show in my mannerisms. Rather, I take a breath and remind myself of my purpose and why I am in that conversation.
>
> There are many communication resources and courses out there. I highly recommend investing in your communication skills, because communication is such an essential competency for you to be a leader, and effective architects are excellent leaders.

There are many different communication styles. A visionary leader is able to use the strength of their convictions to motivate and inspire an audience to achieve an aspiration. A conventional leader dictates what must be done, why, and how, relying on the strength of their own authority to get things done. A collaborative leader establishes trust and shows how diverse perspectives were considered to reach a conclusion.

In practice, I've found myself sliding among all of these styles depending upon the circumstance. Visionary communication suits me well when I am passionate and believe in an idea and I want other people to join me in proactively solving a problem. I tend to use this style when briefing partners and executives. I try to paint a vivid, compelling picture of the future and ensure that they understand what I am saying to get buy-in on the conflict, the destination or resolution, and the journey to get there.

Conventional is helpful when I need to state that a standard is non-negotiable; this was the most uncomfortable style for me to adopt because I had to learn to be OK with not always being liked. Collaborative is probably my most-used style, leveraged during all of the discussions that lead up to formulating an architecture decision or strategy.

Regardless of your communication style, here are some tips for giving effective presentations:

- Speak with confidence and poise, with a respectful tone to instill credibility and trust in your position.
- Speak at a volume and cadence that allows for people to follow along easily. It's OK to let some of your passion through, but don't let excitement make you too loud or rush your words.

- Practice making pauses seem natural so that you don't use filler words like "um."

- Practice in front of a mirror so that you understand your nonverbal cues. For example, sitting straight conveys more confidence than slumping over does. Make eye contact.

- Use your active listening skills to read the audience's reactions and tailor your communication accordingly.

- Pretend you're having a conversation, so that you don't come across too rehearsed.

In addition to using communication to align others, you should also define and execute a communication plan as part of your strategy. This communication plan serves to ensure alignment throughout implementation. Repetition is key; in a wildly changing landscape, reminding people why you are doing what you are doing, and celebrating the wins, is important to sustaining momentum toward your long-term vision.

Now that we've reviewed the 4 Cs framework, let's go back to defining objectives for your enterprise architecture strategy. What kind of goals can your organization set to balance proactiveness and reactiveness? Does your organization tend to operate in firefighter mode, without thinking about the long-term future? If so, a culture shift may be needed to introduce strategic thinking and proactive architecture decisions. What are the strategic problems to solve, and is it clear what roles solve them? If not, you can craft objectives to clarify this.

The case studies in the next section may provide some inspiration for your own objectives and key results.

Case Studies

Let's review a few case studies and examine some thematic dos and don'ts that they reveal. The first scenario is called *the cloud migration*.

The Cloud Migration

EA Example Company watched its competition get into the cloud and decided that the time was right to make a strategic investment in migrating to the public cloud themselves. They declared a vision that they would be a cloud-based company and defined an ambitious timeframe. At the end of the timeframe, EA Example Company was successful in migrating many workloads, predominantly using a lift and shift technique, but experienced major delays in getting new business features delivered, unexpectedly had significantly increased operational costs, and did not fully complete their migration, especially of complex mission-critical workloads.

What happened here?

EA Example Company defined a vision to get into the cloud because they saw the problem as this: they weren't in the cloud when their competition was. However, this wasn't actually solving the right problem. What was the business driver of using a new technology? Perhaps the business driver should have been something around developing more stable solutions in a more cost-effective, scalable, highly perform-ant, agile way. When phrased that way, getting to the cloud would have been part of the solution, rather than the solution itself. In addition, they only declared a time-frame, not an actual strategy that defined the plan to achieve the vision. A strategy would have included tactical aspects such as workload dependency management, cost optimization, workload deprecation, and/or rearchitecture.

Key takeaways from this tale include the following.

Do:

- Use industry trends, market research, and competitive analysis to formulate a proactive architecture strategic direction.

Don't:

- Solve the wrong problem, or solve a problem without considering the business purpose.
- Provide a strategy of proactive architecture without tactics and reactive architec-ture decisions.

The next scenario is the AI inflection point.

The AI Inflection Point

EA Example Company came up with a strategy to unleash potential from their data by making data as usable as possible, and they put an emphasis on machine learning. Thus, when AI came along in the form of large language models, they were well posi-tioned to get onboard with this newest technology trend. However, they assumed that everyone already knew about and was excited about AI, and therefore they had very vague messaging around AI. The one sound byte that developers started to hear was that AI was going to replace menial tasks for developers. Morale and productivity decreased as developers started to fear job insecurity. In reality, EA Example Com-pany was trying to reduce menial work as a way to increase developer productivity—not to replace the developers themselves.

What happened here?

EA Example Company defined a proactive strategy to invest in machine learning and was well positioned to take advantage of the next technology wave of AI. However, their lack of clear, concise, and transparent communication confused developers on what the company was trying to do with AI.

What are the key takeaways?

Do:

- Use industry trends, market research, and competitive analysis to formulate a proactive architecture strategic direction that can withstand changes in the marketplace.

Don't:

- Underestimate the value of good communication. A simple, storytelling narrative that can share strategic intent and a well-thought-out approach—that lets people buy in and assuage doubts—goes a long way.

The last scenario is called *the tactical load*.

The Tactical Load

EA Example Company incentivized and valued short-term wins. As a result, teams solved problems day in and day out, without ever making time to consider the big picture. Architects were incentivized to perform hands-on coding themselves, rather than spend time debating and getting alignment on shared architecture decisions. As a result, the company was able to make progress in delivering features, but it found itself unable to stitch the features together into a cohesive experience for its end users and wound up repeating issues. In addition, as time went by, their competition sped ahead in anticipating consumer demands that changed based on technology advances like AI, while EA Example Company lagged behind, trying to optimize its original offerings.

What happened here?

EA Example Company embraced a culture of fighting fires and focused on being very reactive and tactical only. As a result, the tactical nature of their solutions proved to be too shortsighted to make headway in the changing technological landscape.

What are the key takeaways?

Do:

- Solve problems.

Don't:

- Overemphasize reactive, tactical architecture decisions. A well-thought-out long-term strategy adds inherent value by providing unified direction that can reduce duplicative efforts and bring competitive advantage. Both strategy and tactics are needed.

- Confuse strategy with tactics. For example, although an architect needs to be technically grounded to ensure that their strategic decisions are feasible, emphasizing that they themselves must unilaterally code is missing the point. Architects can code, and sometimes do code to prove out ideas. But to scale, they can also work with other teams to prove out the ideas, while they personally tackle the big-picture thinking and provide the overall strategic guidance as their technical contribution.

Summary

To define and achieve an objective that balances proactive and reactive architecture decisions, and that therefore balances strategy and tactics for your own organization, consider where your organization falls on the proactive/reactive spectrum, and whether or not you would benefit from a change. Consider your talent and whether or not training is needed to increase and improve the number of strategic thinkers.

Establish or promote principles of strategic thinking to help architects understand the right problem, initiate innovation, and be change agents. To further teach strategic thinking, use the 4 Cs framework:

Curiosity
Ask strategic questions to formulate the right business-minded strategic purpose and problem statement. This allows for learning and anticipating the future.

Challenge
Critically analyze inputs such as market research and industry trends to come up with solution options, and then challenge these options to figure out what could go wrong and what can be done to mitigate those risks. This allows for interpreting information to figure out how to navigate the unknown future.

Credibility
Use reactive architecture decisions to define a credible approach to achieving your proposed solution, with clear incremental milestones defined that are designed to build confidence in the strategy through quick wins. This allows for alignment.

Communication

Communicate a compelling narrative to get buy-in on the strategy, and define a communication plan to reiterate the strategy throughout implementation. Determine what communication styles work best in your organizational culture, and coach your strategic thinkers to embody these styles and simplify their messages. This allows for sustained alignment.

Diagnose weaknesses in proactive and reactive architecture decision making that you can strengthen through your enterprise architecture strategy objectives and key results.

Now that I've covered possible enterprise architecture strategy objectives in depth, I'll turn our attention toward understanding key enterprise architecture principles that will guide achieving those objectives for the next five chapters.

CHAPTER 7

A Very Short Manifesto for Effective Enterprise Architecture

The first manifesto that I encountered in my career was the Agile Manifesto (*https://agilemanifesto.org*), when I was working in an organization that was undergoing an Agile transformation. The Agile Manifesto provided several principles that were helpful to guide the numerous decisions that were made to transition from the old way of doing things to the new, Agile way.

Similarly, I believe that the practice of enterprise architecture is also transforming, out of necessity. It is transitioning from the old way of doing things—which was marked by heavy process, governance, and potentially too much theory—to the new way of doing things, which is all about driving business outcomes through holistic problem-solving, value-added standards, and relevant strategic thinking.

In my 20+ years of working, I have experienced all sorts of architecture paradigms and seen firsthand what happens when architecture is perceived to be ineffective.

I have witnessed disdain: "I don't know what those architects do all day." This was from when I was on an engineering team that was lamenting about being hamstrung from being able to use newer technologies that weren't yet approved. The team didn't even know that there were enterprise architecture standards that were supposed to be followed, let alone an extensive approval process to add or change standards, until it ran into a brick wall trying to procure the new technology.

I have witnessed ignorance: "We didn't have architects where I'm from, and we did just fine." This was from when a new leader was hired into my organization, and I had the opportunity to point out that perhaps our definitions of "fine" were different. Although their previous organization did make revenue, it was clear that they lacked architecture direction, given the amount of duplication in their products and services, the lack of interoperability between them, and the disjointed experience across them.

I have also witnessed appreciation: "My architect is essential to my team's ability to operate." This was from a leader who was an experienced architect and who understood the value of delivering technology solutions in accordance with a well-thought-out architectural direction.

I have had the honor and privilege to meet and work with many great architects. When I reflect on what made these architects effective, I realized that they all had a few values in common:

They believed firmly in the collective whole over the individual good.
This is an especially difficult thing to balance when doing the right thing for the collective good is contrary to doing what may be desired for a team's or an individual's benefit. For example, a team may want to skirt standards to get things done and over with, and the architect is in the precarious position of convincing them to do what is right, not just what is quick. Such architects greatly value integrity, and they have learned how to influence others without coming across as bottlenecks themselves.

They were perceived as proactive technology leaders first, and architects second.
This is an important mindset shift because the branding of *technology leader* resonates well, whereas not everyone immediately understands the value of architecture, as discussed in Chapter 1. Also, being a technology leader is important to being an effective architect since that allows the architect to influence changes.

They valued a deep understanding of business needs.
It was this focus on customers and business outcomes that was valued by their organization.

They valued continuous learning.
They were curious and inquisitive, always increasing their knowledge, and were open-minded. They made an effort to keep their technical skills up to date.

They valued collaboration.
They were humble and secure in their knowledge and welcomed diverse points of view. They understood that providing a solution was only half of their work, and that the other half required the ability to build coalitions and manage changes.

There were times when I saw organizations embrace architecture and bring in the right architects with the right mindset to lead effective change. There were times where I saw organizations stumble, confused about the purpose of architecture, much to the detriment of the people performing architecture work. I have seen enthusiasm for the practice of architecture, but without the appreciation for the people that performed the architecture work.

As a result, I have developed a perspective on what makes architecture, and the people performing architecture functions, effective and valuable to an organization. I am sharing that perspective with you now in the condensed form of four principles for effective enterprise architecture. As stated in the Agile Manifesto, "while there is value in the items on the right, we value the items on the left more." Similarly, the following principles, which constitute my very short manifesto here, emphasize the items on the left as more valuable than the items on the right:

- Contextual understanding *over* siloed decision making
- Tangible direction *over* stale documentation
- Driving behavior *over* enforcing standards
- Evolution *over* frameworks

Enterprise architecture as a practice needs to be effective if it's going to be invested in by an organization. It is therefore helpful to be guided by principles, born from experience, of what works well, and what doesn't, when establishing an architecture practice and performing architecture work.

The next four chapters dive into each principle in depth.

CHAPTER 8

Contextual Understanding over Siloed Decision Making

Enterprise architecture principles help ensure that architecture decisions are made consistently. The first enterprise architecture principle in the very short manifesto for effective enterprise architecture is *contextual understanding over siloed decision making.*

Ever make a perfect architecture decision? If so, kudos on an extremely rare achievement. In my experience, architecture decisions require trade-offs, and therefore tend to be merely good enough rather than perfect.

The *good enough* result depends on what considerations are made during the analysis of what to trade off against. Often, the quality of an architecture decision is directly impacted by the experience and knowledge of the person who made it, and what they considered as trade-offs and implications. If trade-offs are improperly considered, the decision is at risk of being shortsighted.

Contextual understanding refers to understanding all the factors that form the problem statement and rationale of the decision, to include background, usage scenarios, assumptions, constraints, solution alternatives, and implications pertaining to the decision. *Siloed decision making* refers to making decisions based solely on one's own experiences and point of view.

Here's a real-world example. My husband and I decided to treat ourselves by not cooking for dinner. Now, if we were to make that decision in a silo, we would consider only what we like to eat, the cost of the meal, and our memories of what restaurants we enjoyed. Ultimately, we would likely go out to a nearby restaurant. However, with the context that our children also needed to eat and have different tastes, that it was a weeknight and therefore we were shorter on time than a weekend, and that we needed leftovers, this resulted in a different decision—ordering in from a restaurant that mostly pleased everyone. As mentioned earlier, decisions tend to be good enough rather than perfect, so the one person who didn't like the food made do with a tried and true alternative found at home.

You'll notice that the word *over* is included in the principle that gives its name to this chapter. This is deliberate, to emphasize the item on the left, contextual understanding, as more valuable than the item on the right, siloed decision making. Thus, the item on the right does have some value, just comparatively less.

You see, being able to make decisions in silo is actually quite important to avoid paralysis by analysis. *Paralysis by analysis* means waiting on analyzing so many factors, and being so concerned with the unknown or unpredictable factors, that no decision is made. Siloed decision making can help with this scenario to build confidence through one's experiences to provide a well-formed opinion even if all desired contextual information isn't available. One mechanism that can help shore up this well-formed opinion is to document all assumptions that are made, such that if any factor does change or turn out differently, it is easier to go back and review the decision and make changes. This helps the decision maker take calculated risks and make forward progress by still making a decision even when not all context is available.

Imagine crossing the street at a crosswalk in an intersection with a stop sign and seeing a car bearing down on you. Without waiting for the context of whether it will stop or not, you will use your experience to get out of its way because you know that in human versus car scenarios, car wins. Time-sensitive decisions tend to timebox how much context can be gathered. As a result, it is also an important skill to be able to prioritize sources of context, such that the most impactful contextual factors are considered.

Decisions made with contextual understanding are likely to be less brittle and more sustainable than those made without it. This is key in architectural decision making since, although architectures do evolve over time, changing certain architectural decisions after implementation can be very painful and very difficult. Enabling flexibility as an outcome is key to evolutionary architecture.

A good example of this concept is in application interface design. Designing this contract between applications to exchange data is an architectural matter that needs to be made with context of usage, performance, and security requirements. Using the interface as an abstraction allows the application to change behind the scenes as it needs, such as adopting a more modern technology stack.

The more painful it will be to change a decision, the more important it is to gather context to make that decision.

Now that I've shared my perspective on the value of contextualized decision making over siloed decision making, I'll spend the next section discussing where context comes from and how these factors can be prioritized.

Architectural Domain Model

To apply the principle of contextual understanding over siloed decision making, it is helpful to define a capability classification model that groups capabilities into architecture domains. This model allows for decisions about those capabilities, and the technological solutions that provide them, to be made in context of the overall domain and any other dependent domains. The domain context itself is defined in relation to the business processes and outcomes that it supports.

Capabilities are enduring in a way that organizational structures that define ownership of technology solutions are not. Capabilities for a core business function typically stay the same, even as technology evolves to provide those capabilities. Capabilities themselves evolve based on business needs or business practices evolving. This is all well and good, but what exactly are capabilities? The next section will clarify.

What Are Capabilities?

Are you wondering if I mean business capabilities or technical capabilities when I say *capabilities*? *Business capabilities* describe the abilities of the business, the organization, to do things. Business capabilities are not tied to any given solution, part of the organization, role, or function. As mentioned earlier in terms of endurance, business capabilities do not change even if the organization splits or changes, or a new technology is used to implement the capability. *Technical capabilities* describe using technology to result in business outcomes. Similar to business capabilities, technical capabilities are also enduring and do not change even when an organization or a specific tool changes. Technical capabilities map to business capabilities. Technical solutions map to technical capabilities. Together, these mappings provide a lineage from technology to business outcomes. Thus, to summarize, I mean both business and technical capabilities.

Figure 8-1 illustrates an example using capability mapping lineage in the context of resiliency.

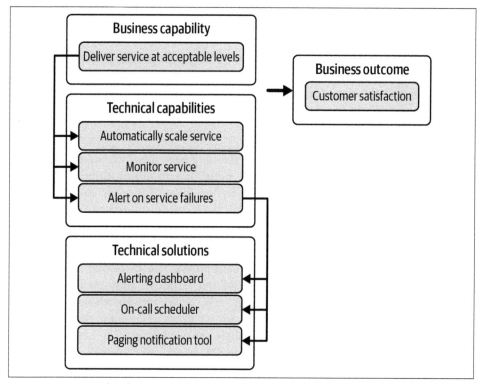

Figure 8-1. Example of mapped business and technical capabilities resulting in a business outcome

One thing you may notice from the example in Figure 8-1 is that a capability defines *what* the ability is, not *how* the ability is implemented. The capabilities are agnostic of the choice of technology solution or tooling.

How Capabilities Fit in an Architecture Domain Model

The architectural domain model should have two levels, a business capability model and a technical capability model, which are tied together. The business capability model typically helps an enterprise better understand its own business functions and abilities, which provides the context necessary to make important strategic decisions such as where to invest. Similarly, the technical capability model typically helps an enterprise better understand its technology solution landscape and how technologies are being applied. It provides the context to make various decisions, including decisions to:

- Overcome gaps and technical weaknesses.

- Overcome arbitrary uniqueness and reduce duplication or converge development efforts.

- Invest in more sustainable solutions rather than bespoke, niche projects.

- Make underlying technology changes and be able to identify implications to the organization or business as a result of the change.

Figure 8-2 illustrates such a layered architectural domain model, using the traditional three-tier application architecture of presentation, logic, and data layers as inspiration.

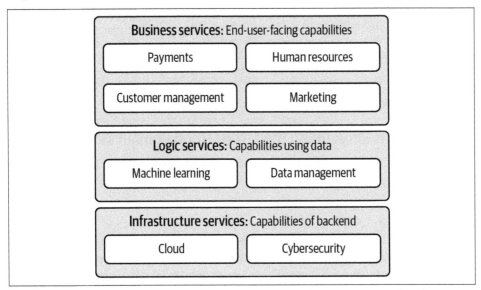

Figure 8-2. Example of layered architectural domain model, where each white box is an architectural domain, a group of business and technical capabilities

Unlike the traditional three-tier model—where the presentation tier at the top and the data tier at the bottom do not directly communicate with one another—in this architectural domain model, the domains and their capabilities can interact with one another to map to a business process. The value of the layer is simply in nesting or categorizing domains for human readability and discoverability.

Figure 8-3 builds on the layered architecture domain model to illustrate emailing a customer as the mapped business process.

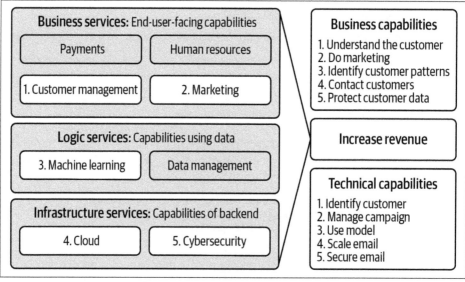

Business services: End-user-facing capabilities

Payments	Human resources
1. Customer management	2. Marketing

Logic services: Capabilities using data

3. Machine learning	Data management

Infrastructure services: Capabilities of backend

4. Cloud	5. Cybersecurity

Business capabilities
1. Understand the customer
2. Do marketing
3. Identify customer patterns
4. Contact customers
5. Protect customer data

Increase revenue

Technical capabilities
1. Identify customer
2. Manage campaign
3. Use model
4. Scale email
5. Secure email

Figure 8-3. Example of a layered architectural domain model

Considerations for Defining the Architectural Domain Model

Defining capabilities—whether business or technical—and defining the domains that group them is more of an art than a science. Here are some considerations for defining capabilities:

Focus on what, not how

For business capabilities, what is the business doing? What can the business do? For technical capabilities, what can the technology do? In the previous section's example, the business is trying to contact customers, and the corresponding technical capability is to email the customers.

Level of detail

Typically, you will find that you end up with a hierarchy of multiple levels. You can have as many levels as make sense for your organization to understand what the capabilities mean, and how they drill down and map to one another. In the previous section's example, the email capability stems from reusable infrastructure services, rather than being a bespoke capability that only services the marketing domain to contact customers.

Common language

Decide on whether you will use verbs or nouns to define your capabilities, and their order. For example, is it *data management* or *manage data*? The goal is to make the domain model self-service so that users of the model who make architecture decisions, be they an architect themselves or a person in a product or engineering role, can understand the capability definition. This common language will also help to create shared alignment across an organization, which is of the utmost importance to establish the architecture decisions related to a domain. In the previous section's example, the "verb first, noun second" order is used.

Here are some considerations for defining architectural domains:

Logical boundary

The capabilities in a group should be related in some logical way to support a given business purpose. In the previous section's example, customer management is distinct from marketing, although marketing is a way to manage customer expectations.

Domain hierarchy

Similar to the level of detail consideration mentioned earlier, groupings can get as detailed as needed to use the domain and their child domains in decision making. Rather than create these domain definitions in the abstract for the sake of having a model, do so with the aim of clarifying ambiguity with the right level of detail. In the previous section's example, customer management implies managing any kind of customer—both prospective and existing—that are used by the marketing campaigns. But perhaps this is a differentiator for your organization, and you would have different domains for capabilities that target prospective customers versus capabilities that target existing ones.

Distributed accountability

The architectural domain model needs to be an effective tool to aid architecture decision making. As a result, it should be very clear what roles are accountable for what responsibilities as related to an architecture domain. For example, someone needs to be accountable for defining the capabilities (usually a business architect), for mapping the technical solutions (usually a domain architect), for the architecture decision (usually the domain architect), for implementing the architecture decision (usually the technology lead of the impacted technical solution), and for prioritizing the architecture decision for implementation (usually the product lead of the impacted technical solution).

Although the architectural domain model is an important mechanism to provide context for a number of architecture decisions, it is not the only one.

Other Contextual Inputs

Context for all architecture decisions includes a well-defined problem statement. Depending on the kind of decision that needs to be made, additional factors are helpful to provide more context, such as principles and constraints.

For example, the architectural domain model should help determine that a decision is needed to invest in a new technical capability. To proceed with this decision may in turn require a build-versus-buy decision. To make a build-versus-buy decision, context typically also includes capturing all identified solution options, architecture principles, and NFRs to assess the solution options against. See Chapter 5 for examples of NFRs; you'll want to define a standard baseline of NFRs to use in architecture decision making.

Some of these solution options may be discovered from what already exists in the architectural domain model, whereas others may come from industry and market research. Context may also include things like whether or not there is budget and capacity to support a new solution or whether or not it is feasible to extend an existing solution.

 Timebox the time spent gathering context to accelerate decision-making progress and avoid analysis paralysis. Capture all trade-offs and implications as the context in which the decision was made.

In summary, contextual understanding includes a well-defined problem statement and all of the inputs that were taken into consideration to make the decision.

Case Studies

Let's examine a few anecdotal case studies and study the themes that they present.

The Aloof Architect

EA Example Company promoted a fast-paced culture where speed and time to market were of the essence. It needed to deliver a critical service, which, because it was critical, needed to be highly available. A seasoned architect, Alice, was asked to design the critical service's high availability (HA) architecture.

Alice had several years of experience in designing technical systems with HA architectures. As a result, Alice assumed the level of HA needed and included proven architectural elements such as redundancy, scaling, and failover for the new critical service to overcome well-known failure modes. The engineering team conducted several performance tests and, sure enough, the critical service was able to horizontally scale to outpace demand, and failover as needed. Alice was proud of herself and did not think to consider how the new critical service would interact in an ecosystem of other services. The critical service went into production only to experience a severe incident a few days later when a downstream dependency failed and impacted the availability of this critical service.

What happened here?

This was an example of the *aloof architect*, who is not interested or involved in collaborating to contextualize decisions, because they are overly confident and certain in their instincts and experiences to make decisions. An aloof architect typically has good intentions, but their self-reliance can lead to missing important considerations that inevitably lead to flawed, shortsighted decision making. In this scenario, the aloof architect, Alice, did design a proven, highly available architecture for this critical service based on her own experiences, but she missed the architectural domain–level context of how this application fit into the ecosystem and failed to consider dependencies as a factor.

Key takeaways include the following.

Do:

- Reuse proven architecture patterns.
- Prioritize the need for more context to make impactful decisions.

Don't:

- Solve the wrong problem, or solve an incomplete problem without considering necessary context.

The Aware Architect

EA Example Company learned from experience and decided that, in addition to time to market, valuing operational excellence was also important. To deliver a critical service, the company relied on another experienced architect, Amanda, to design the critical service's HA architecture. Amanda decided to first confirm the business requirements of what level of HA was needed for this critical service. Amanda first mapped the critical service to EA Example Company's architectural domain model and mapped that in turn to critical business processes. Based on that mapping, Amanda was able to better understand what this critical service was dependent on and what the overall level of service available to customers needed to be.

Amanda asked questions of the architects and engineers of the dependent services to find out what kind of telemetry was available if they failed. She recognized that she was not a monitoring expert, and so she brought in a monitoring subject matter expert to figure out whether the telemetry was sufficient or not. She conducted a failure mode analysis to understand the probability and impact of such failures, as well as failures within the critical service's components. Based on all this context, along with her own experiences, Amanda designed a highly available architecture, which included a caching layer to support acceptable stale data in the case of the loss of the dependency.

Amanda reviewed this architecture with peers and senior engineers, who asked questions and uncovered additional weaknesses that could be strengthened. As a result, she iterated a couple of times before finalizing the architecture. She collaborated with the engineering team to implement and test the architecture, and to tune key pieces such as the monitoring and alerting telemetry used for automation capabilities. It took a bit longer to get to production with their critical service, but the service was performant and highly available and gracefully degraded performance when faced with the failure of the dependent service rather than a full outage.

What happened here?

This example details the *aware architect*, who is consistently able to bring contextual understanding into their architecture decision making. An aware architect provides context from many different perspectives, ranging from business to technical, across different disciplines and subject matter domains. An aware architect is always learning and can bring in their context to inform the decision-making process. An aware architect is also self-aware in understanding their own limits and will bring in additional expertise as needed to supplement their own contextual understanding.

Key takeaways are summarized as follows.

Do:

- Seek diverse perspectives and voices of dissent to bring in varied context and strengthen decision making.

Don't:

- Ignore the value of accepting trade-offs and their implications. In this scenario, the caching layer was an acceptable mitigation for the failure of the dependency, resulting in performance degradation rather than no adverse impact whatsoever.

As demonstrated by these anecdotal case studies, it is better to be an aware architect —aware of your own limitations and seeking to learn context—rather than an aloof architect who relies only on themselves.

Summary

Context is essential for making a high-quality, sustainable architecture decision. This chapter covered the first recommended enterprise architecture principle, *contextual understanding over siloed decision making*, for organizations to output great architecture decisions consistently.

One way to bring context into architecture decision making is through the architectural domain model. The architectural domain model for an organization is a key artifact output of an effective enterprise architecture function. It is a capability classification model that provides a common language for understanding what the business does. It provides traceability across business and technical capabilities to technology solutions in the context of business outcomes. That understanding provides a great deal of necessary context for architecture decisions, including the following:

- Investment in new capabilities or new solutions
- Deprecation of existing solutions
- Build-versus-buy decisions regarding technology
- Decisions on reuse of existing solutions
- Investment into overcoming technical weaknesses or gaps

Aware architects are those who are adept at considering contextual understanding to make architecture decisions. They understand the limitations of their own experiences and point of view, and they actively seek out other points of view and frames of reference for a more holistic context from which to make decisions. Aloof architects are a cautionary tale; they rely only on themselves, their own experiences, and their own point of view to make decisions. They tend to have good intentions but are at risk of delivering shortsighted decisions.

The ability to perform siloed decision making, especially in times of duress or time sensitivity, is still an important skill. The risk of shortsighted decisions can be mitigated in part by understanding how to prioritize contextual factors to gather just what is needed to make a *good enough* architecture decision that takes calculated, documented, and accepted risks.

In other words, this architecture principle values contextual understanding more highly than siloed decision making, yet understands the need to make decisions in silo as well.

CHAPTER 9

Tangible Direction over Stale Documentation

The second enterprise architecture principle in the very short manifesto for effective enterprise architecture is *tangible direction over stale documentation*.

Tangible in the context of this principle is referring to the metaphorical meaning of having a measurable value rather than the literal meaning of being perceptible by touch. *Measurable value* in the context of architecture output is synonymous with business value. The architectural direction must have a clear association with business value to be effective. This association is what transforms documentation, a typical vehicle of delivering architectural direction, into tangible direction.

Documentation done well can provide several benefits:

Enable collaboration and communication
> Documents and diagrams help focus conversations and accelerate getting people on the same page to talk through problem-solving. In addition, documentation preserves a historical record that can help teams avoid rehashing the same topic over and over again. It is typically easier to react to something tangible that is written down and/or visualized than talked about in the abstract.

Provide clarity
> Clear documentation and diagrams facilitate efficient and effective understanding of a technology solution, an architecture domain, or interactions across domains. Clarity reduces operational inefficiency that occurs from misunderstanding or misalignment.

Identify risk-based insights
> Clear documents allow for identifying areas of risk to mitigate them and enable comparison to established patterns. For example, examining a deployment

architecture allows the reviewer to discover whether or not horizontal scaling is possible, and whether or not there are single points of failure that introduce resiliency and reliability risk.

Every architecture document described in Chapter 2 should have an associated business value, as shown in Table 9-1.

Table 9-1. Example of associating business value with an architecture document

Architecture document	Possible business value
Architecture principles	X% increased productivity due to consistent and sustainable decision making
Architecture standards	X% reduction in arbitrary uniqueness, thereby enabling Y% cost savings Z% increased productivity due to conformance and avoidance of compliance issues
Architecture frameworks	X% increased productivity due to clear guidelines
Architecture patterns / best practices	X% increased productivity due to reuse Y% cost savings due to avoiding compliance issues
Architecture diagrams	Depends on the problem being solved as depicted in the diagram—for example, X% cost savings or Y% improvement in risk and compliance posture
Architecture metrics	X% increase in operational efficiency based on data insights

As Chapter 6 discussed, architecture strategy is another key architectural output that uses documentation. It can be very difficult to quantify the impact of an architecture strategy, especially when it can take years to deliver against the direction set out in the strategy. To help overcome this challenge, I recommend getting into the habit of sizing the problem that is being solved by the strategy. If you can size the problem—by understanding who or what is impacted, to what degree, and what is being impeded or lost—then you can say that the strategy will provide quantifiable benefits for solving it.

For example, an architectural serverless strategy could solve a problem around maintaining nonserverless infrastructure and frequent disruptions from needing to patch vulnerabilities, which relates to total cost of ownership and productivity. There could be a one-time trade-off of migration or conversion cost to reach a serverless state for existing systems, but overall the strategic benefit adds up over time. Incremental milestones could be defined to show progress against achieving these benefits.

The rest of this chapter is devoted to concepts that allow for tangible direction to be defined and accepted.

The Importance of Experimentation

One pitfall of architecture is being too theoretical or abstract to be understandable, and therefore being unable to provide tangible direction. Architecture assertions need to be grounded in technical fact for many reasons, including getting alignment based on trust and confidence that the architecture direction is correct.

One popular method to yield technical facts is experimentation. *Experimentation* can take the form of proof of concepts or pilots to prove out the ideas in the architecture. For example, if the architecture direction is to use serverless technology because it will save labor and time, then conduct an experiment to prove that that is in fact the outcome of using serverless technology, and that it is in fact possible to use serverless technology in the current systems. It is likely that there will be lessons learned from such experiments that will strengthen the overall strategy for how to achieve serverless at scale.

Another method is to review proven industry case studies and demonstrations and use these as proof for an architecture recommendation. This method is not necessarily enough on its own. Experimentation in your own organization's environment is more definitive proof that an architectural direction is correct.

It is not always possible to experiment to prove out every architecture decision. While it is advisable to experiment with significantly impactful decisions, where experimentation is not possible due to constraints such as time, progress can still be made as long as calculated risks are accepted and potential failure is tolerated as an opportunity to learn and course correct. This ability to accept risk and tolerate failure is a cultural trait.

Documentation Standards

You'll notice that I qualified the benefits of documentation with the statement of documentation *done well*. Chapter 4 already elaborated on the knowledge management and usability aspects of documentation done well. This section elaborates on documentation standards, which define guidelines that allow for common and consistent communications through diagrams.

Such standards or guidelines should cover the following elements of a diagram:

Symbology
What do all the symbols used in a diagram represent? For example, an arrow: is the arrow documenting a data flow, a network interaction, an ontology, or something else? Is there any meaningful difference between a solid or dashed line used for the arrow? Or how about the type of arrowhead? Is there a specific iconography used? For example, cloud providers such as Amazon Web Services (AWS) provide their own iconography for architecture diagrams.

Colors
Keeping accessibility in mind, define consistent aesthetics and purposes. Try not to deviate from societal norms to avoid cognitive dissonance. For example, red

usually means bad or high risk, yellow indicates medium bad or medium risk, and green means good or low risk.

Granularity

Decide on the level of detail for each diagram type and be consistent. For instance, if a diagram gets too cluttered and is hard to follow, it is likely trying to cram too much information into one visual and should be decomposed. A diagram should be intuitive and speak for itself.

See examples such as the C4 model (*https://c4model.com*) for already defined standards. Let's look at examples of common architectural views. Figure 9-1 illustrates a generic layered hierarchy view, used to show how capabilities or systems are composable. Figure 9-2 illustrates an ontology or interaction view, used to show how systems relate to one other. Relationships can represent flows including but not limited to data, network, or dependencies. Figure 9-3 is a generic example of a deployment view, which ideally would use the industry standard iconography. Figure 9-4 illustrates sequence views, which show step-by-step interactions between systems and/or users.

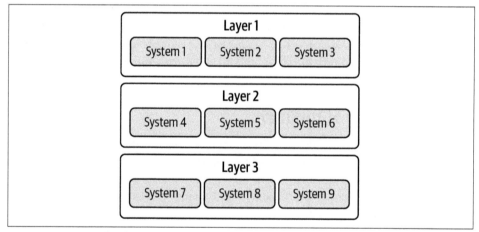

Figure 9-1. Example of a layered hierarchy view

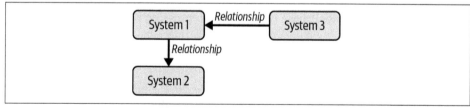

Figure 9-2. Example of an ontology or an interaction view

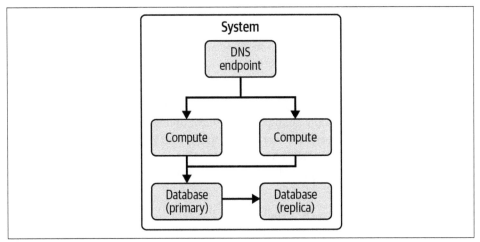

Figure 9-3. Example of a deployment view

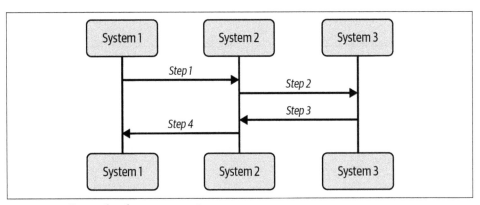

Figure 9-4. Example of a sequence view

Documentation as Code

There are modeling languages for architecture diagrams such as Unified Modeling Language (UML) (*https://uml.org*), PlantUML (*https://plantuml.com*), ArchiMate (*https://oreil.ly/9R6FZ*), Systems Modeling Language (SysML) (*https://sysml.org*), and Business Process Model and Notation (BPMN) (*http://www.bpmn.org*). These modeling languages provide a common, and usually simple, way to describe architectural characteristics of technology solutions and software. In addition, modeling languages are essentially ways to output a diagram through code. As a result, this code can be managed similarly to traditional software code, supporting updates and enabling workflows as needed based on updates and reviews.

To overcome stale documentation, establishing update and maintenance mechanisms that are low effort and responsive to proactive triggers is key. Otherwise, the use of the diagrams in business processes such as architecture decisioning and incident management is suspect.

For example, let's say an architect defined a sequence diagram that described the integration between two systems to support a workflow. Wouldn't it be great if as soon as any elements in that diagram change in real-life implementation, the diagram was also updated? One way to ensure that this happens is to include diagrams as part of release packages, such that when change impact analysis occurs naturally as part of release management, any impacted diagrams are also updated. Essentially, diagrams need to be considered as living documents.

Another practical way that works well to keep diagrams up to date is to autogenerate them. This is not possible for every diagram, but it is possible for diagrams such as interaction views and deployment architectures. This method may still require some human oversight and judgment, but it reduces the manual effort that it takes to create and maintain the diagram.

A more novel idea is to make architecture diagrams queryable through code such that you can add a rules engine to glean insights. For example, let's say you have a dependency diagram that is queryable. Queries can be built that allow you to identify the blast radius of any given dependency and therefore measure the risk and impact of that dependency failing. As another example, imagine that a context view that describes how a system interacts with other systems is queryable. A rules engine could identify whether or not integration patterns are being followed by querying those interactions.

Case Studies

This section examines a few anecdotal case studies and studies the themes that they present.

The Archaeological Architect

Archie was an architect who worked at EA Example Company. Archie worked closely with a software engineering delivery team to understand their software products. He documented the current state of the software product using diagrams such as interaction views and sequence views with lengthy explanations. EA Example Company had a culture of frequent releases, and this team was no exception, releasing nearly every single week. Archie found that much of his time was consumed just keeping the current-state documentation up to date. The software engineering team did not include Archie in any decision making for new capabilities.

What happened here?

Archie is an example of the *archaeological architect*, someone stuck in documenting the current state and who spends more time updating the current state than they do in figuring out the future or target state. Although understanding the current state is important, architecture needs to be future facing and proactive. By only documenting what was or had already happened, Archie was adding limited value.

Key takeaways are summarized as follows.

Do:

- Be selective in what is documented.
- Maintain documentation so that it doesn't get stale.

Don't:

- Only document the current state.
- Rely on manual effort to keep documentation up to date.

The Ambitious Architect

Amber was another architect who worked for EA Example Company. Amber also worked closely with a software engineering team, and she took the time to build a relationship with the product and engineering leads to understand what problems they were facing with their software. She then worked with the team to document their current system architecture and coupled that with the understanding of their problems to put together another diagram with a couple of key changes as a proposal for an aspirational future system architecture. She reviewed the proposal with the team, and they discussed the recommended changes and identified constraints. They deliberated about the constraints to figure out which ones were truly constraints and which ones could be lifted, and then they settled on implementing the changes. She also gained consensus from the product lead to include documentation review as part of their definition of *done* for both feature delivery and product planning. This allowed for the whole team to feel a sense of ownership of their documentation, and for frequent review and incorporation of documentation into product decision making.

What happened here?

This example details the *ambitious architect*, someone who focuses documentation on problem-solving, particularly to define the future. Doing so allows for architecture to be proactive and strategic, to determine what is feasible and what is a constraint, and to define a tangible plan of action to overcome any challenges standing in the way of achieving the future state. The ambitious architect has ambitions to help the team use technology to solve future needs, not just the current-state deliberations.

Key takeaways are summarized as follows.

Do:

- Build a coalition of relationships with product and engineering teams to define value in documentation.
- Use documentation to define future state based on current-state understanding.
- Associate future-state architecture with business value.

Don't:

- Limit the future to today's constraints.

As demonstrated by these anecdotal case studies, it is better to be an ambitious architect, seeking tangible direction for an aspirational future, than an archaeological architect who limits themselves to the current state.

Summary

Documentation is necessary and critical to providing a clear understanding of an architecture. This chapter discussed the second recommended enterprise architecture principle, *tangible direction over stale documentation*, to highlight the need to make documentation as effective as possible.

Tangible direction means that the architecture decision and strategy have a clear associated business value and are grounded in technical fact versus theory. In addition, it is helpful for documentation to adhere to standards for consistent understanding and reduced cognitive load such as symbology, colors, and granularity.

Keeping documentation up to date so that it is not stale is a challenge that can be overcome in a variety of ways, such as defining and executing an update process, using automation to generate diagrams, and making diagrams queryable to allow for rules to prompt an update.

Ambitious architects understand how to use documentation to further their aspirations to achieve future-state architecture. Archaeological architects, on the other hand, spend too much time and effort on the current state without providing direction on the future.

Thus, documentation is extremely important and adds value, but not if it is allowed to get stale, and not if it doesn't provide tangible direction to achieve a business-beneficial future state.

A business-beneficial future state is also characterized by being secure and compliant. The next chapter dives into the third principle of the very short manifesto for effective enterprise architecture to achieve this characteristic.

CHAPTER 10

Driving Behavior over Enforcing Standards

The third enterprise architecture principle in the very short manifesto for effective enterprise architecture is *driving behavior over enforcing standards.*

Chapters 2 and 5 talked about standards and requirements and the importance of both enabling and enforcing them. The principle of driving behavior over enforcing standards emphasizes this idea to say that while enforcement is important and necessary, especially in a well-managed, regulated environment, defining standards and requirements in terms of human behavior is even more valuable. This is because the quality of compliance depends on human behavior.

There are two broad categories for the quality of compliance:

Minimum
> The minimum level of compliance is a pass or fail type of compliance against the minimum level of satisfaction to the standard or requirement.

Optimum
> The optimum level of compliance is satisfying the minimum level and also doing more to get the most benefit out of the standard or requirement. This can get nuanced pretty quickly.

For example, let's say there is an enterprise architecture standard to use a certain software programming language. The minimum level of compliance might be that the programming language is used. A more optimum level of usage might also consider the version used, best practices for managing memory and compute, using the right package manager, and using well-known, highly performant, vulnerability-free libraries.

Both the minimum and optimum levels are accelerated by incentivizing desired behavior.

Driving Desired Behavior

For driving the right behavior, Figure 10-1 provides a simple framework to use.

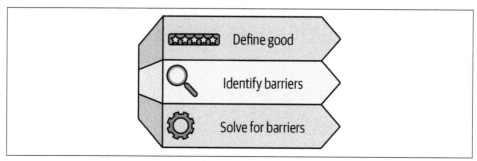

Figure 10-1. Framework to drive desired human behavior

You first have to define what *good* looks like. Is the minimum enough? Or is doing more, the optimal level, necessary?

From the example above, it could be that enforcement focuses on the minimum level to ensure that all software is developed using the standard programming language. While sufficient from a compliance perspective, from a human behavior perspective, it is likely better to go beyond the minimum and use the correct version without vulnerabilities.

After defining what good looks like, you then have to identify the barriers that prevent getting to that good outcome. For instance, why wouldn't a software engineer use the standard software language? There could be many reasons, including but not limited to the following:

- They didn't know they were supposed to use that language.
- They were more familiar with a different language and were more comfortable using what they knew.
- The software application was already written in a different language, and using the standard language would require a refactoring and migration that they didn't have time or priority for.
- It is too hard to use the standard language; the development ecosystem isn't set up to support using it.
- They believe that a different language is better suited for their specific problem.

Last but not least, depending on the barrier, there are different ways to solve for driving the right behavior, as shown by Table 10-1.

Table 10-1. Examples of driving behavior to adhere to standard software language

Potential barrier	Potential solutions
The software engineer doesn't know the requirement.	Implement training. Conduct a communications campaign. Only allow for the required language to be used in software delivery processes.
The software engineer is more familiar with other languages.	Implement a training program to upskill talent.
The software application is already using a different language.	Prioritize refactoring or grant an exception.
The development ecosystem is not set up to support the standard language.	Do not require the standard until the development ecosystem is enabled.
The software engineer prefers a different language for the specific problem.	Allow for a champion/challenger model to allow for differentiated use cases and/or prove that the standard works fine.

Human behavior is a complex topic. In my experience, behavior can be learned and conditioned.

Conditioning Behavior

Humans learn behaviors based on experiences. There are typically two kinds of learning:

Conscious learning
> This refers to increasing knowledge through explicit, deliberate choice. For example, a software engineer taking a training course.

Unconscious learning
> This refers to implicit learning. For example, if a leader talks about the value of well-managed software and the importance of risk mitigation, the software engineer learns to value these things as well.

These types of learning, when coupled with conditioning, are what enable humans to develop habits. *Conditioning* refers to associating consequences to a given behavior:

Positive
> Positive conditioning is often perceived as a reward. For example, if it is easy to complete a task, the human is likely to repeat that task. Positive conditioning could also involve recognition in the form of public appreciation for a job well done.

Negative
> Negative conditioning is often perceived as punishments or friction. For example, if it is difficult to complete a task, the human is likely to look for a

workaround or a way to bypass that difficulty in the future. Or, if credit is misplaced, the human is likely to not want to do the same work again.

Sometimes, friction is used as a tactic to drive the right behavior. Let's reuse the software language example. An organization may focus on enabling the standard software language such that the software engineer does not have to take any extra steps to use that language. They can just write their software, build it, test it, and deploy it. Whereas because the organization does not invest in enabling other languages, using an alternative language may cause friction, such as needing to get exception approvals, needing to follow a custom path to get software library dependencies from the right repository, or needing to work with cybersecurity to make sure their software is scanned. The use of the alternative language may not be outright blocked due to legacy workloads that require it, but the friction induced by using it would help dissuade new software from being built with it.

 Humans tend to be motivated to avoid friction when possible, so use friction with deliberate intent.

The next section looks more closely into motivation.

Understanding Motivation

Human motivation is a key part of human behavior. There are two categories of sources of motivation that inspire humans to take action:

External
> This refers to a source outside of the individual that appeals to pride, sense of accomplishment, and level of effort. For example, external motivation can come in the form of social approval such as rewards or recognition, ease of experience in simplifying effort, and organizational goals.

Internal
> This refers to a source from within the individual that aligns to their values, interests, and sense of purpose. For example, internal motivation can come in the form of wanting to do the right thing, wanting to do fun things, and wanting to make a difference or an impact.

In the previous example, friction was used as an external source of motivation to drive the desired behavior. This is because when a compliance task is intrinsically rewarding or interesting, humans tend to complete it with joy rather than fear. The easier it is to comply, the better off you are in driving the right behavior.

Using Conditioning and Motivation Together

Putting conditioning and motivation together leads to the framework illustrated by Figure 10-2.

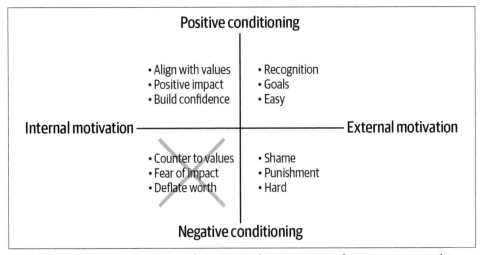

Positive conditioning

- Align with values
- Positive impact
- Build confidence

- Recognition
- Goals
- Easy

Internal motivation ———————————————— **External motivation**

- Counter to values
- Fear of impact
- Deflate worth

- Shame
- Punishment
- Hard

Negative conditioning

Figure 10-2. Framework using conditioning and motivation to figure out ways to drive desired human behavior

While the framework in Figure 10-2 includes four quadrants for completeness, I have crossed out the quadrant in which internal motivation and negative conditioning intersect. This is because I do not recommend any tactics that land there. I believe that all humans have innate worth and deserve respect, and actions taken in this quadrant are counter to that belief.

Let's review an example of applying this framework. Let's say an organization is concerned about the costs of operating applications in the cloud. In the pay-as-you-go model, the cost of using cloud services is very transparent and can get expensive pretty quickly. Using the concepts of conditioning and motivation, an architectural strategy to improve efficiency could include the following to drive desired behavior:

Positive conditioning and internal motivation
Establish a training program to appeal to internal motivation for increasing knowledge, and positive conditioning for providing training.

Positive conditioning and external motivation
Establish and sustain public rewards and recognition for bringing down expenses. Such positive conditioning appeals to external motivation for accomplishment and social awareness. Another tactic would be to heighten awareness of cost efficiency through leadership presentations, which appeals to external motivation for aligning with organizational goals. A third tactic could be to enable

easy access to cost projections and reporting. This appeals to external motivation for simplifying effort and to positive conditioning for making cost management part of business-as-usual activities.

Negative conditioning and external motivation
Define and enforce an automated control that restricts and prevents high-cost instance types from being used. Engineers would experience this consequence during their software build and deploy process, and the negative conditioning teaches them not to repeat this behavior.

Although these are not usually perceived as architecture, they are part of what would drive the desired human behavior to adhere to the architecture standard. As a result, considering human behavior and motivation is quite relevant and beneficial to delivering effective architecture standards and requirements.

Case Studies

Let's examine a few anecdotal case studies and study the themes that they present.

The Administrative Architect

Once upon a time, there was a company that had an enterprise architecture standard around cloud server instance types. With cost in mind, certain instance types were not allowed. For the most part, this worked fine—except for one day, when a machine learning (ML) team came along. They found that their ML workloads were failing. They consulted their architect, Addison, for help, and recommended looking into GPUs.

Addison quickly realized that GPUs were a proven industry recommendation for highly complex ML workloads. However, the standard did not allow for GPUs, and Addison wanted to comply with that standard. As a result, Addison ended up suggesting that the team reduce the complexity of their workload and deal with the lower-cost instance type. Frustrated, the team decided to eschew this guidance altogether and pursue an exception path, but Addison would not approve it. They escalated beyond Addison to their senior leadership, who, when told that the business could not meet their ML aims without this capability, decided to override Addison's objections and grant the exception. The team ended up being able to use GPUs, and not necessarily in the most cost-conscious way.

What happened here?

Addison is an example of the *administrative architect*, someone so focused on compliance to rules, standards, and regulations that they end up not solving problems and business needs. As a result, their guidance is ineffective, and the perception of architecture becomes a negative one. If Addison had instead focused on the desired behavior (spend efficiency) and coupled that with the business need (highly complex ML workloads), she could have perhaps figured out a solution that utilized GPUs in a cost-effective way.

Key takeaways are summarized as follows.

Do:

- Understand the intent of the standard or requirement in terms of the desired benefit, and the desired human behavior necessary to achieve that benefit.
- Understand the business need.

Don't:

- Be afraid to challenge the standard if the standard needs to evolve.
- Enforce the standard to the detriment of satisfying the business need.

The Ambassador Architect

There was another company that was trying to increase the stability of its applications to improve its customer satisfaction levels. As part of this agenda, the company's enterprise architecture defined a resiliency standard that included a declaration that all new cloud-based applications would be *active/active*, meaning that they would be configured in a redundant deployment that could handle loads from either deployed stack.

This company also had data scientists who were supported by an enterprise architect named Ambrose. Ambrose listened when the data science teams came forward to say that active/active didn't work for them. He asked several questions to better understand what the barriers were and determined that the issue was that the active/active pattern was written without understanding the data processing use case. Handling scheduled batch jobs or streaming data processing was a different scenario than a stateless web application, which was where the active/active pattern shined. When it came to these other scenarios, active/active did not make sense due to the risk of data duplication and the complexity of handling data processing events.

Ambrose explained to the team that achieving high resilience was very important, even in these scenarios, but he was open to figuring out a different way to achieve the outcome of swift recovery from failure. He worked with the team to figure out the best way to recover from failures in these scenarios, and he had them prove this method out with one of their batch-processing applications.

He then went back to the rest of the enterprise architecture team with a proposal to both modify the current active/active pattern such that it was clear that it only applied to web applications, and with a new resiliency pattern that was feasible for the batch-processing workloads. Both were approved, which allowed the data science teams to proceed and also achieve greater resiliency.

What happened here?

This example illustrates the *ambassador architect*, someone who brings a deep understanding of the standards and requirements that can guide teams on the expectations of adherence. As an ambassador, the architect understands that their job is to guide the team and drive right behaviors with the flexibility needed to allow for changes—whether that change is to effectively challenge the standard or requirement itself, or to change the team's behaviors, or both. The ambassador architect is willing to take a stance but will also listen to feedback and act on that feedback to evolve and improve the architecture guidance.

Key takeaways are summarized as follows.

Do:

- Allow for negotiation and flexibility to evolve standards as needed.
- View architecture as a way to guide and problem-solve.

Don't:

- Be a pushover.
- Be too rigid.

As demonstrated by these anecdotal case studies, it is better to be an ambassador architect—able to objectively represent standards and solve for business needs—than an administrative architect who can only enforce standards by rote.

Summary

Architecture standards and requirements are a key deliverable of an effective enterprise architecture practice. Enforcement of these standards and requirements is therefore a key piece of architecture governance. This chapter discussed the third recommended enterprise architecture principle—*driving behavior over enforcing standards*—to emphasize the benefits of defining compliance activities in terms of desired behavior.

Driving behavior refers to identifying what *good* looks like for humans to comply with the standard or requirement, and then determining the barriers in the way of performing that good behavior. Overcoming these barriers is possible, and a framework offered in this chapter combines the concepts of conditioning behavior with sources of motivation.

Positive conditioning means associating good consequences with a behavior, whereas *negative conditioning* is the opposite, associating bad consequences instead. *External* sources of motivation are those found outside an individual, and *internal* sources are from within an individual.

Ambassador architects are those who understand how to negotiate between the standard and the business problem at hand. They are unafraid to evolve the standard if that is necessary to solve the problem. On the opposite end of the spectrum are *administrative architects*, those who try to rigidly enforce the standard as a pass-or-fail construct and are unwilling to consider adaptation either by the team trying to comply or by the standard itself.

Thus, enforcement is an essential component of enterprise architecture, as elaborated in Chapters 2 and 5. Enforcement done in the context of driving behavior is what will achieve an optimum level of compliance to standards rather than just the minimum level or no level at all.

This chapter offered a few frameworks to help achieve this optimum level of compliance. As great as frameworks are, the next chapter dives into the fourth and last principle of the very short manifesto of effective enterprise architecture to discuss the power of evolution over frameworks.

CHAPTER 11

Evolution over Frameworks

The fourth and final enterprise architecture principle in the very short manifesto for effective enterprise architecture is *evolution over frameworks*.

It should not be a surprise that in a book full of frameworks that I consider frameworks to be very useful tools. Software development frameworks are typically great starting points that accelerate development through reuse of common elements and reduction of errors. Architecture frameworks help streamline processes, enable consistent output, and provide efficient reuse.

There are well-known enterprise architecture frameworks such as the Zachman Framework (*https://oreil.ly/qBq54*), TOGAF (*https://oreil.ly/8lsJb*), and Open Agile Architecture (*https://oreil.ly/jfzpi*), and specialized ones like the Department of Defense Architecture Framework (DoDAF) (*https://oreil.ly/leFrO*) that define foundational processes, templates, and tools such as reference models. In general, there is typically much more advantage in reusing frameworks than there is in recreating them. Why, then, do I state that evolution is more valuable than frameworks? There are two reasons.

The first has to do with responding effectively to change. In biology, evolution is how species of animals and plants change over time based on natural selection. Environments change, and natural selection is the process by which organisms that adapt to their environment are the ones that survive.

Similar to natural environments, technology is constantly changing. As a result, any enterprise architecture function needs to be able to adapt and stay relevant to business needs. In a world of ruthless prioritization—where businesses are highly concerned with the need to deliver better, faster, and cheaper—the practices of architecture must adapt and evolve, to survive and deliver business value.

The second reason I say evolution is more valuable than frameworks has to do with recognizing diversification. In biology, one output of evolution is diversity. Similarly, in the business world, while there may be similar characteristics across businesses, no two organizations are exactly the same. As a result, using frameworks requires being able to apply them effectively in a specific organizational context. In other words, tailoring frameworks to make them most effective and usable is important. You need to know how to use any framework in the context of your organization to be productive.

Take architecture review boards (ARBs) as an example. Early enterprise architecture frameworks had a clear methodology for instituting a governance process that included architecture review as a checkpoint or a gate. Getting architecture review approval was a necessary step in being able to deliver new technology. Over time, though, as organizations underwent digital transformations, and changed again to use revolutionary technologies such as the cloud, the pace of technological change far surpassed the ability of a manual process based on ARBs to keep up. As a result, more modern implementations no longer have a formal ARB; instead, the architecture governance steps themselves are embedded into software delivery processes.

A Short History of Enterprise Architecture

Enterprise architecture began in the 1980s with the goal of aligning information technology (IT) systems with business strategy. John Zachman is credited with establishing enterprise architecture by articulating a structured approach to achieve this aim with his Zachman Framework.

Then digital IT systems gained traction and swung the pendulum from IT being in a support role to being a critical business enabler. That influenced enterprise architecture frameworks to evolve from being IT-centric to business-centric. And that meant taking a more holistic approach to align technology investment across the whole organization to business goals. The Open Group published TOGAF in the mid-1990s as a standard for enterprise architecture under these circumstances. Enterprise architecture became a strategic way to break silos and integrate across the entire business organization.

Another trend that hit in the early 21st century was the rise of Agile and DevOps for digital-powered organizations. These were quite complementary of enterprise architecture, since they embraced the paradigm of breaking silos to improve collaboration and communication. The Scaled Agile Framework (*https://oreil.ly/IFR5x*) still includes enterprise architecture today as a prominent role and function.

The next inflection point came in the form of cloud computing. Cloud computing disrupted the ways of doing IT by providing a more flexible paradigm to innovate with new technology. No longer was there a need to separate infrastructure from application, to have separate functions of compute, storage, and so on. The cloud enabled unprecedented self-service and full-stack engineering to flexibly innovate.

And for enterprise architecture, this meant tackling the complex challenge of dynamic technology across the full stack along with the opportunity to integrate emerging technologies.

The most recent inflection point is the rise of machine learning (ML) and artificial intelligence (AI). Talk about data-powered insights! This new revolution has the potential to provide unprecedented insights based on real-time intelligence to enable better decision making. For enterprise architecture, this means intrinsically understanding the power of data and using that to fuel strategy—a strategy that also has an emphasis on cybersecurity and data privacy to protect that data.

Thus, in addition to the original and sustained goal of aligning IT strategy with business goals, enterprise architecture has evolved as a discipline to do so across complex organizational and technology landscapes, while also incorporating the flexibility and agility needed to innovate with emerging technologies, and simultaneously judiciously balancing risk, governance, and compliance concerns. As long as enterprise architecture can be dynamic and evolve in response to such transformative changes, it will continue to be an essential strategic enabler of the enterprise.

Let's now take a look into evolutionary trends that help to operationalize the principle of evolution over frameworks.

Evolutionary Trends

Just as businesses rise and fall based on their ability to evolve with the times, so too does enterprise architecture as a function. This section elaborates on evolutionary trends to embrace in establishing effective enterprise architecture practices for your organization.

From Theory to Data

Chapter 9 discussed the importance of fostering a culture of experimentation, of being receptive to learning from fast failure, and of using data to prove out the right path forward. In addition to this paradigm, it is also necessary to be able to communicate the business implications of the recommended architecture decision based on data-driven empirical evidence.

For instance, let's say that the business is interested in acquiring another company. Enterprise architecture recommends an interoperability standard to ensure that existing and acquired systems integrate, but meeting that standard will require several existing systems to upgrade their interfaces. Use experimentation to output data of the average *level of effort* (LOE) to perform such an upgrade and to show the difference between integration efforts before and after that upgrade. Then use these results to discuss the standard in practical business terms—the return on investment (ROI), the effect on mergers and acquisitions (M&A), and the kind of profit and loss (P&L) that is incurred.

Using this technique, enterprise architecture is able to translate business needs into IT standards that are then tangibly associated with practical business benefits. The standards may have been initiated by a theory, but they are driven into reality by data.

From Outsider to Insider

As technology changes, one risk to architecture is to become outdated. For instance, let's say an organization is transitioning from a data center posture to a cloud-based platform. Enterprise architecture standards that worked well in the data center may be wholly unsuited for the cloud. An enterprise architect needs to think like the engineers who have to use and operate the technology to help evolve the standard. For example, a standard around centralized backups using software-defined storage may not make as much sense in a cloud environment where storage and backups are federated commodities.

Architects must be able to establish trust to successfully influence business outcomes and have their standards and guidance be adopted by engineers. Thus, the more the architect proactively learns the technologies that the engineers use, with practical hands-on means rather than just research or theory, the better off they will be in making credible recommendations. This requires a significant investment in continuous learning, and the humility to recognize when one's expertise is stale and in need of refreshment.

Besides obsolescence, another risk is being perceived as too detached from stakeholder needs. Chapter 2 covered the importance of understanding stakeholders and of close collaboration to understand and appeal to their specific needs. The best framework in the world is meaningless if the stakeholder finds it irrelevant. Getting stakeholders involved makes enterprise architecture's value and worth more readily apparent.

For example, enterprise architecture should have inside knowledge of stakeholder needs and solve for them to answer relevant questions like the following:

Product manager
> What applications support their product's capabilities? What technical debt should they be aware of that needs to be remediated?

Senior executive
> What is the technology strategy for their vertical? How does it align with business strategy?

Engineer

What is the modern tech stack? What tools are supposed to be used to support monitoring and logging? What's the standard way to build and deploy software?

 Rather than an outsider parachuting in with little to no relevant guidance, enterprise architecture must seek to be an insider, a member of the same team, adding value through relevancy.

From Blocker to Enabler

Since enterprise architecture defines *standards*, which are essentially *requirements*, and there is a strong governance component to the function, sometimes enterprise architecture is perceived as a blocker. Rather than having architecture governance be a blocker, Chapter 5 discussed the enterprise architecture strategy objective to both enable and enforce, and Chapter 10 covered the principle around driving behavior over enforcing standards. Ultimately, the standards, requirements, rules, guidelines, and best practices that are defined by enterprise architecture need to be integrated with and automated by software delivery tools that can provide developers with rapid, consistent feedback in a helpful way.

In short, an enterprise architect has to think like an engineer to create an effective architecture function. But this isn't the whole story. Standards, if you recall from Chapter 1, are only one (albeit large) piece of what enterprise architecture does. The other is around setting technology direction. For that, an enterprise architect has to think like a product leader and a technology leader to create an effective architecture function. Enterprise architecture has to be able to create new value streams, use new technology, and make the hard decisions around technology portfolio rationalization. It's an extremely delicate balance between blocking new work or investment and guiding the new work or investment toward an aligned direction.

For instance, let's say an application team wants to build a new feature. The architect realizes that that feature is very similar to another feature that is planned to be built on an enterprise platform. The team is not particularly supportive of waiting on the platform to deliver the feature, since the team knows that if they control the feature, they will get exactly what they want, when they want it. Yet, in service of the greater good and technology rationalization, the architect knows that waiting on the platform would be the best thing to do.

A traditional architect might use the power of architecture governance to block the new feature. While this could force the usage of the platform, it is likely to heighten the perception of architecture as a blocker. An architect who embraces the trend to transform from blocker to enabler might instead figure out how the team can develop their feature and then contribute that feature to the platform as a win-win scenario. Or they could work with both the team and the platform team to prioritize the platform's work so that the team gets their feature when they wanted it or maybe only has to compromise a little bit.

 The enterprise architect must lead with enablement to serve both the enterprise and the software delivery application team and satisfy each, especially when one's need is greater than the other's.

Case Studies

Let's examine a few anecdotal case studies and study the themes they present.

The Adamant Architect

Adam was an architect who worked for an organization that was starting its journey to the cloud. As he embarked on the first application migration, he researched the organization's preferred cloud service provider's architecture framework. From that framework, he learned several important and foundational design considerations for performance, reliability, cost, and security. He worked with the application team to apply these considerations to rearchitect their application to perform more optimally in the cloud environment.

The team migrated to the cloud with their rearchitected application based on the framework's recommendations rather than lifting and shifting the original application. Initially, this was successful because the application functioned in the cloud as intended. However, two major issues materialized after the migration. The first was that the application no longer adhered to the organization's regulations for protecting data and created risk for the organization. The second issue was that the application team was ill prepared to sustainably operate the application in the cloud—for instance, managing backups by themselves.

What happened here?

A good framework can provide a clear, reusable methodology to solve problems. The cloud service provider's framework did just that, enabling a solid architecture for the given application. However, Adam was an adamant architect. An *adamant architect* is someone who sticks rigidly to the framework without considering tailoring or trying to change strategy when needed. In this scenario, Adam neglected to consider two major factors:

- The team was used to operating in a data center environment that used an operating model whereby central teams managed infrastructure components such as storage, database, and backups. In the cloud, these became commodities that were self-service; however, this change was not identified by the framework. Adam should have used his contextual knowledge of the organization and his ability to think like an engineer to include this change as part of the architecture plan to ensure sustainable operations.

- The organization was regulated, which meant that there were regulations that applied specifically to data protection. Since the cloud framework was generic, although some protections were implemented, not all of the ones that were necessary for the regulation were considered. Adam should have tailored the framework to his organization's needs.

Key takeaways are summarized as follows.

Do:

- Identify and apply proven frameworks that can help solve a problem.
- Actively learn about new technologies to incorporate them into an architecture.

Don't:

- Be too rigid to tailor the framework to your organization's needs.
- Be too stubborn to raise the need for overall strategic changes.

The Audacious Architect

Audrey was an architect who worked for a software company. The company used the software development lifecycle (SDLC) methodology heavily as a framework to develop its software products. The company wanted to glean insights from data analytics about the usage of the software and also wanted to explore opportunities to incorporate ML into its software products. As a result, a new discipline around data science and ML was born.

Audrey recognized that all software needed to meet the same basic standards from an enterprise architecture and cybersecurity perspective; for instance, the software needed to be developed using approved languages that were within end of life and vulnerability free. However, Audrey quickly realized that the SDLC as defined and practiced by her company was based on assumptions around the type of software being developed—namely, web applications and microservices. It was not purpose-built for software developed by data scientists and ML engineers, which meant issues arose, such as the following:

- SDLC release management processes did not include the right checks for data science and model approval.
- SDLC notions around the stages of development, staging, and production did not fit. For instance, data science and ML had to use production business data instead of test data.

Audrey validated her conclusions by working with the new data science and ML teams. She then took it upon herself to advocate for them by presenting their needs as part of a strategic shift in how the company developed software. At first, these efforts were in vain because there was a lack of understanding about why there were such differences in software development, and a lack of recognition of the severity and urgency of the gaps. Audrey did not give up. She took these challenges head-on to define a business case and built new relationships to gain allies and supporters for this cause. Eventually, her persistence paid off, and an initiative was established to update the SDLC to enable data science– and ML-based software to be developed simply and securely.

What happened here?

Audrey is an example of an *audacious* architect, who understands the framework well enough to focus on the value that it is driving and who can evolve the framework itself as needed to still achieve that value under catalytic circumstances. Audrey took risks to drive the strategic changes she foresaw as necessary. The audacious architect drives bold changes and is courageous enough to do so in the face of resistance.

Key takeaways are summarized as follows.

Do:

- Evolve frameworks as needed.
- Take calculated risks.

Don't:

- Try to lead bold, transformational changes by yourself.
- Accept the status quo when you don't have to.

As demonstrated by these anecdotal case studies, it is clearly better to be an audacious architect, able to boldly evolve frameworks for specific business needs, than an adamant architect who never unleashes the full potential of a framework.

Summary

Architecture frameworks are a cornerstone of an effective enterprise architecture practice. They define reusable methods, processes, and tools to solve common problems. Defining and/or following a framework is, however, not enough for a fully effective enterprise architecture practice. This chapter discussed the fourth recommended enterprise architecture principle, *evolution over frameworks*, to highlight the acute need to evolve so you stay relevant and add value.

Evolving the usage of frameworks with organizational context allows for optimal usage of that framework. Evolving the practice of enterprise architecture itself is necessary to adapt effectively to the ever-present changes in the business and technology landscape.

Enterprise architecture cannot cling to archaic processes and paint theoretical pictures of the future and expect to survive, let alone thrive. Adamant architects are those who resist or are slow to recognize the changes needed—to themselves, to the frameworks they use, and to the practices that they are supposed to embrace.

Enterprise architecture can and should be the strategic problem-solver that guides the organization to a bright future that incorporates new technology, rationalizes the existing technology portfolio, and delivers innovative products and services founded on proven standards. Audacious architects are the bold drivers of the changes necessary to achieve this aim.

CHAPTER 12

Assessment Framework

So far, this book has covered effective enterprise architecture, including key concepts, key objectives, and key principles. To apply this knowledge to your own organization, you first need to know where your organization currently is on its journey to establishing effective enterprise architecture, and for that you will conduct an assessment.

Maturity models are a fairly common type of assessment tool, made popular by *capability maturity models* (CMMs). Typically defining five levels—from initial to optimal—CMMs help simplify complex topics into a series of linear steps and benchmarks to assess performance. This process can help organizations understand the level that they are currently at, and what remains to get to where they want to be.

I have used maturity models to assess the current state of an organization, with an emphasis on process maturity and quality. In this experience, I did see some benefit to identifying the level that the organization was at and creating a roadmap to increase that level. I have even developed my own maturity models for things like platforms and have found benefit in determining what nonfunctional requirements (NFRs) needed to be in place for what level. In a similar vein, Figure 12-1 shows a high-level example of what an effective enterprise architecture maturity model could look like.

Using a step-like progression, this maturity model shows the clear difference from starting with nothing to ending with something quite optimal. However, I have come to realize that maturity models as assessment tools all too often fall short.

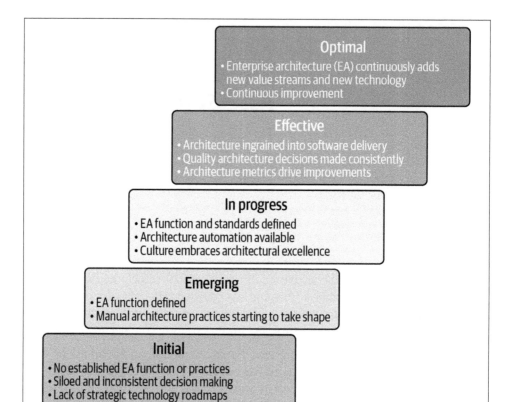

Figure 12-1. Example enterprise architecture maturity model

Wait, what? Yes, you read that right. Here's why I have come to this, perhaps startling, conclusion:

They are static.

Maturity models are static things, a snapshot of the time during which they were defined. As technology and business needs change, they may not go far enough to address the real gaps, the true competencies the organization needs to establish. They also imply that there is an end stage when you are done. This is a misnomer, because as technology changes and businesses evolve, so too should enterprise architecture.

They lack context.

With the diversity of organizations across industries and their usage of technology, it is highly improbable that a single maturity model could have enough context to be useful for all of them. In fact, interpreting the maturity model can lead to inconsistent results depending on the specific organizational context used for the interpretation.

They are linear.
> Maturity models assume linear growth for all phases, yet reality is never a straight line. What happens when the assessment results are scattered across multiple levels?

They have a terminology problem.
> Intended or not, they impart a negative connotation to the areas that are assessed as immature. Negative connotations can lead to defensive reactions rather than to constructive behaviors to fix the gaps.

So, what do you get instead of a fully baked maturity model? You get an assessment framework that relies on an outcome-based capability model.

Conducting an Enterprise Architecture Assessment

Unlike a maturity model, an outcome-based capability model doesn't define the bar for all of the practices that you should seek to achieve in striated levels. Instead, it is meant to be used as a dynamic aid to identify capability areas for continuous improvement. The enterprise architecture assessment framework adds to this concept by including a prioritization schema to focus on improving capabilities that will bring the most benefit. Figure 12-2 visualizes this assessment framework.

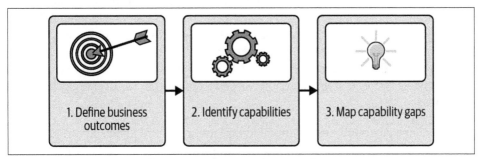

Figure 12-2. Enterprise architecture assessment framework

The first step of the enterprise architecture assessment framework is to figure out what business outcomes need to drive the capability model.

Define Business Outcomes

The first step is to *define business outcomes* as quantitatively as possible. Since enterprise architecture needs to have alignment across the enterprise to be successful, I highly recommend defining your business outcomes in collaboration with your key stakeholders to ensure a shared understanding of what enterprise architecture will seek to support and achieve. Thus, the business outcomes should be traceable to the results of an effective enterprise architecture function and practice.

Chapter 1 hit on a few general business outcomes of effective enterprise architecture:

Improved efficiency and optimize investments by avoiding silos
> Providing collective goals in the form of a shared destination state that crosses organizational boundaries will reduce duplication and align and focus priorities.

Increased customer satisfaction and improve brand and reputation by avoiding chaos
> Providing clear standards with requisite enablement and enforcement allows for accelerated delivery of consistent, cost-effective, well-architected software products and services that are more stable and provide better experiences.

Improved agility and enable innovation by avoiding technical debt
> Making better architecture decisions enables responding to changes in a cost-effective way.

Although these could apply to your organization, there may be some specific other outcomes for your particular organization. For example, perhaps your organization is considering a merger or acquisition; that would be a key initiative for enterprise architecture to bolster. Or perhaps it is undergoing a major technology transformation, such as moving to the cloud. The major transformation would yield business outcomes that should be directly supported by enterprise architecture.

For example, an organization transitioning to the cloud could define business outcomes around migrating application workloads to the cloud, accelerating agility of application development, improving scale and resilience of applications, and improving spend efficiency. In this scenario, enterprise architecture can provide the holistic strategic thinking necessary to provide a data-driven approach to cloud migration. In more tangible terms, enterprise architecture can provide the cloud strategy to do the following:

- Develop a powerfully secure, scalable, and resilient cloud platform.
- Create reusable reference architectures and patterns to accelerate and streamline migration.
- Identify interdependencies to determine the sequencing of migrations.
- Define strategic roadmaps for new or enhanced technology capabilities needed to support the cloud and migrations.

By concentrating on the shared business outcomes, you can then figure out what needs to be true to get there, which brings us to the next step of the enterprise architecture assessment framework.

Identify Capabilities

The next step of the enterprise architecture assessment framework is called *identify capabilities*. Just as Chapter 8 discussed capabilities in an architectural domain model providing key context, this step of the assessment framework is considering enterprise architecture itself as a domain. So, now you're defining all the capabilities necessary to achieve the desired business outcomes that pertain to an enterprise architecture function and architecture practices.

Figure 12-3 shows an example of such a capability model. Using people (culture), process, and tools as broad categories, this capability model can be used to figure out the specific capabilities that an organization needs to strengthen to establish an effective enterprise architecture function and practice.

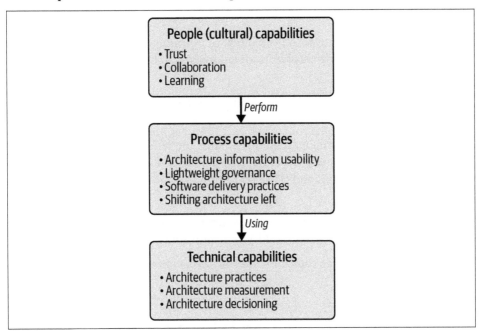

Figure 12-3. Starting point of an enterprise architecture capability model

This capability model can and should be expanded and tailored to your organization based on analyzing people, process, and tools.

For example, let's go back to the scenario of an organization going through a transformation to cloud technology. A major business outcome is to migrate applications to the cloud, as quickly and cost-efficiently as possible. As a result, enterprise architecture functions as defined in Chapter 1, of strategy, enablement, and oversight, may need the following tailored capabilities:

People
> Cloud architecture skills

Process
> Cloud governance, cloud application standards, and cloud application modernization disposition framework

Tools
> Cloud migration

Effective architecture practices in the context of operating and using the cloud could include the following nonexhaustive list of tailored capabilities:

People
> Cloud application architecture, cloud engineering, and cloud certification

Process
> Cloud standards for FinOps, cloud standards for resiliency, cloud configuration management using enterprise architecture metamodel, cloud network management, cloud monitoring, and cloud security

Tools
> Cost management, cloud billing, cloud service discovery, software-defined networking, cloud provisioning, cloud automation, and cloud policy controls

Once you have your tailored capability model, you can move on to the next step.

Map Capability Gaps

The next and final step of the enterprise architecture assessment framework is to perform a *gap analysis* using the capability model developed in the previous step. You may have to conduct research and interview several stakeholders to find out where there are capability gaps, with questions like the following:

- What is challenging across the dimensions of people, process, and tools that makes it hard to achieve the desired business outcomes?

- Do all the capabilities that you identified in the previous step have solutions?

- Are any solutions suboptimal and, if so, why?

For example, for the enterprise architecture functions as defined in Chapter 1 of strategy, enablement, and oversight, questions might be similar to these:

People

Are they staffed with the right talent, which has the right skill sets to lead technology changes? Is the organization structured to use that talent effectively?

Processes

Are there well-defined and clear architecture standards? Are there well-established and easy-to-follow architecture processes? Is architecture information readily available? Are architecture templates reusable?

Tools

Are there easy and automated tools to support the architecture standards and processes? Is architecture governance automated?

For assessing enterprise architecture practices, an analysis could take a form like this:

People

Are roles and responsibilities in architecture decision processes clear and well understood? Is your talent equipped with the skills they need to be successful in fulfilling the role that they play in the enterprise architecture ecosystem? Do you have an organizational culture that is founded on trust and receptive to collaboration and reuse? Do stakeholders understand the roles of architects and the value that they bring? Do stakeholders adequately use architecture information?

Processes

Are there clear processes around making architecture decisions? Are architecture standards incorporated into software delivery processes? Is architecture ingrained into the fabric of the software delivery processes?

Tools

Are there tools that make it easy to perform architecture work? Are standards automated in terms of adhering to them and measuring compliance?

Once you have identified capability areas across people, processes, and tools that are weak and hinder the success of enterprise architecture, you then need to map these gaps to the following to prioritize them:

Impact

Determine which capability gaps, if remediated, provide the greatest benefit.

Effort

Determine the work necessary to solve for the gap.

Impact and effort can be quantified with the scoring scale defined in Table 12-1.

Table 12-1. Scoring scale

Score	Description	Impact (benefit)	Effort (duration + labor)
1	Low	Negligible (e.g., benefits are hardly felt and are not sustainable)	Minimal (e.g., within a few days, one person)
2	Medium-Low	Limited (e.g., benefits affect only a small population or are small improvements)	Small (e.g., within a few weeks, a few people)
3	Medium	Moderate (e.g., benefits are broader and are more noticeable)	Moderate (e.g., within a month or so, a team or so)
4	Medium-High	Broad (e.g., benefits affect a wide population and are sustainable)	Trending toward higher (e.g., within a quarter, a few or more teams)
5	High	Game changer (e.g., benefits are transformative, with huge return on investment)	High (e.g., several months, several teams)

Applying this scoring scale to the identified capabilities results in the capability gap analysis. Using the earlier cloud example, this analysis could produce something like Table 12-2.

Table 12-2. Example capability gap analysis

Dimension	Capability	Gap	Impact	Effort
People	Cloud architecture	Talent lacks skills in developing cloud applications.	5 - High	3 - Medium
Process	Cloud governance	Governance processes exist for security and data, but not for how they apply to the cloud.	5 - High	4 - Medium-High
	Architecture reviews	Architecture reviews currently do not look for cloud-specific elements and lack reference patterns.	3 - Medium	4 - Medium-High

As this brief example shows, a quick scoring based on estimated impact and effort allows for priorities to take shape. It is likely that the skill deficiency would be the first capability area to be tackled, followed by the governance process.

Summary

Evaluating the state of your organization in the context of effective enterprise architecture is necessary to determine an enterprise architecture strategy. Maturity models are one form of assessment tool, but they are static, lack context, and can be oversimplified and prone to misinterpretation. Thus, instead of relying on a maturity model as an assessment tool, this chapter presented an assessment framework that relies on an outcome-based capability model.

By starting with defining shared business outcomes and tracing that directly to enterprise architecture efforts, you have begun to articulate the business case of how enterprise architecture will provide value to your organization. Next, by focusing on these outcomes to identify the capabilities needed to achieve them, and then performing a gap analysis, you will have produced a clear, holistic view of the capabilities that make the most sense in your organizational context to invest in.

Assessment durations can vary depending on the level of detail, engagement, and collaboration necessary. Typically, assessments of this nature should be timeboxed within one month, and done as part of an annual strategy cycle. Speaking of strategy, the next chapter discusses how you can build on your assessment to establish your own enterprise architecture strategy.

CHAPTER 13

Framework to Define Enterprise Architecture Strategy

Chapter 1 shared how enterprise architecture is supposed to define the strategic north star that guides solving enterprise-wide complex problems and transformations. Enterprise architecture also defines the principles, standards, and best practices that enable all software engineering teams to deliver high-quality, resilient, cost-effective, and secure software.

Just as enterprise architecture defines the strategic north star for business and technology initiatives, enterprise architecture needs its own strategic north star to establish itself as an effective function. *Dogfooding* is the practice of using your own products and services to see how well they work and identify opportunities. This chapter discusses how to dogfood strategy by pulling together everything this book has covered so far into a framework to define your own enterprise architecture strategy.

Defining Enterprise Architecture Strategy

Defining the strategy for a strategic function may sound a bit meta but is really quite essential to provide enterprise architecture's value proposition and focus efforts. Figure 13-1 illustrates a framework for defining such a strategy.

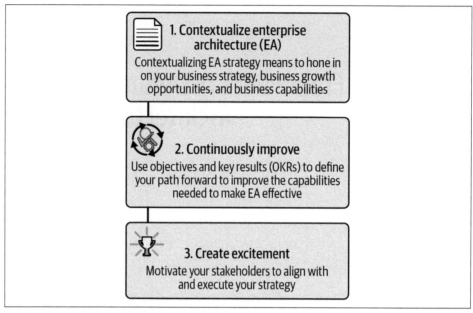

Figure 13-1. Enterprise architecture strategy framework

The enterprise architecture strategy framework has three steps:

1. Contextualize enterprise architecture.
2. Continuously improve.
3. Create excitement.

Let's now look deeper into the first step.

Contextualize Enterprise Architecture

It is important to recall that enterprise architecture is broader than information technology (IT). Enterprise architecture is effective and successful when it can provide a holistic, feasible strategy for delivering business outcomes through the usage of technology. That holistic strategy has to cover all the aspects of the enterprise, from operations to delivery and compliance, in terms of alignment and evolution of people, processes, and tools.

This strategy must occur in the context of your own business needs. Chapter 8 discussed the principle of contextualized understanding. Hence, the first step in defining your own enterprise architecture strategy is to deeply understand your business strategy, business growth opportunities, and business capabilities.

How do you go about understanding your business growth strategies? Well, it's likely that there is a corporate business strategy that is well defined and iteratively changing each year in response to new information. First, you need to comprehend what that is by partnering with your corporate strategy group and/or discussing with your senior leadership.

Generally, corporate strategy includes a business model. A *business model* describes how the business delivers products to the market and drives profit and growth. It defines the customer base and unique business characteristics for competitive edge, and it determines what products and services make up the core business revenue streams. Enterprise architecture doesn't usually own the business model, but if a business model is lacking, enterprise architecture can drive the need and collaboration to define it.

Enterprise architecture can further contribute to the business model by staying on top of technology trends to figure out how they should be incorporated into business growth. Ways to do that include learning from industry research firms like Forrester and Gartner, and from industry conferences that pertain to your technology areas. For example, in the cloud industry, major public cloud service providers such as Amazon Web Services (AWS), Microsoft Azure, and Google Cloud Platform (GCP) hold their own conferences.

Enterprise architecture does own the business capability model, which describes the capabilities necessary to support delivering the products and services to the customers defined by the business model. Business capabilities were covered in Chapters 8 and 12. Speaking of Chapter 12, based on the enterprise architecture assessment framework described there, you would have zeroed in on the desired business outcomes and capability gaps that need to be overcome to achieve those outcomes, which brings us to step 2 in the enterprise architecture strategy framework.

Continuously Improve

The understanding of business growth strategy, business outcomes, and capability gaps is key to informing your enterprise architecture strategy, as defined by objectives and measurable objective key results (OKRs). These objectives are twofold:

- One set focuses on what enterprise architecture as a function and enterprise architects as a role need to do to drive strategy.
- One set focuses on architecture practices to enable software delivery and includes all the necessary components of architecture decisioning, such as standards, templates, processes, and tools.

Chapters 2 through 6 described a set of sample OKRs based on similar analysis to establish an effective enterprise architecture strategy. These OKRs related to the principles established by the very short manifesto defined in Chapter 7 and explored in Chapters 8 through 11:

Create shared alignment.
> This OKR is all about establishing a culture of trust, identifying and working with stakeholders to get them to agree with—and implement toward—a stated direction. It relates to the principle of contextual understanding over siloed decision making described in Chapter 8.

Make architecture information embedded and accessible.
> This OKR covers the importance of integrating intuitive and usable architecture information with software delivery processes. It relates to the principle of tangible direction over stale documentation described in Chapter 9.

Enable and enforce standards.
> This OKR emphasizes the duality of effective standards in needing to be both easy to adhere to and governed to ensure adherence. It relates to the principle of driving behavior over enforcing standards described in Chapter 10.

Instill proactive and reactive architecture decisions.
> This OKR addresses the nature of architecture decisions and the need to balance strategic and tactical decisions. It relates to the principle of evolution over frameworks described in Chapter 11.

An additional tool that you can use to inform your OKRs is a *strength, weakness, opportunity, and threat (SWOT) analysis*, as illustrated by Figure 13-2.

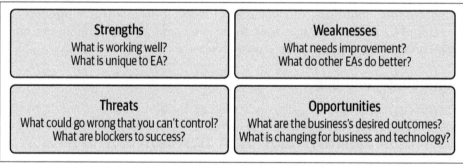

Figure 13-2. Enterprise architecture SWOT analysis template

The SWOT analysis should also be conducted in collaboration with enterprise architecture's key stakeholders across the enterprise, inclusive of business, technology, operations, and compliance organizational units. To perform a thorough SWOT analysis, consider both internal and external factors. For instance, when brainstorming strengths and weaknesses, consider not just what enterprise architecture would say about itself, but what others say about enterprise architecture. Also, keep in mind that strengths are what provide advantages or benefits, whereas weaknesses result in risks.

For opportunities, consider changes to policy, regulations, and trends in technology and industry to identify opportunities that enterprise architecture can exploit in a positive way. Some opportunities can also be threats, such as technology trends that aren't capitalized upon. For instance, are there new technologies that could be used? How about your competitors—are they using new technologies that give them an edge on their products and services? Are you at an inflection point, with disruptors on the horizon?

 Limit your SWOT analysis to the top 5–10 specific ideas in each quadrant. A lengthy analysis can become unwieldy.

Any OKRs that you define should demonstrate progress toward your desired business outcomes. While any given key result may make only an incremental improvement, the combined results should drive transformative changes. You can revisit KRs year to year, and even the objectives themselves, to select the specific capabilities to focus on improving.

As a result, your OKRs become your three-to-five-year roadmap. Showing the top items that did not make the prioritization cut can also be compelling. It can be eye-opening for stakeholders to realize what you're not going to be able to do due to constraints in resources and dependencies. OKRs also help set their expectations for what is achievable and where stakeholders are a dependency to make an OKR successful. That brings us to step 3 in the enterprise architecture strategy framework—creating excitement.

Create Excitement

Much of what enterprise architecture does depends on others, and a strategy for effective enterprise architecture is no different. Thus, keep in mind that a strategy that stakeholders rally around is a strategy that will deliver results.

Communication and marketing therefore make up the last step of the framework to define enterprise architecture strategy, and they must be done deliberately and continuously in the lifecycle of both defining and executing the strategy. Chapter 6 discussed communication in the context of gaining alignment; this step in the enterprise architecture strategy framework goes further to say that you also need to create excitement. Genuine excitement and caring about the outcomes are key to enabling sustained stakeholder engagement through the long haul of multiyear execution.

What gets people excited? *Relevance* and *incentives* are what come to my mind. If you can show that your strategy is relevant to stakeholders' desired outcomes, their needs, and their specific pain points, you will be in a good position to appeal to them. Answer the question, "What's in it for them?" Why should they care, when there are a thousand other things for them to take care of?

Reiterate that you are making stakeholders' lives easier.

In this step, you should establish a communication and marketing strategy. Go on a roadshow to socialize the enterprise architecture strategy with your key stakeholders, at both senior and junior levels. Identify or establish common forums where you can return to provide updates.

Determine the brand identity that you want to associate with enterprise architecture. If you personified enterprise architecture, what values or adjectives would you use? *Trustworthy*, *friendly*, and *productive* come to my mind. Starting with values is important because you want to appeal to people's sense of why enterprise architecture exists, along with the enterprise architecture value proposition, rather than what or how enterprise architecture fulfills it.

You want to preempt the notion that you are adding bureaucracy or unnecessary complexity as part of your *what* and *how*. Rather, you want to sell your brand and showcase that you are adding value for stakeholders and are ultimately making their lives better. As a bonus, it happens to be true: enterprise architecture's value is in enabling everyone to build better software as one team, for the good of the enterprise as a whole.

Your branding will come through as part of your communication and marketing strategy and will help to create excitement around enterprise architecture and what enterprise architecture is doing to help. It may be odd to think about branding a function rather than a software product or service, but it is in fact the same technique. And in a function that depends on humans to align and engage, branding is a powerful way to instill trust and build excitement.

If your enterprise architecture is associated with a negative brand, declare a reset as part of your strategy. Resetting and reinventing your brand are very possible and just need consistency and repetition to change people's perception.

In branding, appeal to people's sense of why enterprise architecture does what it does, not what or how it does it.

Share wins periodically to demonstrate tangible progress and to prove that the needle is moving in the direction of forward progress. This part of the story is easier if you can quantify gains with metrics that people care about.

In addition to the specific metrics tied to your OKRs, are there any additional metrics that tell the story of enterprise architecture's value that you can share? For instance, consider the functions of enterprise architecture:

Strategy
Are strategies being produced and operationalized? For example, if enterprise architecture has driven a resiliency strategy, can you show with data that applications are improving their resilience? Maybe applications are recovering from failures faster, or maybe they aren't even experiencing failures as often.

Enablement and enforcement
Can you show that more applications are meeting architecture standards? Better yet, can you show progress in the business benefits of those standards, such as reduction in labor, improvement in cost efficiency, and/or reduction in risk?

By taking a deliberate stance on enterprise architecture's branding, quantifying outcomes and making them relevant, your communication and marketing of your enterprise architecture strategy will help to make it successful.

Summary

Just as enterprise architecture delivers strategy for the enterprise, so too does enterprise architecture need a strategy for itself in order to be an effective function of the enterprise, for the enterprise.

The enterprise architecture strategy framework is comprised of three main steps:

1. Contextualize enterprise architecture.
As mentioned in Chapter 12, context in the form of understanding business needs, business outcomes, business strategy—and the business capabilities that power that strategy to achieve those outcomes and solve for those needs—is essential to ground the enterprise architecture strategy. In fact, Chapter 12's framework to assess enterprise architecture's current state would be an input into this step.

2. Continuously improve.

In a modern organization, business needs are fluid and technology is dynamic. Therefore, enterprise architecture itself must also be continuously improving to thrive as the strategic leader of an organization. The OKR framework provides a structure to define a strategic roadmap with measurable outcomes demonstrating incremental improvement. The specific OKRs are informed by the context defined in step 1.

3. Create excitement.

Given that enterprise architecture cannot operate in a silo—and in fact is chartered in part to break silos—it is essential that stakeholders are aligned and moreover truly motivated to engage in helping enterprise architecture's strategy be successful. By developing a strong brand for enterprise architecture, and ensuring that communication and marketing emphasizes the relevancy of enterprise architecture to stakeholder needs, the enterprise architecture strategy is likely to gain support.

You can use the enterprise architecture strategy framework to establish your own tailored strategy for establishing an effective enterprise architecture function and effective architecture practices for your organization. A key output of effective architecture practices is high-quality decisions. The next and final chapter provides a framework to enable high-quality architecture decisions.

CHAPTER 14

Framework for Architecture Decision Making

Effective architecture decisions are the heart and center of everything that enterprise architecture does. After all, what is a strategy or an architecture if not the culmination of several architecture decisions?

It is one thing for one team to make good architecture decisions. It is entirely another thing to accomplish this feat at scale—every team, across every organizational unit, making high-quality, consistent architecture decisions. Check out industry guidance from AWS (*https://oreil.ly/RcWHX*) and GCP (*https://oreil.ly/8hsGx*) for more perspectives on why architecture decision records are so important for an enterprise.

To help solve the scaling challenge, this chapter covers a framework that equips decision making with clarity and transparency.

Let's start with the prerequisites required to apply this framework effectively.

Building a Foundation for Architecture Decision Making

Architecture decision making is a process. A very important process, but nonetheless, a process. A process's efficiency depends on the tools that support it, the sequence and content of process steps, and the people executing it.

Thus, first let's take a look at the primary tool needed to support the framework for architecture decision making: the architecture decision registry.

Providing an Architecture Decision Registry

While making the best choice under the circumstances is front and center in architecture decision making, architecture decisions also provide a historical record of the rationale behind them. This record enables any team member or stakeholder, including new ones, to understand what decisions were made and why. To get the most value out of this record, it is important for enterprise architecture to determine what repository solution fits their user needs the best.

For instance, an organization that is used to software practices may prefer to maintain architecture decision records as markup files stored in the source code repositories, accessible from a developer portal. An organization that is used to more traditional documentation may look for a knowledge base or wiki type solution.

The key considerations that factor into the decision of solution selection for a repository include a few that were elaborated in Chapters 2 and 4 as being necessary for any architecture information:

Accessibility
> The repository must be easily available to all the end users that need to interact with the architecture decision record.

Usability
> The repository must be easily searchable for end users to find the specific records that are relevant to them.

Auditability
> As a historical record, the repository must preserve record immutability and provide an auditable record of approvals and timestamps.

Regardless of the specific solution used for the repository, architecture decision records should be immutable once approved to preserve an accurate historical record. That means that in the scenario that something changed and an architecture decision needs to be revisited, a new record should be created with the original one being preserved and deprecated.

Speaking of creation and deprecation, that brings us to the next prerequisite: the process around lifecycle management.

Managing the Architecture Decision Lifecycle

All architecture information has some sort of lifecycle applied from cradle to grave. Figure 14-1 shows the typical lifecycle of an architecture decision record.

Figure 14-1. Lifecycle of an architecture decision record

The first step is simply to start the architecture decision record as a *draft*, preferably using a standard template such as the one provided in Chapter 1. This is the shortest step, unless there is contention over who owns the decision to begin with.

The second step is to move the record to *in progress*, which means adding to the architecture decision documentation with research, data, and feedback.

There is a feedback loop between this step and the next one of *review*, due to the need to collaborate and iterate on the record based on input from others. This feedback loop can repeat as often as needed to cycle through all the stakeholders that are needed to consult on the decision.

It is during this feedback loop that I recommend finding the stakeholders that are most likely to disagree with your recommendation. They are the ones that ultimately strengthen the decision because they allow you to understand their concerns and proactively assuage them or document the concerns as a risk. Getting alignment may require compromise and remembering that no decision is perfect, it just needs to be good enough based on the information that is known at the time that is captured as assumptions and implications. See Chapters 2 and 3 for more on stakeholder alignment.

The final review is conducted by whomever has the authority to *approve* the decision. After approval, the decision is completed, until the time that something has changed that either invalidates it or requires a new decision. Either way, this decision's last step is to *deprecate* in favor of a new decision; in fact, the link to the new one should be documented as well, in order to allow for traceability.

The specific nature of who has approval authority and steps of approval depend on the architecture decision workflow, discussed in the next subsection.

Defining the Architecture Decision Workflow

The architecture decision *workflow* is what governs the architecture decision-making process.

Since this process shows what leadership roles were involved, it directly affects how they are perceived and impacts perceptions around autonomy.

For instance, an autocratic culture would retain decision-making autonomy only at the most senior levels, resulting in teams needing to wait on others' directions and acting as directed. In contrast, a culture that is based on empowerment would distribute decision-making autonomy.

Can you guess which cultural philosophy I would prescribe? If you guessed the second one, you are right. I have found that autonomy coupled with right-sized governance works well to encourage the right decisions.

 The architecture decision-making process shines the light of truth on empowerment and autonomy; so, consider carefully what statement your decision workflow makes in terms of who is allowed to decide what.

To determine that right-sized governance, it is first necessary to consider that architecture decisions are not homogenous. Figure 14-2 illustrates the degrees of architecture decisions and how they differ.

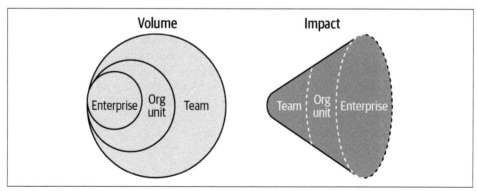

Figure 14-2. Degrees of architecture decision making based on volume and impact

---

As shown in Figure 14-2, there are three broad categories of decision makers:

Team
> This is a single project, product, platform, or application team.

Org unit
> This is an organizational unit, which may contain many teams.

Enterprise
> This is the whole organization, which contains all of the organizational units and all of the teams.

The volume of decisions, indicating frequency and number, is highest at the team level and lowest at the enterprise level. Yet the impact of the decisions made greatly differs. Each decision maker can make a decision that impacts at any broader level.

Teams typically make decisions that only impact themselves. These decisions usually pertain to specific application architecture details such as their high availability deployment architecture or choice of software language. Sometimes, though, their decisions can be more far-reaching. For instance, a team that decided to use an enterprise data warehouse service that pumps it full of data beyond initial projections may very quickly exceed the cost and performance that enterprise service was expecting to deliver. A team that decided to improve their own code quality may influence their org unit to define quality standards for their whole unit.

It is the potential impact of the decision that significantly influences the governance process and approval workflow. Figure 14-3 illustrates an architecture decision-making hierarchy that allows for decisions to be made at different levels based on differing impact.

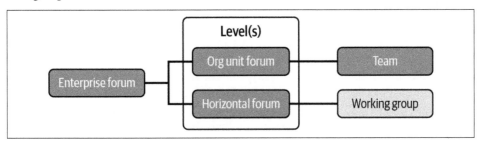

Figure 14-3. Hierarchy to support architecture decision making

As shown in Figure 14-3, the team represents the local level. The team is the smallest atomic unit of decision making. Dynamic, ad hoc, cross-functional working groups are a common structure to support multiple kinds of decision-making forums, and they are shown as well.

The middle level is the most nebulous and depends on the specific organizational details. Essentially, this is where in the simplest form it is the main organizational units, such as lines of business. There may be horizontals at this level that stretch across the organizational unit, such as an architecture team or a somewhat centralized site reliability engineering function.

The enterprise-level forum is accountable and responsible for enterprise-impactful decisions, such as a whole new enterprise technology standard. These can also be viewed as horizontals that stretch across all organizational units in terms of their impacts, such as cybersecurity. Figure 14-4 expands on this notion to show how the enterprise architecture governance model needs to include multiple horizontals.

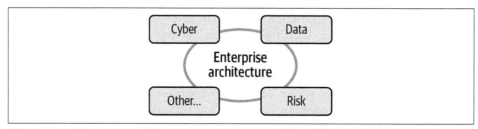

Figure 14-4. Enterprise architecture governance model with horizontals

The Other label in Figure 14-4 is a placeholder for whatever other governance forums an organization may have that would need to provide transparency to the enterprise architecture decision-making forums, such as Procurement or Legal.

Each entity in Figure 14-3's hierarchy has autonomy to make the decisions that are within their scope and impact. Entities on the left have broader scope and impact than entities on the right. Transparency must occur at all levels such that those on the left understand what decisions are made on the right, and vice versa.

Once impact goes beyond a single entity's impact, the decision is escalated to the broader entity for decision-making power. For example, say a team or horizontal made a decision to use a new third-party vendor that required a whole new connectivity pattern. That decision would get escalated all the way to the enterprise level to ensure that the pattern is valid. On the other hand, if an organizational unit defined greater rigor around technology standards than the enterprise, that would not need any further escalation.

All of these entities are made up of people who are conducting the architecture decision-making process. These people should be trained, which brings us to the last prerequisite: architecture decision training.

Avoid prolonged stalemate by ensuring that each forum has a clear charter with an explicit purpose and chair. That allows the forum to be results-driven in making decisions rather than just having a lot of conversations.

Offering Architecture Decision Training

Education is a great aid to empowerment and efficiency. Targeted training is recommended for roles like enterprise chief architect (ECA), divisional chief architect (DCA), solution architect (SA), and application architect (AA). These roles are regularly accountable and responsible for making architecture decisions and may also chair the decision-making forums, as shown in Figure 14-5.

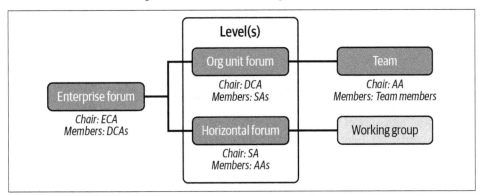

Figure 14-5. Architecture decision-making hierarchy overlaid with specific architecture roles

In Figure 14-5's example, the ECA chairs the enterprise-level architecture forum, which includes representation from DCAs and also should include representation from other horizontal groups as illustrated in Figure 14-4. Each DCA chairs a forum for their own organizational unit. SAs could then chair forums as needed for horizontals related to their architecture domain. Although a team doesn't formally have a chair, Figure 14-5 shows the AA in that role to note that the AA is accountable for architecture decisions at this level, working in partnership with the team.

Depending on the nature of the forum, partners from business/product and technology groups would be included as stakeholders. The charter for the forum can further elaborate on the roles and responsibilities supporting that forum. In addition, there should be targeted training for partners who need to be involved both in making the decision and in executing against that decision. This training should be part of onboarding for those roles, or if there is no role-based training, part of general onboarding.

Consider tailoring terms from architecture decisions to the broader technology decisions to appeal to business/product and technology partners in the training.

The enterprise architecture function should provide targeted training for all roles to effectively use these forums to identify impactful decisions that need escalation and to make decisions within their own purview. Training should also cover how to use the architecture decision template and repository, along with best practices to include considering nonfunctional requirements (NFRs) for a given decision type. (See Chapter 5 for more details regarding NFRs in decision making.)

With the prerequisites of tooling (accessible and usable repository), process (lightweight lifecycle and governance), and people (training) realized to build a solid foundation for architecture decision making, we are now ready to discuss the actual framework.

Framework for Architecture Decision Making

The desired outcome of this framework is to scale throughout the entire enterprise to produce consistent, high-quality, transparent decisions.

As illustrated in Figure 14-6, this framework includes three phases that overlap and relate to each other in a continuous, integrated feedback loop:

1. Satisfy prerequisites

2. Monitor execution

3. Evolve and enhance

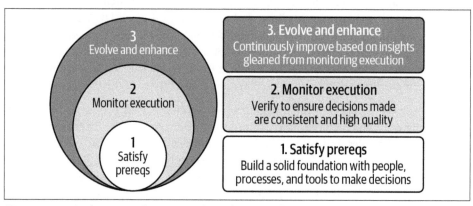

Figure 14-6. Architecture decision-making framework

The first step, satisfying prerequisites, was elaborated upon earlier in this chapter. So let's move on to the second step: monitor execution.

Monitor Execution

Each of the prerequisites needs to be monitored to ensure it's effective. For instance:

Architecture decision repository
Is the repository being used as intended, or are there grassroots alternatives being used to store decision records? Are users happy to use it?

Architecture decision lifecycle and workflow
What is the duration of each stage—are there any bottlenecks? Are the feedback loops working as intended?

Architecture decision training
Is there coverage for all roles involved in the decision-making processes? Are any refreshers needed?

In addition to monitoring the processes of making architecture decisions, you also need to monitor the effect of those architecture decisions once implemented. Figure 14-7 pictures the process associated with monitoring implementation.

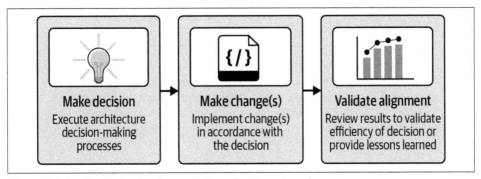

Figure 14-7. Monitoring implementation of architecture decisions

As shown in Figure 14-7, once a decision is made, a change or many changes are implemented as a result of that decision. Once these changes are completed, alignment to the original decision needs to be validated, and a quick postmortem should be conducted to review the efficacy of the decision. Was it spot on? If not, why not?

Celebrate successes and treat failures as learning or growth opportunities.

Architecture fitness functions, defined by *Building Evolutionary Architectures* by Neal Ford et al. (O'Reilly, 2017), have gained traction in recent years as a way to measure and validate alignment. For instance, say you're looking at an application architecture decision on solution selection for the database, because you were solving for specific data access, consistency, availability, and performance requirements. Once that database is implemented, over time you should be able to get measurements on its usage to validate whether or not it is meeting the requirements as intended.

All of the insights gleaned from monitoring execution are input into the overarching phase of evolve and enhance, discussed next.

Evolve and Enhance

Having devoted Chapter 11 to evolution, it should come as no surprise that I have found the ability to evolve and enhance to be crucial to effective scaling in architecture decision-making practices. It takes time, repetition, and incentives to create new habits, and instilling architecture decision-making practices is no different.

Any insights gleaned from monitoring execution should be fed right back into continuous improvement and the strategic OKRs that become a blueprint for effective enterprise architecture in your organization. In addition, these insights can be leveraged into the communication and marketing arm of enterprise architecture to provide customer-centric transparency.

For instance, enterprise architecture tends to walk a fine line between bureaucracy and value-add. Despite best intentions at establishing lightweight governance, imagine that the monitoring reveals that there are bottlenecks based on how a certain decision-making process is being run. Control the message and perception around this pain point to either acknowledge the pain point and show that it will be resolved, or explain why the pain point is necessary due to the risks involved that require such rigor.

Summary

When enterprise architecture flourishes, it enables great architecture decisions to be made. This means great architecture decisions that clear the way toward a grand future, a future that is defined by a clear and cogent architecture strategy that marries business goals with technology. And great decisions that meet business goals, make customers happy, reduce risk, proactively drive innovation, and bring people together to work toward shared outcomes.

Architecture decision-making practices get better over time through practice and refinement. Do it, and do it again, and do it better than the time before. This chapter covered the prerequisites needed to build a solid foundation for architecture decision making through proper tools such as an architecture decision repository, streamlined processes around decision lifecycle management and right-sized governance, and strengthening people through training.

Satisfying prerequisites was the first step in the framework for architecture decision making covered in this chapter. The second step was to monitor execution, both of the prerequisites and of the decisions themselves, as they undergo implementation. The third and final step was to evolve and enhance, in the spirit of continuous improvement, using the data-driven insights gleaned from monitoring execution.

This was the last framework in this book. This book has aimed to provide you with the ability to establish an effective enterprise architecture practice, which is essential for a modern organization to thrive using technology to meet business outcomes. While it is my sincere hope that this book has provided helpful frameworks and guidance, effective enterprise architecture is not possible without strong enterprise architecture leadership and unyielding commitment from the senior leadership team to support enterprise architecture.

I can't say this enough: enterprise architecture, being an enterprise-wide phenomenon, needs the backing of the enterprise, and an influential leader, to be successful. Apathy to enterprise architecture is destructive and must be countered with demonstrated value. Value is both tangible and intangible.

The tangible piece is measurement and relevancy, which is why Chapter 1 started with the value proposition using business terms, and Chapter 2 emphasized metrics. Know your *why* to inform your *what* and *how*, which takes the form of the strategy to establish enterprise architecture, first introduced in Chapter 2, expanded in Chapters 3 through 6, and presented as a framework in Chapter 13. Inform your strategy through an assessment, as covered in Chapter 12.

The intangible pieces of value in this context are perception and caring. Use the principles first introduced in Chapter 7 and elaborated upon in Chapters 8 through 11 to establish a culture that values architecture and the architects who perform architecture.

It is this value that I prize so highly that I now leave you with. Value architecture. Value the practice, and more importantly, value the people.

Index

A

AAs (see application architects)
abstract knowledge, 87
access control, 123
accessibility
    of architecture decision repository, 224
    in knowledge sharing and UI/UX design, 98
accessible (embedded and accessible OKR), 40
active/active, 191
adamant architect case study, 200
adaptability, 122
administrative architect case study, 190
Agile, 196
Agile Manifesto, 161
agility, 118, 142
    improved with better architecture decisions, 208
    inhibited by technical debt, 5
    needed to innovate with emerging technologies in enterprise architecture, 197
    quantum of deployment and, 119
    reduction of through lack of technology standards, 4
AI (artificial intelligence), 146
    AI inflection point case study, 156
    rise of, 197
alignment, 59
    (see also shared alignment)
    in high-quality targeted architecture, 51
all-in-one deployments, 118
aloof architect case study, 172
ambassador architect case study, 191
ambitious architect case study, 183
application architects, 229

    role of, 12
application target architecture deliverable, 22
approval stage (architecture information), 85
    knowledge of many over knowledge of few, 95
approved (architecture decision records), 225
archaeological architect case study, 182
ArchiMate, 181
architects
    comparing typical roles, 13-17
    effective, common values of, 162
    proactive and reactive, 140
    typical architecture roles, 11-13
architectural domains, 12
    architectural domain model, 167-171
        capabilities, business and technical, 167
        considerations for defining, 170
        how capabilities fit in, 168
architectural mindset, 89
architectural views, 180
architecture
    about, 1
    conceptual, logical, and physical, 13
architecture decision making, framework for, 223-233
    building a foundation, 223-230
        defining architecture decision workflow, 226
        managing architecture decision lifecycle, 225
        offering architecture decision training, 229
        providing architecture decision registry, 224

for cloud services, 43
bureaucracy and value-add, enterprise architecture walking fine line between, 232
business benefits of solving a problem, 68
business capabilities, 167
in layered architectural domain model, 168
model of, 217
business lead, 20
business model, 217
business needs
discussing standard in terms of, 197
enterprise architecture strategy in context of, 216
business objectives, 71, 162
of solving a problem, 68
business outcomes
defining in enterprise architecture assessment, 207
mapped business and technical capabilities resulting in, 167
understanding the right problem, 141
Business Process Model and Notation (BPMN), 181
business value
associating with architecture documents, 178
tying architecture work to, 29

C

C4 (Context, Containers, Components, and Code) model, 21
canary deployments, 118
capabilities
business and technical capabilities, 167
capability target architecture, 34
how they fit in architectural domain model, 168
identifying in enterprise architecture assessment, 209
mapping gaps in capabilities
example capability gap analysis, 212
impact and effort to resolve, 211
mapping in enterprise architecture assessment, 210
model grouping them into architecture domains, 167
new capability, architecture decision for investing in, 46
capability maturity models (CMMs), 205

capability target architecture deliverable, 22
capacity, 121
case studies
in contextual understanding over siloed decision making, 172-174
aloof architect, 172
aware architect, 173
in driving behavior over enforcing standards, 190-192
administrative architect, 190
ambassador architect, 191
in embedded and accessible architecture, 105-108
best practices, 106
new enterprise architecture standard, 105
static artifact, 107
in enable and enforce, 133-137
the free-for-all, 134
the reporter, 136
the suffocation, 135
in evolution over frameworks, 200-202
adamant architect, 200
in proactive and reactive architecture decisions, 155-158
AI inflection point, 156
cloud migration, 155
tactical load, 157
in shared alignment, 76-80
mandate, 76
never-ending debate, 79
relitigation, 77
silo, 78
in tangible direction over stale documentation, 182-184
ambitious architect, 183
archaeological architect, 182
proven industry case studies, using as proof for architecture recommendation, 179
center of excellence (CoE), 127
versus community of practice, 127
centralized architecture organizations, 17
centralization in hybrid architecture, 19
challenge, 148, 158
questions to challenge assumptions and proposed solution, 148
champion/challenger model, 124
change agents, 144
change, evolution responding to, 195

G

gap analysis for capabilities, 210
GitOps workflows, 146
    use to improve quality, 149
good enough architecture decisions, 165, 175
governance, 10
    architecture review boards and, 196
    from blocker to enabler, 199
    difficulties of with different technology
        choices, 4
    enterprise architecture governance model
        with horizontals, 228
    typical governance document ontology, 113
GPUs, 190
granularity of diagrams, 180

H

HA (see high availability)
hierarchy supporting architecture decision
    making, 227
high availability
    designing architecture for, 172, 173
    enabling teams to achieve, 130
high availability design, application architec-
    ture decision made around, 46
high-quality target architecture, 50
    lagging indicators for, 51
horizontal scaling, 119
hours spent finding architecture information
    (KPI), 42
human behavior, driving (see driving behavior
    over enforcing standards)
hybrid architecture organizations, 19

I

identifying, integrating, and inferring policy
    enforcement points, 132
immutability, optimize for immutability princi-
    ple, 55
impact of architecture decisions, 226, 227
    going beyond single entity, escalation of
        decision, 228
impact of capability gaps if remediated, 211
implicit knowledge, 88
in progress (architecture decision records), 225
incentives, creating excitement with, 220
incidents caused by application, 51
inductive reasoning, 142

logical thinking with, 143
industry research firms and industry conferen-
    ces, learning from, 217
ineffective enterprise architecture, pitfalls of, 6
informational listening, 147
innovation, 112
    initiating, 142
    respecting, 53
    stifled through excess standardization, 6
interaction points, in define stage, 101
    user personas or roles engaged in, 102
interfaces, 122
    application interface design, evolutionary,
        166
internal motivation, 188
    positive conditioning and, 189
interoperability, 121
interoperability NFRs, 121
    goals of, 121
    key application architecture decisions for,
        122
    loose coupling versus tight coupling in
        applications, 122
    summary of, 123
invisibility and intuitiveness (in UI/UX), 98
IT systems, aligning with business strategy, 196
ivory tower architecture, 6

J

just in time (architecture information), 95

K

key performance indicators (see KPIs)
key results (see KRs)
knowledge management, 83-91
    benefits of, 90
    goal of, 84
    lifecycle of, 85
    types of knowledge relative to architecture
        information, 87
    and UI/UX design principles, 94
KPIs (key performance indicators), 30, 57
    architecture standard KPIs, 50
    defining and measuring, necessary informa-
        tion, 31
KRs (key results)
    sample KRs for embedded and accessible
        OKR, 40
    sample KRs for enable and enforce OKR, 49

shared alignment OKR, sample KRs for, 34
types in OKRs, 30

L

lagging indicator KPIs, 31
   example for embedded and accessible OKR,
      42
   example for high-quality application archi-
      tecture, 51
   example of, 37
   examples for enable and enforce OKR, 49
layered hierarchy view, 180
lead with why principle, 52
leaders (enterprise architects), 15
leading indicator KPIs, 31
   examples for embedded and accessible
      OKR, 41
   focusing on business benefits, examples of,
      35
learning, 162
   conscious and unconscious learning, 187
level of effort (LOE), 197
lifecycle of architecture decision records, 225
   monitoring execution of, 231
lift and shift, 5, 142
listening, 73, 146
   active, 34, 155
   types of, 147
load balancing, 116
logical architecture, 13, 22
logical thinking, 142
   with inductive and deductive reasoning, 143
loose coupling, 122

M

machine learning (see ML)
make it easy to do the right thing (principle), 53
management decisions for applications, 121
mandate (case study in shared alignment), 76
manifesto for effective enterprise architecture,
   161-163
marketing, 219
maturity models, 205
   example of effective enterprise architecture
      maturity model, 205
   shortcomings as assessment tools, 205
mean time to detect (MTTD), 115
mean time to repair (MTTR), 114
measurements

key characteristic in OKR framework, 29
   measuring to improve, 104
   outcome-based and effort-based in OKRs,
      30
   using to improve consumption of architec-
      ture information, 99
metamodel (enterprise architecture), 124
   illustrative example of, 124
metrics
   architecture, 45
   blindly mandating, avoiding, 77
   quantifying gains with, 221
   things not to measure, 31
milestones, 150
minimum level of compliance, 185
mission statement, 8
ML (machine learning), 190
   incorporation into software products, 201
   rise of, 197
modularity, 122
   in high-quality targeted architecture, 51
motivation
   understanding human motivation, 188
   using with conditioning to drive behavior,
      189
MTTD (mean time to detect), 115
MTTR (mean time to repair), 114

N

negative conditioning, 187
   using with external motivation, 190
net promoter scores (NPS) KPI, 41
network functions in architect roles, 16
new enterprise architecture standard (case
   study), 105
nonfunctional requirements (NFRs), 113, 172,
   205
   for architecture decisions, 230
   interoperability, 121
   operational efficiency, 119
   release, 117
   security, 122
   stability, 113
north star, 7
NPS (net promoter scores) KPI, 41

O

observability, 115, 116
OKR (objectives and key results) framework, 29

V

value of architecture, 29
value of enterprise architecture, 233
verifiability, 123
vertical scaling, 119
views (architecture), 180
vision and strategy, 140
vision statement, 7
visionary communication, 154
volume and impact, degrees of architecture
 decision making based on, 226

volume of architecture decisions, 14

W

weaknesses, 218
whole over individual good, 162
workflow (architecture decisions), 226

Z

Zachman Framework, 195
Zachman, John, 196

About the Author

Tanusree (Tanu) McCabe is an executive distinguished engineer (EDE) who leads enterprise architecture strategy at Capital One, positioning the company to take strategic advantage of modern technologies such as cloud. Her experience with enterprise-wide transformations such as moving to the cloud and adopting Agile, and her technical expertise with modern architecture styles such as microservices and serverless, gave her firsthand insight into what is necessary for an effective enterprise architecture practice. Tanu has presented at conferences such as AWS Re:Invent and ServerlessConf, covering topics such as architecting for resiliency and serverless applications.

Tanu is driven to inspire positive innovation to allow creative freedom to flourish, and this book is a way to do just that—it provides knowledge to empower others to practice enterprise architecture effectively to yield business outcomes and unleash technical innovation. This knowledge has been gained through her own trials and tribulations leading enterprise architecture strategy.

Colophon

The animal on the cover of *Fundamentals of Enterprise Architecture* is the crested oropendola (*Psarocolius decumanus*), or crested oriole.

An icterid, or New World blackbird, the crested oropendola is a common sight in its native South America, where it may be spotted alone or in small flocks foraging in trees for insects, fruit, seeds, and nectar.

Crested oropendolas are colonial nesters, building their large, woven, hanging nests in close proximity to one another. Each colony typically has one dominant male, whose distinctive songs include a descending call reminiscent of sliding one's hand down a piano keyboard. Females of the species lay two blotched blue-gray eggs that hatch in 15–19 days, with another 24–36 days to fledging.

The crested oropendola has been listed by IUCN as of least concern from a conservation standpoint. Many of the animals on O'Reilly covers are endangered; all of them are important to the world.

The cover illustration is by Karen Montgomery, based on an antique line engraving from Wood's *Animate Creation*. The series design is by Edie Freedman, Ellie Volckhausen, and Karen Montgomery. The cover fonts are Gilroy Semibold and Guardian Sans. The text font is Adobe Minion Pro; the heading font is Adobe Myriad Condensed; and the code font is Dalton Maag's Ubuntu Mono.

O'REILLY®

Learn from experts.
Become one yourself.

Books | Live online courses
Instant answers | Virtual events
Videos | Interactive learning

Get started at oreilly.com.

Milton Keynes UK
Ingram Content Group UK Ltd.
UKHW050105100924
448103UK00003B/7